"THAT NEW VISION OF THE WORLD WON THROUGH HARDSHIP . . ."

Antoine de Saint-Exupéry

Wind, Sand, and Stars

High & Wild

Essays and Photographs on Wilderness Adventure

Galen Rowell

SPOTTED
DOG PRESS®

BISHOP, CALIFORNIA

High and Wild: Essays and Photographs on Wilderness Adventure by Galen Rowell

Cover and title page photographs by Galen Rowell

Front cover: Cerro Torre at dawn from the summit of Fitz Roy, Patagonia.

Inset: Self-portrait in the Dry Valleys, Transantarctic Mountains, Antarctica.

Front flap: Crescent moon behind the ridge of an unnamed Karakoram peak near K2.

Front flap inset: Self-portrait atop Cerro Madsen, with Fitz Roy in the background, Patagonia.

Back cover: Across the Kern Plateau beneath a full moon on the John Muir Trail.

Half-title page: High winds on Anye Machin in Eastern Tibet.

Verso half-title: Dave Sharp skiing around a bristlecone pine in the White Mountains, California.

Title page: Ned Gillette and the view toward Mount Foraker from high on Mount McKinley, Alaska.

Published exclusively by Spotted Dog Press, a registered trademark of Spotted Dog Press, Inc.

For information about this or other books by Spotted Dog Press, please visit our website:

www.SpottedDogPress.com

To order this book, please call us toll-free at: 800-417-2790

Contact us by email: info@spotteddogpress.com, by FAX at 760-872-1319, or by mail at:

Spotted Dog Press, Inc., P.O. Box 1721, Bishop, CA 93515-1721

Please include your name, mailing address, and daytime phone.

We welcome your comments about this or any other title published by Spotted Dog Press.

Spotted Dog Press, Inc., First Edition 2002

Edited by Galen Rowell

Book design and production by Wynne Benti

Printed in China by C&C Offset Printing Co., Ltd.

Library of Congress Cataloging-in-Publication Data

Rowell, Galen A.

    High and wild: essays and photographs on wilderness adventure / Galen Rowell.-- 1st ed.

        p. cm.

    Originally published: San Francisco : Sierra Club Books, c 1979.

    Includes index.

    ISBN 1-893343-08-1

    1. Mountaineering--United States. 2. Mountaineering--Canada. 3.Mountaineering--Himalaya Mountains. 4. Mountains--United States--Recreational use. 5. Mountains--Canada--Recreational use. 6. Himalaya Mountains--Recreational use. I. Title.

    GV191.4 .R68 2002

    796.52'2'0973--dc21   2002021844

High & Wild

Essays and Photographs on Wilderness Adventure

Table of Contents

	PAGE	7	*Foreword by Robert Redford*
		9	*Preface*
CHAPTER 1		13	The New Age of Mountain Exploration
2		25	Alone on Bear Creek Spire
3		33	An Early El Capitan Epic
4		45	The Great White Throne
5		51	Layton Kor's Last Wall
6		57	The South Face of Half Dome
7		67	The Seventh Rifle
8		73	A Winter Traverse of the White Mountains
9		81	Yosemite's Other Valley
10		87	The Moose's Tooth
11		95	Free Climbing Keeler Needle
12		105	Skiing the High Desert
13		113	A Vertical Mile in the Alaska Range
14		123	The Cirque of the Unclimbables
15		133	Around Mount McKinley on Skis
16		141	A One-Day Ascent of Mount McKinley
17		149	Man and Beast in the Karakoram
18		159	Topping the Trango
19		169	Skiing the Karakoram High Route
20		179	Cholatse: Last Virgin of the Khumbu
21		189	A Night Out on Fitz Roy
22		203	The Highest War
23		213	The John Muir Trail in Winter
		221	*Photographic Notes*
		223	*Index*

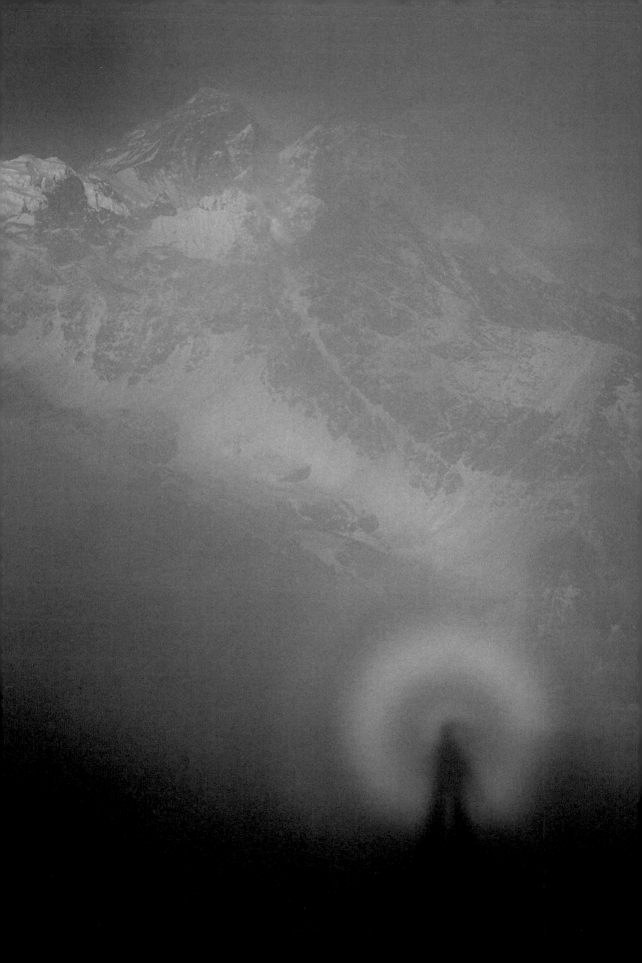

Foreword

There is a symbiotic relationship between nature and art. Every now and then someone will emerge who embodies this alliance. Galen Rowell is one. Photographer, essayist, naturalist, opportunist. He is all of these. But more. In his life, his work, his spirit, he suggests something new—a composite. That rare breed that combines these qualities to bring us a new light—a gift.

In the fall of 1982, I had the pleasure of meeting Galen Rowell— a willing guide to the high Khumbu region of Nepal, in the intense, solitary atmosphere of a culture old and a space remote from the complications of a mechanized society. On a late afternoon somewhere around 15,000 feet I had the privilege of witnessing something awesome. We stopped, an extra sense signalling that high above us on a steep hillside was a mountain tahr, scarce and elusive. Rowell sensed his presence. I had no clue. He loaded his camera with blurring intensity, never taking his eyes off the animal that I still had trouble finding. Then Rowell was gone—off the trail and up the cliff—quickly. And quietly. I watched as he stalked the reluctant animal, moving with great speed and agility at an altitude that doesn't allow for it. He seemed to contradict gravity and physical law. He would wait and watch and move and disappear and reappear—always closer. The animal was grazing and standing still. Finally I saw that the man and the animal were practically face to face—a great sensitivity prevailed as Galen shot picture after picture, always watching and the animal calmly watching in return. The pictures were taken. Rare. Beautiful. How did it happen? I sensed respect and understanding and felt a positive joy to be able to be there to see it.

In this new edition of *High and Wild*, the most personal of his books, Rowell gives us an opening to that amazing grace —the ability to move through nature and capture moments seldom seen. He takes us beyond, to a rarified place that our own eye cannot spot and does so without disturbing what is there. I feel his work is about to happen—the apprecation now to expand. I am grateful for his talent, his mind, and his sensitivity. And for that which he shares with us.

ROBERT REDFORD
Sundance, Utah

Above: On the way to Mount Everest.
Opposite: Spectre of the Brocken beneath Mount Everest.

Preface

I felt the need to begin the preface of the first edition with the disclaimer, "This is not a guidebook." Back in the seventies, Sierra Club Books had tried to convince me that a book like this would never sell. They wanted me to produce a handbook of American climbing that would weave information about the best climbs and the latest techniques with my personal experience. It took me years to convince them that a more philosophical look at my own mountain adventures would have anything more than a very limited appeal.

I remember a tense editorial meeting after years had passed since signing a book contract and I had yet to write a single word. Was I going to do this book or not? Their consensus was that climbers, armchair explorers, and editors alike wanted how-to information, not historical and ethical ramblings, especially by a guy in his thirties who might not be venerable enough in the eyes of reviewers. My response was that if this was true, why were major magazines, such as *National Geographic* and *Outside*, publishing my adventure narratives, complete with philosophical and environmental ramblings?

Someone asked, "Could we assemble some of those under one cover and use your photographs to create a coffee-table book instead of a handbook?" Thus the 1979 first edition was born.

My stated goal was to provide "a more immediate and intuitive view of the activities that form the basis of wilderness exploration: mountain climbing, backpacking, skiing. And thinking." I wanted to emphasize that even as climbing and skiing have become ever more recreational and technical, their roots as methods to explore otherwise inaccessible areas of the wild Earth remain very much alive. They are dependent on wild places, often extremely wild places, and as I said then, "Wilderness is more than a physical place; it is a state of mind . . . the original state of mind—the one in which we evolved."

As this expanded third edition by a third publisher goes to press twenty-three years later, little has changed for me. At sixty-one, I'm still bucking the latest fads of climbing and skiing in favor of adventures that offer a genuine wilderness experience. My fondest memories of climbs and expeditions around the world are far more about the wild places themselves than the technical difficulties I overcame on rock, snow, and ice. This explains why some of the "failures" mentioned in these pages—the Moose's Tooth, K2, and a Ruby Mountain ski traverse—rate right up there for me personally among my life experiences.

Opposite: Galen Rowell beneath a roof high on the Salathe Wall, 1967. Photo: Layton Kor
Above: Recent portrait by Barbara Cushman Rowell.

This new edition in a more readable size includes ten more chapters than the original thirteen. Five were added to the second edition and five more appear here. The latest additions include two early ascents of El Capitan in Yosemite that helped shaped my philosophy as well as more recent explorations in the great ranges of the world.

What saddens me is the way that some of these essays have become historical documents of change, like photographs in an old scrapbook, in just twenty to thirty years. Many of the most exotic and remote areas I describe here have been forever transformed, and not for the better. What I called "some of the wildest country I had ever seen" on the trailless west side of the Bugaboo Spires of British Columbia now has clearcuts and frequent arrivals by upscale "helicopter hikers." The incredibly remote Siachen Glacier that I traversed on skis

in the Karakoram Himalaya with a permit from Pakistan has been occupied by Indian troops for the past 18 years, as the highest war in history continues on. Where I camped in a wild meadow below Fitz Roy in Patagonia in 1985, the ramshackle town of El Chalten has since sprung up within a national park.

The majority of the exceptions that are little changed from the time of my earliest adventures are in the High Sierra, where Bear Creek Spire, Keeler Needle, and the John Muir Trail remain as pristine as I found them, despite more foot traffic through areas formally preserved as Wilderness.

After exploring on all seven continents and reaching both poles in the nineties, it became ever more clear to me that the Eastern Sierra is my favorite place on Earth. Though many of the ranges that I have visited are much higher than the Sierra Nevada, and some hold isolated clusters of mountains that are more spectacular, no other place has such a readily accessible diversity of well-preserved wildness and natural beauty. The proof is in my photographs. Far more of my most memorable images have come from here, rather than from more exotic locations. The diversity of light and landforms amidst a favorable climate in North America's largest area of contiguous designated wilderness outside Alaska is simply unbeatable for what stirs my personal passions.

In 2001, my wife, Barbara, and I moved full-time to the Eastern Sierra and opened a photo gallery on Highway 395 in Bishop. I often arrive to work late in the morning, having watched the sunrise on Mount Whitney on my way to scramble up the east face, or perhaps from 10,000 feet through the limbs of a bristlecone pine. I don't arrive so late on other mornings when I've been photographing alpenglow on the peaks from a wild pond near my home, running a trail through the Buttermilk Rocks, or tracking mountain lions or bighorn sheep before dawn with zoologists. I would no longer be regularly doing such things at my age, were it not for the decades of wild experiences chronicled in words and images in these pages.

GALEN ROWELL
Bishop, California · 2002

*Above: Galen photographing beside Upper Yosemite Fall with Half Dome in the distance, 1992. Photo: Ron Kauk
Opposite: Ed Ward high on Mt. Dickey.*

"I BECAME LESS AND LESS CONCERNED WITH THE MASTERY

OF TECHNICAL DIFFICULTY,

OR EVEN THE ASCENT OF INDIVIDUAL PEAKS,

BUT MORE AND MORE ABSORBED

IN THE PROBLEMS AND DELIGHTS OF MOVEMENT

OVER WIDE AREAS OF MOUNTAIN COUNTRY."

Eric Shipton

~

That Untravelled World

1

The New Age of Mountain Exploration

When this chapter appeared as the introduction to the first edition, the essays about wilderness adventures in the sixties and seventies contained in these pages were quite contemporary. It was written to explore the common philosophies behind all types of climbing, from ice mountains to bouldering, and to set them in the greater context of exploration. My predictions about solo ascents of Yosemite walls and alpine-style climbs in the Himalaya are now read with an historical eye, rather than as visions of a yet-to-be-realized future.

Like aging snapshots in a scrapbook, all these essays have come to represent visions from the past, rather than the present. Thus this chapter takes its rightful place among them to begin a celebration of some of the episodes in the ongoing drama of mountain adventure in which I was privileged to participate. That many of these wild places remain virtually unchanged allows today's adventurers to experience them in ever more creative ways.

Nine men gazed at an endless panorama of snowy mountains glowing in the evening sun. Giant glaciers dropped from the flanks of the peaks, covering hundreds of square miles with ice. Except for the men and their equipment, the entire tableau could have been transported from the ice ages of the Pleistocene. The scene's splendor was much more than mere prettiness; it reflected the free expression of natural forces—forces at odds with the men standing for the first time on the summit of Canada's highest mountain, Mount Logan.

A storm was brewing. Black sky oozed toward the men, and they dared not linger at the top, an elevation of nearly 20,000 feet. Mount Logan is more like a range than a single mountain; an eleven-mile section lies above 16,000 feet.

The storm overtook the party as it descended in the subarctic twilight, forcing a bivouac in the open at 19,000 feet. The next day they reached their high camp, only to find it torn apart by the blizzard. Another night was spent in the open. When the frostbitten men finally reached their base camp, they found it, too, ravaged by the storm.

At this point, a modern expedition would have radioed a bush pilot, flown out to civilization, and received hospital treatment for frostbite. Even without a radio, the expedition

Skiers watch an avalanche cross the Kahiltna Glacier on the first circumnavigation of Mount McKinley within the limits of its glacial systems.

would have faced nothing worse than a boring, painful wait for an aircraft to arrive at a prearranged time.

For the nine men of Albert MacCarthy's successful expedition, however, the ordeal was far from over. The year was 1925, and they were 150 miles from civilization: only a handful of humans had ever seen Mount Logan from closer than 50 miles. In summer, the approach to the mountain had been far too rough for pack animals, so MacCarthy and his companions waited until winter snows had carpeted the rugged canyon floors and glacial moraines, and then spent seventy winter days laying in caches over 130 miles of the route. In temperatures that often dipped to –40° F, he and three others slowly worked their way toward the mountain, first using horses, then dog teams when the going got rougher.

Only Greenland and Antarctica are more heavily iced than the thousands of square miles of glaciated highlands surrounding Mount Logan, and both the approach and retreat were like a polar expedition. After forty-four days of ice and snow, MacCarthy's weary party finally touched earth again in June, but the ordeal continued. The expedition decided to speed its retreat by floating the rapids of the Chitina River. Makeshift rafts were built with frostbitten hands, but soon one overturned with men, food, equipment, and cameras aboard. The men swam to safety and completed the long journey to McCarthy, Alaska, on foot.

Since 1967, a high-altitude scientific research camp, supplied by helicopter, has operated each summer at 17,600 feet on Mount Logan. The advent of air travel and modern communication systems have made remoteness increasingly difficult to attain. Remoteness, after all, is more than mere physical distance; it is also a function of psychological and technological separation from the rest of humanity. In time, in isolation, in everything but measured distance, the Logan climbers were more remote than astronauts on the moon.

We are now witnessing the slow death of exploration on earth, and with it the ethos that powered the early polar expeditions and the Mount Logan pioneers. Exploration on foot has become a nostalgic anachronism. Most scientific endeavors associated with it— mapping, surveying, prospecting, photographing, biological research—have welcomed mechanization with open arms. Contemporary climbers use modern transportation and communication to reach the mountains, but they generally agree that the climbing itself must be kept free from motorized or highly technological equipment.

The experience of the first Mount Logan climbers can never be duplicated. Too much of the mountain and its surroundings are too familiar to too many people. But regardless of civilization's encroachment on even the wildest mountain areas, mountaineering has remained essentially a wilderness activity, and its natural setting is all important. If this were not the case, climbing would be merely an athletic event, as satisfying on tall buildings or inside gymnasiums as on mountains.

It is no accident that many key people in the environmental movement have strong backgrounds in mountaineering, where the very essence of the experience depends on the natural character of the terrain. John Muir, David Brower, Dick Leonard, and Ansel Adams are just a few of the prominent conservationists who climbed mountains extensively, making tangible contacts with the current of evolution and deriving self-knowledge from personal interaction with the harsh, tilted world of rock, snow, ice, and sky. The birth and early years of the Sierra Club took place in this mountain crucible.

For many years, I assumed there must be a direct connection between Western culture and climbing. Conditioned by American public education, I contented myself with suppositions as arrogant as any entertained by pre-Victorian biologists. I placed great importance on the notion that mountaineering achievements paralleled the growth of industrialized and urban societies. I assumed that climbing was a triumph of rationality over primitive superstition and was the epitome of a goal-oriented society in which events and discoveries had a cumulative value. After all, I had been taught that mankind mastered the world by passing information from generation to generation, enabling modern Western man, the latest beneficiary of this process, to understand the basic principles of nature. Armed with such notions, I concluded that only men in this highly evolved and obviously superior state would knowingly expose their mortal bodies to the terrifying forces of nature. I saw climbing as an expression of modern man's understanding of these forces.

I noted that dogs who follow their masters in the mountains seem to have an instinctive sense of where to stop. They might climb one small cliff, but balk completely at one only slightly higher. I attributed this innate prudence to all living things and reasoned that natural selection might favor it. (If this were true, the best climbers would be those with perfectly ordered, logical minds. The opposite is closer to the truth.)

Several events made me re-examine my assumptions about climbers—both animal and human. One occurred in Alaska as a bush pilot flew me to a remote mountain. We flew past the last spruce trees, beyond the final green splotches of alpine vegetation into an Arctic world. Wolverine tracks began in the snow and continued for miles to the head of a large glacier, far beyond any source of food. Like our own advance into a hostile environment the tracks seemed unexplainable. I thought I had witnessed an isolated event, but later I talked to a climber who had seen a single wolf at 10,000 feet on Mount McKinley. Searching for a motive but finding none, I supposed the wolf and the wolverine had merely been lost.

Then I spent a day watching a mountain goat in a wild range of mountains in the Canadian North, and for once I felt I had a clear understanding of nature's logic. Goats climb to avoid predators and to feed on the lush alpine vegetation. I was not at all surprised when my actions in a meadow frightened a goat onto a steep cliff. I watched him run across a headwall on which my companions and I had used ropes and pitons only a few days earlier. With almost sadistic pleasure I approached the bottom of the cliff and guarded the only possible descent from the bulging, 2,000-foot rock face. The goat tried every conceivable way of climbing down, but instead of stopping at a point where he began to feel uneasy, he pushed himself, as a climber would, trying something one grade above his standard. I nervously watched him pivot on a hopelessly narrow stance and attempt a traverse that eventually ended in flawless granite. While wandering around the base, I made a discovery: the broken, mummified body of another goat that evidently had fallen from the same cliff. After several hours of watching, I returned to camp, still in sight of the goat, but half a mile away.

Instead of immediately descending and continuing in the direction he was originally headed, the goat stayed on the wall for quite some time. When he did come down, he looked to see if we were still watching. We were too far away to offer any threat to his passage, but he followed the base of the cliff in the direction opposite to where he was originally headed. At the first crack system he began to climb again, this time a flashy, three-hundred-foot romp. At the top of a pedestal he pivoted a full circle, like a fashion model, then bounded down the cliff again. He repeated his climbing antics in other spots, seeming always to make sure that we were watching. Finally, he ambled off in the direction he had originally taken. Where was the instinctive animal prudence I had posited?

The goat's antics appeared to have no survival value. If anything, I thought they were the dangerous frolics of an alpine show-off, but on further reflection I realized my response to the goat's climbing was similar to the public's reaction to human mountaineering. Products of the technological age, we are always ready to condemn as frivolous any activity whose purpose cannot be explained with reason and logic. I knew why I climbed, even if I couldn't express it in words. But as a prisoner of the modern, I believed that the urge had to be logically explainable. "Because it is there!" is a useless platitude. An answer closer to the truth came from a glider pilot who was asked by a television interviewer why he liked to do loops fifty feet above the ground: he simply answered, "I guess I'm just an adrenaline freak!"

Mountaineering may be the final step in terrestrial exploration, but it is increasingly becoming an end in itself. It is futile to explain climbing as either the triumph of rationality over superstition or the triumph of primitiveness over an increasingly artificial world. It is at once neither and both. It is MacCarthy's party on Mount Logan in 1925; crag climbers in New York in 1979; de Saussure making scientific observations on Mont Blanc in 1787; sourdoughs climbing Mount McKinley's north peak in 1910; Whymper, who longed to be a polar explorer, climbing the Matterhorn in 1865; Whillans, a Manchester plumber, on Mount Everest in 1972; two children scrambling in a national park campground; Toni Egger disappearing on Cerro Torre in icy Patagonia; an Indian hunting party on top of Mount Whitney; a solo climber on Yosemite's El Capitan.

The common thread of these diverse experiences is human interaction with mountains. But not all such interaction is considered mountaineering. The north wall of the Eiger is one of the most famous climbs in Europe, but those who traverse it via the railway tunnel that pierces its face can hardly be called mountaineers. Climbers adapt their behavior to wild surroundings rather than changing the face of the land to ease their passage. Most questions of climbing ethics and style revolve around this concept. Techniques that alter the environment—even temporarily—are not considered as good style as those that leave no sign of passage. Examples of environment-altering techniques are step-cutting in ice; expansion bolts, which require holes drilled into rock; expeditionary climbing, which depends on establishing temporary tent cities at strategic locations and moving a pyramid of men and supplies upward until the summit is within easy striking distance; and the use of fixed ropes, which enable climbers to ascend the rope instead of the rock or snow.

Mountain goat powering up a cliff in Canada's Cirque of the Unclimbables.

Unlike skiing, kayaking, and many other outdoor sports, climbing is not fundamentally dependent on equipment. A skier can't ski without skis, but a climber can climb without ropes or pitons. Much climbing is done without any special equipment at all. At least half of the five hundred "technical" climbs in Yosemite Valley could be climbed solo, unroped, and barefoot, by a highly skilled climber, although this would be as risky as a circus acrobat performing without a net. The next step beyond climbing without equipment is to carry it only for safety—as an acrobat uses his net for security—rather than for direct climbing aid. This is often the most satisfying kind of climbing: raw adventure achieved with a few classic tools. Simplicity is the hallmark of good climbing equipment. A nylon climbing rope is a simple tool that does a complex job. It is a flexible, portable, energy absorbing device capable of diffusing sudden shock loads of thousands of pounds. Similarly, an ice axe serves as a step-cutting tool, a walking stick, a handhold for technical ice climbing, and a braking mechanism for a climber falling on snow. By shifting the emphasis from working with the natural scene to tinkering with gear, equipment fetishists alter the basic character of the mountaineering experience.

Collecting an excess of fancy new equipment, however pointless in itself, is only one symptom of a more serious ailment. Perhaps because they can no longer look forward to the rewards of explorers, modern climbers feel compelled to measure themselves in other ways—usually not so much by skill and dedication as by lists of conquests. Climbs are numbered, measured, and categorized and for many, the goal becomes all important, the game only secondary. What Aleister Crowley, the eccentric Englishman, stated early in the century holds true today: "Climbing itself is being very much spoilt by the attitude of the [British] Alpine Club in insisting that the achievement, not the enjoyment, is the important thing. This is the American Spirit, to count and compare instead of being content with spiritual satisfaction."

Crowley may have overstated his case, for spiritual satisfaction is a synergism involving both self-experience and achievement. And competition is often a necessary catalyst for the biggest climbs, providing motivation for an activity that is useless in practical terms. But he is right that the self-knowledge derived from personal interaction with natural forces is a more important component of alpinism than is competition with the rated and timed achievements of others.

The renowned British climber A.F. Mummery, who climbed in the Alps a century ago, once wrote:

> The true Mountaineer is the man who attempts new ascents. Equally, whether he succeeds or fails, he delights in the fun and jollity of the struggle. The gaunt, bare slabs, the square, precipitous steps in the ridge, and the black, bulging ice of the gully, are the very breath of life to his being. I do not pretend to be able to analyze this feeling, still less to be able to make it clear to unbelievers. It must be felt to be understood, but it is potent to happiness and sends the blood tingling through the veins, destroying every trace of cynicism and striking at the very roots of pessimistic philosophy.

Previous: Sunset after the ten-day storm that pinned down Warren Harding midway up El Capitan's Dawn Wall in November, 1970.
Opposite: Nancy Feagin leads 5.11 on the first free ascent of the Direct Northwest Face of Half Dome, 1993.

Mummery sounds a theme that is becoming increasingly popular today: the true mountaineer, whether he succeeds or fails, delights in the struggle. Of course there is some extra elation in a hard-won achievement, but the emphasis is more on the effort itself than on its ends. The first ascent of a mountain is only the beginning. Almost endless variations are possible: new routes, solo climbs, winter climbs, all-free ascents, pitonless ascents, alpine-style climbs of mountains previously climbed by expeditionary sieges. Many of the adventures described in this book represent "new twists" to old challenges and are all the more rewarding for being so.

Many young climbers feel unlucky not to have been part of the so called Golden Age, roughly from 1860 to 1960, when most of the world's important mountains and rock walls were climbed for the first time. These particular achievements can never be repeated, but a mountain or cliff is never conquered, though one party of climbers or many manage to sneak through its defenses. Crowley's "spiritual satisfaction" and Mummery's "delight in the struggle" are still available for the modern generation, for the two-thousandth person on top of Mount McKinley as well as for the first, and for the unnumbered person who solves a boulder problem in a city park.

Every present-day mountaineer is a frustrated explorer at heart, secretly envying the struggles of the Mount Logan climbers and other pioneers of the high wilderness. He intuitively comprehends the mysterious attraction of alpine sanctuaries for the

W.E. Smoke Blanchard, Bishop's only Bhuddhist truck driver of the 1960s, introduced the sport of bouldering to the Eastern Sierra in his favorite Buttermilk Rocks.

wolverine, the wolf, and the mountain goat. Also intuitively, he plays the climbing games of style without ever having been taught the rules. If he were told he must play the games according to a fixed set of rules, he would surely rebel. He values first ascents, but is more often found doing "old classics" for the sheer joy of climbing. His experiences, not medallions, are his achievements. When he does throw his heart and soul into an especially difficult climb, he feels not only joy, but also regret when it is over. Like Mummery, he delights in the struggle, and many lowland hours are spent in contemplation of his next objective.

The remoteness of Mount Logan in 1925 is gone forever, but a glimpse through the window of the past is still possible. A glint is returning to some climbers' eyes as they go after famed Himalayan mountains in self-contained, alpine-style groups. The trend of not using hammers in rock climbing leaves many newer routes with no signs of human passage; every person who repeats these climbs can discover them anew, as did the first ascent party. The limiting factor in mountaineering is not first ascents but wilderness, and prime experiences will always be dependent on the preservation of the environment.

2

Alone on Bear Creek Spire

I had already fallen in love with the Eastern Sierra as my favorite place on Earth when I fled Yosemite Valley for this wild weekend adventure. Though my narrative focuses on the differences between climbing the known features of the Valley and an unexplored rock wall in the nearby High Sierra, the experience set the tone for major changes in my life. Just a year later, I sold my auto shop in the city and began a new career as an outdoor photographer and writer. That same year, I visited the wilds of Alaska for the first time, which whetted my appetite for the Himalaya.

The passion for the landscapes of the Eastern Sierra that I describe in these pages led me to purchase half interest in a tungsten mine with log cabins inside the John Muir Wilderness later in the seventies and to eventually live full-time in the Owens Valley town of Bishop. The Pine Creek Tungsten Mine, once the town's major employer, has long been closed and mountain tourism is now at the center of the local economy.

On a Friday evening in 1971, I drove two hundred miles east from Berkeley, California, on a road as familiar to me as my home street. It led to Yosemite Valley, where I had been climbing on weekends for a decade. As the winding road enters the national park, it parallels the Merced River through a deep gorge before the canyon opens into a flat valley surrounded by cliffs that rise to the stars.

Even to those who have been there hundreds of times, the first glimpse of Yosemite is overwhelming. As a child I imagined that the valley at night looked like a movie set. Moonlight reflected from the massive granite forms made them appear too stark and simple to be big; the valley seemed like a small model of itself. I felt I could almost reach out and touch the tops of cliffs three thousand feet overhead.

I stopped at Yosemite Lodge, where I met a group of climbers who gathered there every weekend. Within minutes, I was invited to join friends on a route I had done many times before. Though I had intended to climb in Yosemite, I felt a sudden urge to change that plan and suggested an alternative—the south face of Bear Creek Spire in the John Muir Wilderness adjoining Yosemite National Park. No interest. I might as well have suggested Patagonia.

South face of Bear Creek Spire in winter.

I sat and thought for a while about why I had lost enthusiasm for a Yosemite climb, and soon realized that I felt a need to escape the security Yosemite represented. It was home—familiar walls, faces, sounds, smells—and I was already part of an earlier generation, from a time when climbers knew the wonder of gazing at great cliffs still untouched by the hand of man. When I first climbed in Yosemite in 1957, none of the big walls had

been ascended. Since that time, all of Yosemite's major cliffs had been climbed by at least one route; El Capitan now had eleven; the front face of Half Dome, four. The simply joys of exploration were on the wane; in their place was a trend to count and compare experiences with those of others who had climbed the same routes. I had no doubt that many Yosemite climbs demanded greater skill than the hardest routes of the highest ranges, but a big red flag went up when I saw climbers far more talented than myself unwilling to test in the nearby wilderness the skills acquired in this fair-weather womb. There was little I could do personally to reverse what I considered an unfortunate trend, except to bow out of it. I decided to go to Bear Creek Spire, alone. The decision to solo did not come from any high motive; quite simply, no one would go with me.

I slept fitfully in a crowded campground before driving at dawn toward Tioga Pass, on the park's eastern boundary. The pass, at almost 10,000 feet, was just below timberline and though summer was nearly over, the meadows were still lush. My climb would begin in just this sort of terrain, but farther south, where not a single road crossed the rugged Sierra crest for two hundred miles. To reach my starting point I drove another hundred miles, first dropping thousands of feet to the desert floor of the Mono Basin, then along the base of the mountains until a deadend side road brought me back up to 10,400 feet.

Here I locked my ten-speed bicycle to a tree in the woods not far from the roadhead. My plan was to drive on to another trailhead farther south, walk eight miles in and 5,000 feet up to the base of Bear Creek Spire, climb it, traverse the north side to pick up my bicycle, and ride forty miles back to my car.

From where I cached my bike, I could see Bear Creek Spire about ten miles away, and before turning around to continue south, I took a long look at it. I had once wondered why this undistinguished 13,713-foot peak, which had been climbed from the west by a moderate scramble in 1923, was named a spire. The answer was clear when I first saw its south face from the ridge of another mountain. The face is a pointed blade of granite, which to the best of my knowledge had never been attempted.

Above: Boulder trapped in weathered whitebark pine roots.
Opposite: Lone shooting star beneath Bear Creek Spire in Little Lakes Valley.

I drove on into America's deepest valley, the Owens Valley, created by a massive fault block between the 14,000-foot summits of the High Sierra and the White Mountains twenty miles to the east. An earthquake greater than the one that almost destroyed San Francisco in 1906 shifted the valley twenty feet in 1872. I took a side road up Pine Creek to the largest tungsten mine in North America. Outwardly it looks like a normal mining operation in a mountain valley; actually, it is upside-down. Shafts climb from the tunnels up into the mountains, and one penetrates Bear Creek Spire, four air miles away.

I left my car and began hiking away from the creaks and whines of the milling operation. I soon came upon what looked like a natural marble quarry: glacial polish had combined with frost-heaving to segment white aplite into piles of burnished blocks that gleamed against the surrounding granite. By noon I left the last whitebark pines below and set out across a barren moraine composed of loose granite boulders. When I saw the vivid green of a tiny lake set amid the glacial debris, I knew that ice somewhere beneath the surface was still carving the landscape. Glacially scoured rock dust—"glacier milk"—accounted for the water's tint.

My memory of how impressive the south face appeared from a distance had been tempered somewhat by a recent look at the contour map, which showed the wall to be about 800 feet high and not particularly steep. Now, at close range, my original impression returned; the face was fully 1,200 feet high, without a single large ledge. The situation gave me pause. It was two o'clock in the afternoon, and I was carrying only minimal equipment: a 9mm rope, one quart of water, some food, a short, half sleeping bag, and a handful of pitons and carabiners. I foresaw a demanding afternoon on the face under a hot sun, but nothing to make me seriously consider giving up the ascent.

The climbing began with deceptive ease. I didn't even rope up for several hundred feet, because cracks and handholds kept appearing in just the right places. A squeeze chimney at nearly 13,000 feet left me panting, however; and I used rope and pitons for safety on the steep face above. I made steady progress until I reached a small pedestal beneath a smooth headwall; I tried to free-climb it with the rope for safety, but failed. The only crack I could spot was separated from better terrain above by about eight feet of blank overhanging rock.

Dropping back to the top of the pedestal, I drank the last of my water and thought about Yosemite. My bright idea of a remote climb was losing its luster rapidly. I could picture my friends in the Valley, who had probably come down from their routes before the afternoon heat and were now sitting in the restaurant with a drink or cavorting in

Above: Endangered Sierra bighorn rams.
Opposite: Climber on Pratt's Crack in Pine Creek Canyon, Eastern Sierra.

Camp Four, the Yosemite climbers' camp. I, on the other hand, contemplated a cold night at 13,000 feet and an arduous descent in the morning.

After a brief rest, I clipped a sling into my highest piton and stood in it. The over-hanging wall pushed me out, and after a futile effort to surmount it, I descended again. The sun was about to leave the face, and I knew that my best chance was to give it every-thing I had while the rock was still warm. This time I put the shortest possible loop into the piton so I could stand a bit higher than before. The headwall had a shallow vertical groove; I worked, with my elbow pointed skyward, to secure an arm lock between my inverted palm and shoulder. When I tried to move my free leg, I felt completely helpless, but I made one final attempt. Dangling from the overhang by the arm-lock, I pulled my foot away from the security of the loop and up onto the eye of the piton. The extra inches let me move the arm-lock higher. I was now out of balance, but very near a wide crack, and a desperate lunge took me high enough to jam a fist into the bottom of the crack.

Relief surged through me, as though a gun aimed at my head had just misfired. The danger was not entirely over, however; I knew that my adrenaline-stimulated strength would be short-lived. I continued up, fist-jamming thirty feet to a narrow ledge, and panted there for long minutes. The ledge traversed the steep headwall for a hundred feet and then connected with a chimney system. It was a lucky break: I wouldn't need to bivouac on the cliff if I could move efficiently in the minutes remaining before dark.

The day's harsh sunlight gave way to dusk, and in the indirect light I could see into the shadowy north faces of an endless sea of peaks. It was a more rugged Sierra vista than I had ever known in summer. At my feet were alpine flowers; this very contrast of life and barren rock had led John Muir to call the range "the gentle wilderness."

Stormy sunrise above Buttermilk Road in the Eastern Sierra.

All along the ledge yellow hulsea and purple polemonium were still in bloom. Sierra bighorn sheep depend on them as an important part of their summer diet. In Muir's day, the flowers might have been nibbled down to the roots. Weathered horns and ancient Indian hunting blinds attest to the fact that the bighorn, now a threatened species, once ranged as high as the very tops of most mountains along the crest. I could imagine a ram profiled on the summit ramparts only a hundred feet above me as I hurried along the ledge below.

Having reached the chimney, I climbed steadily with the pack suspended below me, and within minutes I was standing on the summit, still lit by the last rays of the sun. I would have liked to linger, but it was late. I scrambled toward the shadows of the north side, heading down the broken face toward a tiny meadow with a stream. An hour later, in the dark, I bent down for my first drink in many hours.

I had planned to stop by the stream for only a minute, then descend in the moonlight to the forest below, but after eating a package of freeze-dried hash mixed with cold water, I realized that my legs didn't want to support my body any longer. Without standing up again, I crawled into my half-bag. Though extremely fatigued, I lay sleepless for hours, still carried along by the forced awareness the day had demanded. I felt lucky to have made the climb and to have gotten down safely. I no longer envied the climbers loafing around the Yosemite campground. I was content where I was, alone under the stars on a clear night.

I set off again before dawn, walking through Little Lakes Valley toward the roadhead. After a single day high in the mountains, the well-used trail and established campsites seemed like civilization. At sunrise I reached the trailhead where my bicycle was cached and soon reveled in a 6,000-foot downhill ride. From the floor of Owens Valley I had to climb again, struggling up a 3,000-foot grade in desert heat that was already intense. I stopped half a dozen times to plunge my upper body into mountain streams. At nine that morning, less than twenty-four hours after starting up the trail toward Bear Creek Spire, I reached my car, with barely enough energy left to lift the light ten-speed inside.

A solo climb such as the one I had just made is not a logical extension of Yosemite technique, which stresses extending limits of ability while protected by equipment. Nor is solo climbing simply the means to an end, for there are far easier ways to reach summits. It is a form of private, heightened awareness—something that anyone who has spent time alone under stress can understand. What makes it different and desirable is doing so by choice.

3

An Early El Capitan Epic

My early ascent of the Nose of El Capitan was a rite of passage that brought invitations to climb with some of the best climbers in America, both in Yosemite and in more remote areas, but that wasn't my motivation. I was drawn inexorably toward the rash decision to attempt the face in winter with a partner I hardly knew by a spiritual connection with the great rock that began in early childhood.

That we managed to survive a major storm without proper bivouac gear or a rescue was a life-changing experience for both of us. For more than a decade, I never wrote about it, even though I kept extensive notes and soon became a full-time outdoor journalist. The experience was too far away from what I wanted to communicate about climbing. Rather than play into the public penchant for life-threatening suffering and tragedy, I wanted to share the life-enhancing bliss and satisfaction of my mountain adventures. On this climb, the all-important state of optimistic expectation that normally pervades my being vanished midway up the face into the curtain of blowing snow that whited out our world.

My fascination with the face of El Capitan began in the summer of 1943. World War II was raging, gasoline and tires were rationed, yet my parents went to great effort to introduce me to Yosemite Valley before I turned three. We had the serene valley to ourselves as we slowly cruised beneath El Capitan in the moonlight, never meeting another car in the park. It had taken most of three days to travel less than 200 miles from our home in Berkeley.

How do I remember what happened to me at such a tender age? I'm not sure that I do. My own experience soon merged with my mother's frequent recountings, which became deeply ingrained into our family's lore well before I became a Yosemite climber. She wanted me to share her deep passion for Yosemite and the High Sierra, and she succeeded beyond her wildest dreams.

In the early sixties, when I began climbing Yosemite cliffs and hanging out in Camp Four with climbers subsisting on virtually nothing, my mother saw it as the natural progression of my father's frugal influence. He was born in a log cabin in 1884 and lost his life savings during the Great Depression. When I came along in 1940, he was trying to

Clearing storm on El Captian.

continue living on a professor's salary in the large Berkeley Hills home he had built in the Roaring Twenties. When the war began, he devised a way to preserve the original tires on his Studebaker coupe throughout the years of rationing. He picked up some junk inner tubes, cut them into strips, and glued them over his tire treads with a special adhesive he found in the Sears Roebuck catalog. After lots of trial and error, he found he could drive a steady 15 miles per hour without the rubber falling off. That's why we were cruising so slowly beneath El Capitan so late in the evening.

My mother fell in love with Yosemite on a visit with her parents in an open touring car in 1916. For a decade after college, she performed the first regular broadcasts of live classical music on national radio several times a week from San Francisco, but she talked her women's trio into spending a month each summer in Yosemite, where they played evening concerts after daytime rambles on the trails and peaks.

Despite her recountings, my youthful introduction to "her" El Capitan would surely have faded from my memory were it not for all the visual reminders. There were photographs in books by Ansel Adams on our mantel. One snapshot in our family albums show a miniature Yosemite Valley set atop a picnic table in Berkeley's Tilden Park for my sixth birthday party. I helped my mother select just the right boulders to represent El Capitan and Half Dome.

The two great rocks became enduring entities of my childhood. As my secret trails and hideaways around our isolated home in the wild hills gave way to new houses on all sides, El Capitan and Half Dome remained the same on every visit. I sensed that the great, unexplored faces of these immutable constructs of nature would remain invincible. The summer of 1957 changed all that.

For six years, my family had joined two-week Sierra Club pack trips in the heart of the backcountry. The 1957 outing took us through the ghost town of Mammoth into what is now the Ansel Adams Wilderness. At the remote camp we learned that our young cook, Jerry Gallwas, had just spent five days and nights making the first ascent of the sheer Northwest Face of Half Dome. His team had purposely avoided publicity, so this was the first we'd heard of it.

When Jerry and another young climber, Mike Loughman, showed me their techniques for climbing with ropes and pitons on cliffs behind the camp, the experience felt very different than practice sessions on Bay Area rocks with the Sierra Club Rock Climbing Section. Instead of waiting in line to do short rappels while watching those who carried the most ropes and hardware from the trunks of their cars receive the most admiring glances, we selected the bare minimum of equipment needed to move safely *up* the rock.

Mike was planning a sixty-mile solo cross-country trek to Yosemite Valley at the end of the outing. Though he was only nineteen, he was on the outing by himself working as a climbing guide. At sixteen, I envied his independence and displayed as much enthusiasm and skill as I could muster until it happened: Mike asked me to join him trekking to Yosemite and climbing there for a week.

Together, we asked my mother's permission—a clever ploy since she, too, had gone out of her way to impress the two climbers with her passion for adventure. With a mixed expression of joy and trepidation, she had to say yes.

When we reached the rim of the valley and looked across at Half Dome, something seemed very different than looking up from our car on all those previous trips. Knowing that Jerry had just climbed the great face, the dome no longer looked immutable, and I wondered if I would ever have enough courage and skill to climb it. I had the strong urge to walk over to its base and just touch its vertical granite.

We spent a week doing short climbs before going home to the city, where my life was forever changed. When I went out on the local practice rocks, it was with the sole objective of acquiring enough skills to climb Yosemite's greatest walls. At the end of October 1962, I made the ninth ascent of the face of Half Dome, later in the year than it had ever been climbed. I most enjoyed spending days and nights on walls in the off seasons, when the air was cooler and my partner and I had whole rocks to ourselves. I wondered why others had not made this discovery.

Over the next three years, I climbed many face routes up Yosemite's major features, but never attempted El Capitan. I was all too aware of the epic nature of its 1958 first ascent, just a year after my first climbs with Mike. All but a few Valley climbers considered El Cap out of their personal realm of possibility. Warren Harding had succeeded in climbing directly up the Nose of El Capitan after a total of forty-seven days on the face.

When I befriended Warren and did some wall climbs with him, I couldn't help but compare his abilities to my own. He was sixteen years older, and I was by far the better free-climber, able to ascend more difficult rock more quickly using only natural holds and a rope for safety. Yet I recognized that Warren had something that couldn't be measured on practice rocks or shorter climbs. His legendary guts and endurance had more to do with why he was the first to climb El Cap. I wasn't at all sure that I had what it took to repeat his route.

By the time I attempted the Nose in early 1966, it had received just three more ascents in the eight years since the first climb. All were by the very top rock climbers in America. They were the exceptions to the group of climbers with deep-seated fears about attempting the big walls who lived all year in Yosemite, hiding from the rangers in caves behind Camp Four. In contrast, both Warren and I were somewhat marginalized by the Valley locals as weekend warriors who arrived in fancy cars to energetically attack the rocks for a few days before returning to work in the city. Though my mother was convinced that my natural kinship with Camp Four climbers was related to my father's frugal lifestyle, I was out on the fringe because I represented the establishment to them.

The plus side was that neither Warren nor I felt particularly influenced by what other climbers thought. We climbed for our own personal rewards, often violating unwritten Valley codes that forbad publicity, use of fixed ropes, and attempting big routes beyond your level of experience—a classic catch 22. Steve Roper's 1964 first edition of *A Climber's Guide to Yosemite Valley* listed drilling expansion bolts for direct aid to bypass blank areas

Galen takes a drink midway up El Capitan before the storm, 1966. Photo: Tom Fender

of rock as the number-one subject of ethical debate. His guide also stated in no uncertain terms, "Ethically, it is wrong for a person who should be doing Grade IVs to lay siege to a Grade VI."

A Grade IV is a long climb that can be done in a day, and laying siege is what Warren did on the Grade VI ascent of the Nose for 35 days spread over a year with a number of different partners before going on the wall for a final 12-day push just before Thanksgiving in 1958.

On a cold November evening, Warren reached the base of the summit overhangs with his two remaining companions, Wayne Merry and George Whitmore. Only a hundred feet above them a celebration was under way. An assorted group of friends, lovers, media, and hangers-on had hiked miles up the back side with a feast of hot food and wine. Cheers of well-wishers eager to celebrate the greatest rock climb in history wafted down the cliff. Someone tossed a rope that dangled within Warren's reach and yelled, "Warren, prusik on up and let's get on with the party."

Warren ignored the rope. He had begun drilling and wasn't about to take the easy way out. Finding no continuous cracks in which to hammer pitons in the massive and nearly flawless overhangs, he was drilling holes by hand with star drill and hammer. Under ideal conditions he could drill an inch-deep hole for an expansion bolt in fifteen minutes, then attach nylon slings and step up five feet to place another. Hanging out in space from the overhang with arms overhead, it took him at least forty minutes to drill a hole. On the tiny ledge below, Wayne and George belayed his safety rope and waited patiently for the ordeal to end.

Darkness fell and Warren kept on drilling. When a hole was completed, he would insert a bolt, attach a sling with a carabiner, move up, and renew drilling. The night was marked more by the passage of bolts than time. Five . . . ten . . . fifteen . . . twenty . . .

Dawn arrived while the drilling marathon continued. At 8 a.m., seventeen hours after he began drilling, Warren crawled from a sling attached to his twenty-eighth bolt onto the summit. "It was not at all clear to me," he later reflected, "who was the conqueror and who was the conquered: I do recall that El Cap seemed to be in better condition than I was."

Though the climb took a hallowed place in the written history of mountaineering, the oral tradition of Yosemite climbing was highly critical of that final bolt ladder up the tip of the Nose. The idea that novices could simply clip their way up Harding's bolts, rather than work with the natural weaknesses of the rock to figure out their own passage, outraged many residents of Camp Four.

I noticed a considerable overlap between those who seemed the most outraged and those who seemed the most intimidated to try their own hand at climbing the thirty-three rope lengths to get into position to clip up those bolts. I was among those intimidated by the sheer size and verticality of El Cap, but I had no problem with the idea of clipping up Harding's "easy" bolt ladder.

Thus when El Cap seemed to be in perfect condition with dry rock under clear skies in the late winter of 1966, I set out to make the fifth ascent with a marginally experienced younger wall climber from Colorado named Tom Fender. Harding's bolt ladder proved to

Tom Fender leads the pitch below Dolt Tower in the morning sun.
on the fifth ascent of the Nose of El Capitan, 1966.

be the most difficult climbing obstacle I had ever encountered when we reached it in a snow storm on our fifth evening. No one had ever been rescued from a Yosemite big wall, and we did all we could to survive.

Though El Capitan climbs soon became commonplace in the seventies, they were considered extremely serious business in the sixties. Before going on the climb, I left a handwritten will in my car. As we walked to the base of the cliff, I knew better than to look up. I'd walked in the predawn twilight toward other walls with well-known climbers who had looked up for a few moments too long and lost their nerve. They would conjure up a sudden excuse to retreat: a moving cloud, a worn haul bag, a missing piton we might need—things that would give no more than a moment's hesitation to wall climbers in the near future, who broke so far through the sixties' fear threshold that they weren't aware it ever existed. In those days before El Cap had many ascents, no helicopters buzzed in the back of our consciousnesses. No mid-wall rescues had ever been made, and if we got into trouble, we would be entirely on our own.

Yosemite climbers tended to intellectualize and philosophize a way of life that they considered to be closer to an art than a sport. We walked around knowing that we were involved in something so special that debates about rating systems took on more immediacy than debates about Vietnam. One climber backed off a half-day climb six times. When he finally succeeded, he proudly wrote home, "I have mastered the realm of the Yosemite Grade IV!"

We were definitely far above average in intellectual powers, but far below average in academic success. One evening, four of us sitting in a booth in the old Yosemite Lodge restaurant discovered that we all were National Merit Scholarship finalists in high school, yet we all had dropped out of college to climb. The odds of us randomly meeting in one place were beyond astronomical, but the counterculture selection for Yosemite climbers in the sixties was anything but random.

At the time, none of the above foursome had attempted El Capitan. We were students of the written word, and our abilities to project ourselves into imagined situations were finely honed. When Royal Robbins, the greatest wall climber of the Golden Age of Yosemite, wrote about taking two long leader falls above insecure pitons on the first ascent of Arches Direct, we privately vowed never to climb that route or anything that resembled it.

It slowly dawned on me that the prime movers of Yosemite wall climbing were really the anti-intellectuals who remained undaunted by intimidating language. Robbins, a high-school drop-out, knew how to use strings of complex words to advantage, writing directly to an audience of his peers in such a way as to plateau the more intellectual of us right where we were. He badly wanted to make the first ascent of all the big walls in Yosemite, but while he was ascending Half Dome with Jerry Gallwas and Mike Sherrick, barely beating out a team already assembled by Warren Harding, he returned to find Harding, a no-nonsense construction worker, firmly ensconced on the Nose of El Capitan with fixed ropes and gear.

It was no coincidence that my attempt on the Nose in 1966 was prompted by a splendidly anti-intellectual bricklayer from Colorado named Layton Kor. In the winter of 1965, the immense and powerful Kor made his annual pilgrimage to Yosemite with a slightly shorter six-foot-four teenage protege named Tom Fender. Like his mentor, Tom laid bricks, drank lots of beer, and climbed with raw intensity. One evening, Tom and I talked about the dreaded west face of Leaning Tower, a severely overhanging 1100-foot wall that had only been done a few times by pre-eminent valley climbers, such as Harding, Robbins, and Kor. The first ascent party had ominously written that normal retreat by rappel was impossible and that future climbers should carefully consider the risks before committing themselves. Layton overheard our trepidations and suddenly interrupted, "Bullshit! You guys can climb the Tower right now, no sweat. And when you're done with that, you're ready for El Cap."

Within a few days, Tom and I made what we called the first "podunk" ascent of the Tower. We found it strenuous, but well within our limits. Once we spread the word that the likes of us could do it and feel comfortable about it, there was a virtual line-up among Valley climbers for the rest of the season.

Even with our success on the Tower, we felt intimidated by the hallowed ground of El Capitan. We decided to ask a third climber, but after we began climbing direct aid for a few hundred feet, his nerves got the best of him and we lowered him to the ground. After a brief discussion, we, too, gave up with the lame excuse that we had lost too much valuable time.

A week later, we went back in perfect early-March weather. It hadn't stormed for 45 days. We started in the dark again, before the harsh light of day on the great face could strike fear into our hearts. The climbing went so well that after two days we were halfway up the wall with reasonable certainty of completing the climb faster than the five full days it had taken Royal Robbins' second ascent party.

Our main concern was getting too hot and dehydrated. The sun's heat at midday reflected from the curving walls of granite as if from inside an oven, causing us to sweat heavily as we hauled our army-surplus duffel bag of gear and water up every pitch. Yvon Chouinard, another of the big-wall gurus who later founded Patagonia, had written, "Bad weather in California means hot weather . . . the threat of stormy weather is not serious." Thus Tom and I didn't take it seriously when warm rain began to fall as I nailed my way underneath the infamous Great Roof. Later in the day, a cold front arrived and we were enshrouded in a quiet mist of snowflakes. We talked about descending, but feared trying to reverse the seven pendulum traverses we had already made. What if we couldn't get across one of them in icy conditions? We had no drill or expansion bolts.

Throughout the afternoon, the vertical veil of snow became increasingly horizontal in strong winds. The coming of darkness was disguised until suddenly we could no longer see to climb. We drove pitons and strung out open hammocks, which soon filled with snow and soaked me to the skin. I didn't sleep a wink.

At the first inkling of light we were off and climbing. Though snow pelted our faces and numbed our hands, the climbing itself was easy. We were in a single crack system bound toward the summit. We moved, not with the grace of acrobats or athletes, but with the jerky, repetitive motions of common laborers. I would bang in a piton, clip in my safety rope and a sling, step up a few feet, and bang in another. When I reached the end of the rope, I would tie it to several pitons, sit in a nylon seat, and haul up the bag while

Tom used Jumar ascenders to come up and join me, removing the pitons I had placed on the way. Then we would switch leads and Tom would play sky carpenter for the next 150 feet. It seemed like boring, repetitive work that anyone could learn to do. But then there was the cold.

At each belay, we were most eager to switch leads. The previous leader always needed to thaw cold hands, while the previous belayer always wanted to get moving to warm up a body chilled from inactivity. Both of us began shivering involuntarily minutes after stopping each lead, and we weren't sure how many more hours we could take before lapsing into hypothermia. Had we been winter climbing in the High Sierra or Canada, we would have brought along proper tentage, waterproof garments and boots, plus a stove to make warm drinks. Here in our vertical world, we had nothing except the wet clothes on our backs and soaked down sleeping bags with no more loft than cardboard.

A hundred feet from the summit our crack system ended. As we contemplated the summit overhangs from the same point as Warren Harding eight years earlier, I breathed a sigh of relief. All that separated us from the summit was that controversial "easy" bolt ladder, a simple matter of clipping slings up existing anchors for a few minutes.

Somewhere behind the clouds the sun had sunk below the horizon and the temperature was rapidly falling. Our wet ropes began to change from the consistency of spaghetti to that of steel cable. As I ascended the bolt ladder, I only clipped my safety rope into every other anchor with either double carabiners or a nylon sling plus a carabiner in hopes of lessening the amount of rope drag. Even so, the drag became increasingly great as the rope froze into dog-leg bends where it ran through anchor points. Soon it took all my strength to pull through enough rope to move up to the next bolt. And then the rope wouldn't budge at all.

I was only halfway up the overhang with darkness almost upon us and my headlamp shorted out by the wetness. Tom was urging me to move faster because he was shivering uncontrollably. A wild idea came to me as I looked down at the thick climbing rope uselessly frozen into the anchors and the thin rope dangling out of sight from my waist toward the haul bag clipped into the anchor beside Tom. I asked him to clip all the extra climbing gear to the haul bag and cut it loose. After pulling it up hand over hand, I hung it from my waist by a short tether. I then untied my safety rope in the middle of the lead, breaking the cardinal rule of technical climbing, and tied it to the loose end of the thin haul rope, with the other end tied to my waist. Now I could move again with 150 feet of slack.

Even with the ungainly weight of the bag tugging at my midriff I could climb much faster than before. Within minutes, I was standing in the highest loop of my sling from the last expansion bolt with my hands touching the top. But the climb was not over.

Instead of being home free, where in summer I could have walked off onto moderately inclined rock slabs, I was hanging from the lip of an overhang with my hands digging through two feet of slippery snow. A slip would mean a 300-foot fall if my thin rope held, or 3,000 feet if it didn't.

At the top of Harding's final bolt ladder, I had no sense of success or victory and felt myself to be in greater danger than ever in my life. For five days my world had been 3,000

El Capitan relfected in the Merced River.

feet of granite. At the end of each lead, I had calculated how much farther we had to go. Now I was there. Winds twisted over the lip of the cliff, creating a ground blizzard. I doubted that I could survive an hour or two, much less the night, even if I did make it onto the relative security of the summit slabs.

Digging through the snow in a whiteout that was growing darker by the minute, I found no crack suitable for piton anchors to belay Tom up, but I managed to hammer in just the tip of an angle piton and tie it off with a sling. It held enough of my weight to move over the top onto my knees, but I was still on steeply inclined rock from which I would slide off without anchors hammered into cracks.

For the next hour, I continued digging through the snow with my bare hands and placing more marginal pitons in a shallow crack in the darkness. Finally, the angle lessened enough for me to stand up. As I walked toward the nearest tree, the rope caught me up short. Even by adding all my direct aid slings, runners, and carabiners clipped together I couldn't reach it. Then I spotted the sapling.

Within reach of my rope, a tiny Jeffrey pine was growing out of a crack. Less than waist high, it was barely an inch in diameter above a lumpy, gnarled base emerging from the rock. Even in the freezing conditions, I could bend its skinny trunk to the ground with one hand.

Casing out the situation, I set the haul bag on a narrow ledge just above the tiny tree, laid down on it, then untied from the rope. I reattached it to the base of the sapling, clutched the trunk with both hands so it wouldn't bend, and yelled down, "Off belay! The rope's tied off. You can come up now."

Long minutes passed while I heard only the whistle of the wind. Then came faint moans and groans and silence again. "I can't make it," Tom yelled up. "My Jumars are slipping. The teeth are frozen up." The rope went slack, and I waited, hearing no further cries of distress and no answers to my yells as full darkness descended upon us.

I thought Tom couldn't possibly make it, but I was determined to hold onto the tree with hands that could no longer feel until I knew for certain. If Tom fell, I planned to hang on long enough to see if the tree would hold, but be ready to let go quickly and save myself if it pulled out.

I clearly couldn't wait out the night where I was, and neither could Tom. Since I now had all the bivouac gear, food, and water, his only hope was up. My choices were staying put and trying to survive the night or trying to walk seven miles through several feet of deep snow in the dark to the Valley floor.

Suddenly, the rope went tight and the sapling began to bend. I held on with added strength and felt the rope quiver as a shadow appeared on the horizon. Tom was coming over the lip of the overhang with his full weight on the rope. When his Jumars froze up, he had put them away and clipped directly to the bolts without a safety rope. Now, he had reached the lip and grabbed the rope with all his remaining strength to pull his way over the top.

I was concentrating on holding onto the sapling when Tom's eyes met mine. He glanced over at his pitiful anchor point, but didn't say a word. When he did talk, it was about the future: what should we take with us and where should we head? We left all our gear except clothing and packs, then walked in a straight line away from the edge. Soon we were in powder skier's dream of several feet of bottomless snow, but without skis, in the dark, totally fatigued, and with no idea where we were going except uphill away from the edge.

Tom led the way as the angle lessened, the mist became strangely darker, and wind began to hit us from below. Suddenly he grabbed me and said, "We're walking off the West Buttress!" Once again we tried to find our way off the top of El Cap, but within minutes the strange darkness and wind from below returned. This time we were at the lip of the North American Wall.

The top of El Capitan is a peninsula that juts out a full quarter mile into the valley. After many tries and failures to get off the top without walking off a cliff, we gave up and dug a trench beside a tree in the snow. We lay down beside each other to share body heat inside sleeping bags that were little more than thin sheets of nylon over freezing lumps of goose down.

We stayed awake all night, telling stories of other times we had been cold, but never so cold for so long. In the morning the clouds lifted briefly, and we saw our way off the top to the main rim of the valley. By the time we began to parallel the edge, it was snowing again. We never found the summer trail leading to the top of Yosemite Falls as we wallowed through endless fields of sharp manzanita branches that would have been a masochist's delight, were it not for the fact that we felt no pain on our numb skin.

Four hours later, we reached the valley floor. I staggered into a long waiting line of high-heeled women and sport-coated men at the registration desk of Yosemite Lodge. My clothes were badly torn and covered with leaves and blood. A pool of muddy water ran onto the clean floor as the snow and ice inside my pants melted in the heated lobby. By the time I finally checked into a room, my unfrozen pants had become so loose that I had to hold them up with one hand. I'd lost twenty-five pounds in six days.

Tom declined my invitation to share a room or even take a shower. He bundled up on the seat of his old truck and instantly fell asleep. The next morning he was gone, on his way back to Colorado to lay bricks with Layton. It would be his last Yosemite wall climb.

I returned to my family and small automotive business in the city with satisfaction for having finished the climb, but disappointment that climbing the biggest Yosemite wall did not leave me with the kind of fulfillment I had expected. Despite the challenges of the weather, the climbing itself was remarkably unchallenging. I figured that any reasonably fit person could gain enough skill to do El Capitan after just a few months of practice, yet so many very talented climbers remained afraid to attempt it.

I might have given up Yosemite wall climbs then and there, in favor of wilderness climbs I'd begun doing in the High Sierra and Canada, were it not for an invitation from Layton Kor to climb another route on El Capitan the following spring. On that climb, described in chapter five, he confided doubts about the value of climbing one wall after another, year after year, and it became his last major wall climb.

4

The Great White Throne

When Fred Beckey, America's most prolific rock climber, invited me to make the first ascent of a Yosemite-sized wall of sandstone in 1967, I wasn't sure what to think. No big walls had ever been climbed in Zion, and pitons didn't work very well in soft sandstone. After hammering them deeply into cracks where they would have held up a tank in granite, we could pull them out with our fingers. Clean climbing with nuts and camming devices had yet to be developed. When these new tools began to be used in the seventies, sandstone climbing blossomed throughout the Southwest, since the devices were far more secure and caused no damage to the rock.

I had previously sought out only the firmest granite, yet I found the challenge and beauty of spending many days on a big wall in the slickrock landscape of the Southwest too alluring to pass up. Since then I've made dozens of trips through the Southwest to climb, photograph, trail run, and explore remote canyons and valleys.

During the 1960s climbers who wanted to ascend the legendary sandstone towers of the American desert faced almost as many restrictions as travelers wishing to visit Tibet. Access to the best climbs was forbidden by either government agencies or the Navajo tribe, which, after a century of oppression, had begun to reassert itself. Visitors were required to pay a fee to enter reservation lands, and climbing was outlawed on the sacred cliffs of Monument Valley and Shiprock. The 2,000-foot cliffs of Zion Canyon, in southern Utah, were also off limits because of a ruling by the National Park Service. Although roped ascents of the easiest sides of the formations were permitted, attempts on the great walls had been banned; park rangers judged the soft sandstone unsafe for Yosemite-style sieges, during which climbers must live on a wall for days.

Fred Beckey was the most ubiquitous North American climber of the postwar era. The veteran of a thousand routes—mostly first ascents—Fred had a reputation for succeeding through persistence rather than by unusual skill. Difficulties that held back other climbers—trailless approaches, blank headwalls, miserable weather—seemed only to increase his determination. Fred wanted to climb the 2,200-foot northwest face of the Great White Throne, Zion's most famous landmark. He first applied for permission in 1965 and was turned down, but this failed to deter him. Reasoning that bureaucracy

The 2,200-foot Northwest Face of Zion's Great White Throne.

thrives on a constant diet of paper, he began a stream of correspondence to the park service director, the regional office, the superintendent, the chief ranger, assorted secretaries, and undoubtedly a garbage collector or two. Each letter was duly and courteously answered, and Fred in turn would respond, *ad infinitum*. Ultimately, he wore down the agency's resistance, and special permission was granted on the conditions that the climbers maintain radio communication with the ground and have a rescue party available.

In early April of 1967, I joined Fred and Pat Callis in Zion. Our support party consisted of Pat's wife and Harry Woodworth, a friend of mine from California. Their job was to operate the ground radio and to call the Tacoma Mountain Rescue Team if necessary.

We were gratified to find firm rock on the cliffs at the bottom of the canyon. The same rock, Navajo sandstone, is found in varying degrees of hardness throughout the Southwest. During the Permian period, the Zion area was covered by an inland sea. When those waters retreated, one of the world's largest deserts began to form. For millions of years, however, the climate was still wet enough to leach iron oxide from the distant mountains. Great sand dunes covered the landscape, and sedimentary rock formed at their bases as calcium carbonate—lime—mixed with iron oxide to weld grains of sand together. Later on, the climate became drier; rain no longer washed iron oxide from the hills, and only pure carbonate glued the particles together.

The Great White Throne stood before us like a cross-sectional illustration in a textbook. Shaped like a brick standing on end, its lower third was fiery red, and the upper sections were whiter than Yosemite granite. At its base was the tiny Virgin River, which had cut two thousand feet through rock over eons of time. Smaller side streams had carved the other sides of the Throne, creating a monolith that stood independent of the other canyon walls. All the cliffs were striped in white and red bands, and we understood why the tourist brochures proclaimed Zion "Yosemite Valley in Color."

We didn't expect the quality of the rock to match the area's scenic beauty, but we were pleasantly surprised to begin the climb on firm rock with continuous cracks. On the first lead I protected a long lieback with several pitons driven as solidly as possible. Pat had trouble hammering them out, which increased our confidence in the rock's strength. Higher up, I drilled two expansion bolts into crackless rock and found that it took nearly as long as it would have to drill into granite. We came down that evening, leaving fixed ropes up to our high point. The next day we reached a forested ledge in the center of the face late in the day. Since the weather had begun to look bad, we descended again.

A fast-moving cold front passed through that night, covering the mountains with snow, and we awoke to clearing skies in a fairyland of frosted sandcastles. Two days later we started our final push. Several hours of climbing brought us to our old high point, where Fred began leading a vertical crack using direct aid. The character of the rock changed abruptly. Gone was the hard red sandstone, and now we encountered gray rock that crumbled to pieces in our hands. Fred's pitons sank like nails driven into soft bark. When he could no longer make a piton hold his weight, he drilled a hole for an expansion bolt. The quarter-inch drill made a rounded pit big enough for his little finger. "This stuff is like brown sugar," he yelled down. "There's no way we can continue with the equipment we have."

Our afternoon radio call brought a forecast of a series of storms. We descended again and called a council of war. Apparently, the impure lime that held together the white sandstone of the upper cliffs was partly water soluble. The red rock was far more sound to begin with and relatively unaffected by the moisture. Fred had tried the old desert trick of drilled-in angles—driving a three-quarter-inch, sawed-off piton into a quarter-inch drilled hole—but the sharp edges of the piton broke the rock away, and none of us felt safe trusting our lives to such devices. We decided to go home for a few weeks and return when the weather had stabilized and the rock was dry. I would make up a batch of new anchors that could be twisted into drilled holes where the rock was soft. Fred would monitor the weather and call us when the time was right.

I had the opportunity to observe one of Fred's weather checks when he visited my automotive shop shortly after we returned to California. Never one to waste money, Fred used a pay phone to make a toll-free call to directory assistance in southern Utah. When the operator came on, he asked her what the weather was like. She replied that she didn't have that information and offered him the weather number. "No, no, I don't need that," Fred told her. "Just look out your window and tell me if there are any clouds. And is it windy? How warm is it? Operator? Operator?"

The operator hung up, but Fred patiently tried again and again, until he persuaded someone to look out the window. He repeated this process daily, and also checked the newspaper weather maps. It proved to be the worst spring in thirty years. The usual high pressure zone over the Great Basin never became established, and a battery of storms from the Pacific marched continuously inland.

Fred sounded the bugle at last in early May, and we met in Zion under clouds. With a prediction for clearing skies we returned to our high point, where Pat took over the lead on Fred's "brown sugar" pitch. It was overcast and still as Pat climbed Fred's ladder of pitons, but as soon as he ventured onto new ground we witnessed the most sudden change in weather I had ever seen. Pat described his experience:

The sky became dark and from far below came the wailing of a violent wind rushing up the canyon floor, bending the trees and whipping the water of the river. Lightning, thunder, and suddenly the air was full of swirling snow. I stood in my slings as though in a trance, fascinated and frightened by the swiftness with which the storm had transformed our world into a hostile place. The storm seemed to magnify the distance between my belayer and myself, and I felt alone and frail. Meekly, I retreated down the snow-choked crack in a puppet-like response to the beckoning of my companions.

Pat Callis pounds pitons for direct aid into the soft sandstone of the upper face of the Great White Throne.

In a matter of a few minutes, the fierce squall moved on and the sun came out. Pat finished his lead, and I spent several hours working up a straightforward crack with direct aid. Such a stretch could have been climbed in minutes on Yosemite granite. Tap a piton a couple of times; clip in the rope and a sling; stand higher; tap another. Here, each piton placement had to be laboriously prepared. Sometimes I would beat on a piton for several minutes, only to have it fall out loosely in my hand. Then I would drive a bigger one into the slot. At best it took about a hundred hard bashes to drive a two-inch blade into a crack, and we were both exhausted by the end of the day. We rappelled 400 feet and joined Fred in a camp with a fire on a spacious ledge.

The following day we hauled loads of food, equipment, and water up to "Last Chance Ledge," 600 feet from the summit. Above, lay the crux of the route. A curving open book stretched from the summit to about 250 feet above our ledge, but the area in between was overhanging and quite blank. We were gratified, though, to find thin cracks leading up the headwall. Fred and Pat spent the remainder of the day on two painfully slow leads. Fred just reached the open book as alpenglow turned the upper face into the color of a living ember.

We returned to Last Chance Ledge that night, and in the morning I went up to take the first lead. On the overhanging soft rock I had considerable trouble finding decent cracks for pitons. Fred persuaded me to use nylon loops tied around the inch-thick trunk of a decaying juniper that stuck out of a crack, claiming that any tree with greenery on it would hold a man's weight. I put a tie-off loop around the trunk, cautiously pulled on it, attached a sling, and stepped up. At first, the tree held my weight—but just as Fred was telling me that the more I climbed, the more I would learn to trust trees that grew on cliffs, there was a loud snap. The tree broke off, and I flew through the air with it attached to the rope just above me. Fred's belay through a lower piton stopped me after a thirty-foot fall. Since the face was overhanging, I was unhurt, except where the tree slid down the rope and scratched me. I untied it and watched it fall the full distance to the desert floor below.

I tried the same spot again and took another fall when a soft foothold broke. On the third try I slowly drilled my way past the tree stump using lag screws. Three hundred feet of easier climbing put us on a big ledge near the top. The last lead went up steeply for fifteen

Fred Beckey

feet, and we expected it to gradually round off onto the summit. At the top of the little headwall, our climb ended with stunning abruptness. One second I was over the big drop; the next I was walking on a plateau. By sunset we had all of the party and equipment on top.

We had never visited such a mountain summit. Inaccessible except by technical climbing, it was a level island of desert, half a mile wide. It had been reached only a few times by 700 feet of rock climbing from the south side. Park rangers had told us a little about the natural history of this lofty mesa. A lightning fire here a few years back had been allowed to burn itself out, leaving the top more barren than the surrounding high desert plateau. Somehow, several species of mammals frequented the summit. One party had sighted a bobcat. We saw chipmunks during the day and a kangaroo rat at night. The scuffling sound of a larger animal near our fire led us to the tracks of a ringtail cat.

The top of the Throne was quite a liveable place except for the absence of water. Only small rodents, specially adapted to extracting liquid from their food, could live here year-round. We wondered how these animals, residents and visitors alike, had come here. One biologist has theorized that predatory birds carried up any rodents that now live on top. Although none of us had degrees in natural history, our experience led us to distrust complex solutions that ignored the obvious. We suspected that, rather than being airlifted, these animals had simply done as we had—climbed under their own power. Climbers in every part of the world have come back with unusual animal sightings. The yeti tracks found by Eric Shipton in the Himalayan snows have yet to be satisfactorily explained, but there is little doubt, for example, that a large climbing party on Mount Rainier really did watch a black bear casually step onto the summit, turn around, and head back down the miles of crevassed glaciers. We all had seen rats high on Yosemite cliffs, even in the middle of El Capitan where crack systems didn't appear to connect.

In the morning, we set up seven 150-foot ropes to descend the back side. Reaching the main valley would have taken twenty more rappels, so we traversed across the high country toward a highway four miles away. Following heavily used deer trails over exposed sandstone, we could easily imagine a desperado behind every rock. At one spot that would have been perfect for a B-movie ambush, I came across a freshly killed deer and cat tracks as big as my fist angling toward a ravine. A mountain lion had made the kill and was probably watching us from a safe distance, waiting to return when we left.

The transition to civilization was as abrupt as reaching the summit had been. Around a corner, sage and trailless sandstone ran smack into a highway. That evening we were treated to a victory dinner by the only restaurant in the nearest town, and on the way out I passed Fred Beckey using the pay phone. "Anchorage information? What's the weather like up there? No, just look out your window . . ."

5

Layton Kor's Last Wall

This essay first appeared in BEYOND THE VERTICAL, *a 1983 Alpine House book that celebrates the climbing career of Layton Kor in photographs and writings by twenty-two of his partners. After I sent his publisher my essay, Layton wrote me: "I read it over and over again. . . . Your thoughts immediately brought back the flavor of those great times in Yosemite."*

My essay appeared last in the book, introduced by Layton with the following words: "The last major climb I did in Yosemite was the Salathe Wall with Galen Rowell. Galen was an auto mechanic at the time, living in Berkeley. He was an excellent, strong Yosemite climber with muscle to spare. We arranged that Galen would lead all the hard free cracks, and I would lead the hard nailing. As his account of the climb tells, this arrangement was to work out admirably."

In the early 1960's, Layton Kor was the only one of us who really seemed to enjoy climbing the big walls. At the time, Camp Four was inhabited by trailers, dogs, and climbers, with priorities considered in that order by the National Park Service. Layton was an obvious exception among the scrawny group of college dropouts who literally lived in fear of the big walls they so badly wanted to climb.

Steve Roper described their situation best: "Caught between two influential ways of life, i.e., the parental ideal that one must go to college and become successful, and the instinctive desire of all animals to be free and wild and to do what they want, these climbers give the impression that they are waiting, patiently waiting, for some unlikely and ill-defined miracle to transform them from their free yet unhappy and wretched existence into an existence of security, complacency, and pseudo-happiness."

Layton was a definite anomaly. At a time when out-of-state climbers were not accepted by the xenophobic tribe that inhabited Camp Four, he became an instant insider. His presence was so powerful, his personal integrity so obvious, that he escaped most all the infighting and petty jealousies of the times.

Layton and Royal Robbins both stood apart from the social pressures of Camp Four. They managed to get up a tremendous number of climbs while climbers of nearly the

Layton Kor at the top of the Salathe Wall, 1967.

same technical ability sat out their days in camp or made short, relatively insignificant climbs that did nothing to further the Valley's potential as the greatest pure rock climbing area in the world.

The two men had nearly opposite mental attitudes, however, Robbins saw his triumphs as intellectual, the result of applying his imagination to the sport. He willed his body to follow his mind's course, which was freer than that of others, partly because it was not constrained by academia. Robbins had dropped out of school earlier and more decisively than most of the Yosemite crowd. Where he saw a clear course toward self-education, other climbers were still paralyzed by real and imagined ties with academia. Many of them had gone to top colleges, only to drop out of society and attempt to devote their young lives to climbing.

Layton remained apart from the mental agony that characterized Camp Four, making jokes with short punch lines to poke fun at those who took life too seriously. When Robbins made a multi-day first ascent on the north wall of Sentinel Rock, he wrote that the sunrise was "better than Mozart." Layton climbed a new route next to Robbins', returned to Camp Four, and described the sunrise as "not as good as Fats Domino."

When Layton invited me to climb the feared West Face of Sentinel with him in March 1963, I was proud to be chosen as his partner. As we walked to the base, I thought about how I had passed muster by leading a hard jam crack with him a few days before. Or had I?

Walking up the trail, head bent low so as not to be terrified by the shadow of Sentinel looming in the moonlight, I remembered the conversations of other climbers around the fireplace in the Yosemite Lodge lounge: "Robbins is the best in the world. Just look at the routes he's done!"

"Pratt's a better climber."

"But he does his best climbs with guys like Royal. I think Kor's the best. He gets up anything with anybody. He just goes through camp and picks up anyone who can belay him and drags the guy up route after route. Kor wears out partners several times a month."

I had been picked up in Camp Four. Somewhere in the back of my mind I feared death on Sentinel, and I made a mental inventory of my possessions and what my parents would think and who would call them. But I feared not doing Sentinel far more than death. I was absolutely fixed on not turning back, on supporting Layton, on doing my share of leading if he let me.

On the way out of camp I had to skip every third step or so to keep up with Layton's enormous gait. I was 5'8" to his 6'5". His pace remained rapid through the forest, across the thick, frosted grass of a meadow, over a bridge, and up the steep switchbacks of the Four Mile Trail under Sentinel Rock.

I thought of the day before, and how Layton had asked Eric Beck to climb the West Face with him. The West Face was almost virgin territory, unexplored except by a few rock gods like Robbins, Chouinard, and Frost. Everyone dreaded a long jam crack with a twist in it midway up the wall. Beck, not one to be martyred, replied, "Do you wish to see my blood run from the Dogleg Cracks?"

Galen with a full rack of pitons high on the Salathe Wall. Photo: Layton Kor

Beck liked to call life 5.6—just hard enough to need protection, but not very interesting. A year earlier on a cold April morning, Layton had similarly dragged Beck onto Middle Cathedral Rock, where they made an astounding one-day first ascent of a hard Grade IV.

Sweat poured down my brow as I tried to keep up with Layton. I held his tall frame just far enough in front of me to block the view of the narrow face. I planned to walk up to the wall without looking up, and to start climbing without looking down. That way I'd be committed before I got too terrified.

Fear was a normal part of climbing conversation in those days, so I told Layton just how I felt. He said he was scared too, both of the climb and the fact that he felt sick. It was his first mention of not feeling well. We arrived minutes later at the base and uncoiled the ropes. Suddenly Layton said, "We're going back."

As a consolation we climbed Sentinel by the Steck-Salathe Route a few days later. Layton didn't fit through the narrows, an extremely tight chimney. I stood above him, put the rope over my shoulder in a crouch, then stood up with great force whenever he yelled "Pull," at the end of a total exhale.

In June 1967, the man who had asked me to climb the Salathe with him was quite different from the boisterous Layton of the early days. He'd stopped his incessant pacing, but the look of a caged lion was still in his eyes. At the first bivouac on Heart Ledge he told me of his frustration on the Eiger, how the Europeans thought he was a quitter each time he descended thousands of feet to the Kleine Scheidegg Hotel, and how he actually did far more work going up and down than the other climbers who hung heroically in bivouacs each night to the delight of the media.

Then came the accident. A broken fixed rope sent John Harlin to his death. The Germans stripped some of the fixed ropes high on the face and Layton was cut off from the summit team. He watched them finish the climb without him.

Layton expressed no bitterness, but his pain was obvious. He had lost a friend, a climb, and a connection to the other climbers as well.

Layton was quieter than I had ever seen. Occasionally he would rage about, as if to prove that he was his old self, but he acted like a man who had lost the love of his life. I didn't understand what was happening. I expected life in the Valley to go on forever, with no beginning and no end, just people climbing together, joyfully scaring themselves. I saw myself and Layton as part of a flow that I expected to continue as long as I lived.

Layton Kor above Heart Ledge.

Layton had seen a different world, one of finality and agony, and it had changed him. If we had done the Salathe a year before, he would have wanted all the best leads. We would have argued for them until he found a polite excuse to devour as much of the route for himself as possible and a way for me to save face. This time he just wanted to get up the route. He asked if I could lead all the free climbing. The stores were out of my favorite Pivetta Spiders, and the only decent shoes I had were a pair of leather mountain boots I used for High Sierra climbs. I said yes, confident that once on the wall he would take over as usual.

At that time there were many more aid pitches than free pitches. With his extreme reach, Layton could cruise up aid cracks with far fewer placements than I would need. On the lower part of the wall I actually seemed to benefit from wide, stiff boots that fit perfectly in many of the cracks. Higher, however, I stepped into the worst climbing situation of my career.

Far above protection in a 5.9 off-width crack, my foot jammed. When I tried to force it, the rigid sole kinked, slid down, and locked. I pulled, pounded with one free hand, and began to whimper shamelessly. I had a vision of my tibia remaining in the crack after I fell out.

Ten agonizing minutes passed. Layton told me to stop thrashing and hang on. Without a belay he nailed up to me and began hammering on my foot. It wouldn't budge. Finally he figured out that he could move it upward an eighth-inch at a time by hammering first under one side, then under the other. My arms began to feel like two feather pillows, and I doubted I could continue to wriggle up as my foot crept higher with each blow. Finally it came loose. I held on in desperation as Layton clipped me in, lowered me, then led the rest of the pitch.

I was able to continue my share of the leads, and we made good time to our last bivouac just half-a-day below the top on our third night. A few raindrops hit us as we fought for territory on top of a desk-sized ledge. Layton grabbed me in a bear-hug and jokingly said, "We're going to have a lot of fun tonight!"

We wriggled, couldn't get comfortable, and ended up sitting most of the night. Layton talked not of what he was going to do, but of what he wasn't going to do.

He wasn't going to do alpine climbing. He wasn't going to waste another year in Camp Four. The first inkling that I had that he might stop serious climbing altogether was an off-handed comment that the Salathe might be his last wall. His words drifted out of my mind as I watched him unwind at daybreak into slings and begin nailing a head-wall with jerky, rapid motions like a locomotive getting underway.

In the early afternoon I photographed Layton coming over the top. He stayed there—body below the edge, head above—with a look of serenity I had never seen.

6

The South Face of Half Dome

In the summer of 1970, I made the first ascent of this wholly unclimbed and rarely seen side of Half Dome with Warren Harding. We made many attempts over a period of six years, beginning in 1965 after the two of us had climbed the classic Northwest Face together and compared it to the slightly longer face on the opposite side that had far fewer natural cracks and features. Another essay about this climb appeared in THE VERTICAL WORLD OF YOSEMITE, *an anthology of writings by Valley climbers that I edited and published in 1974. That one was written immediately after our rescue in November 1968—the first successful rescue from a major Yosemite wall. This account tells that story and continues on to describe our future attempts and eventual success two years later.*

Half Dome is not really half a dome. From every point in Yosemite Valley one sees the perfect image of its name, but viewed from the rear its true form becomes apparent. Instead of the rounded south wall one expects, there is a steep cliff, slightly higher and far more flawless than the famous front, or northwest, face. Half Dome actually is a whole dome with a character unlike any other dome in America.

Until 1870, geologists argued convincingly that Yosemite's cliffs had been formed by the bottom dropping out of the valley and that Half Dome must have been whole until one side was sheared off in some primeval cataclysm. After John Muir studied Yosemite, however, he wrote that the "Master Builder" had chosen "not the earthquake nor lightning to rend and split asunder . . . but tender snowflowers falling noiselessly eon after eon, the offspring of the sun and the sea." Muir's glacial theory proved closer to the truth than the cataclysmic one, but modern geologists have discovered that the greater part of Half Dome was never glaciated. Ice gave the dome its clean appearance by scouring debris from the base, but its basic form is the result of gradual processes that were well under way before the ice ages.

Half Dome can be likened more accurately to the last joint of a thumb than to the cleaved hemisphere the name suggests. The textures of its sides are as different as a thumbnail and fingerprint. The northwest face is laced with crack systems produced by

The South Face of Half Dome, Tenaya Canyon, and the Yosemite high country from the air in winter.

vertical joints—lines of structural weakness—cast into the granite as it cooled. The incredibly smooth surface of the south face is due to the total absence of such joints. The northwest is shady and streaked with lichens; the south bakes all day in the sun.

I was introduced to the true character of the south face by Warren Harding, who had made first ascents of many of the biggest Yosemite faces. By 1965, the back side of Half Dome, unseen except from trails above the Valley, was the last major unclimbed cliff in the park. Warren invited me to join him on a winter reconnaissance that he hoped would lead to a full-scale attempt on the face later that year. We planned to scout a climbing route by observing where fresh snow demarked cracks and ledges on the face, but after a four-mile walk to the base, we found ourselves staring at a vertical desert. No snow clung to the wall. It was featureless except for a single overhanging arch that ended in blankness.

Though Warren and I suspected that the south face might be the smoothest big cliff in the world, we never imagined that the ascent would ultimately require six attempts spread over five years— more actual climbing time than any of the dozen Himalayan or Alaskan climbs I've taken part in since. It was also an ascent that violated many of mountaineering's unwritten rules about style and technique. Climbs considered classics are rarely the most difficult routes but rather are ones that follow unexpected geologic weaknesses through seemingly impregnable terrain. The climber's joy in a classic first ascent has much in common with that of the research scientist who has made a ground-breaking discovery: it rests chiefly in the "elegance" of finding a simple solution to a complex problem. To preserve this experience, climbers have generally agreed that drilling ladders of bolts is justified only to connect natural weaknesses, not as a major element of an ascent.

Warren never believed in following a prescribed ethic; he thought each person should choose his or her own brand of mountain madness. He had used over 100 bolts on otherwise unclimbable sections of the first route up El Capitan in 1958, and he estimated that 150 or so might be needed on the south face of Half Dome. We both considered this technique justified in making the first route up an especially blank wall.

On the first attempt in June 1966, we were joined by Yvon Chouinard and Chuck Pratt. After a close look at the face's terrible smoothness, Chouinard wanted to withdraw—not because of the difficulty but because of his dislike for the amount of artificial aid that would be needed. He stayed for the first pitch, during which he took a short fall, complained of an injured shoulder, and quit. A week later, with Gary Colliver along, we made another attempt. Gary rappelled down after one bivouac, but Warren and I continued on for three more days, following a crack system on the underside of the Great Arch. We felt as though we were ascending the inside of a 900-foot peaked roof. Our reward for surmounting this obstacle was a two-day wait in a storm, hanging inside an

Above: Warren Harding beneath the top of the Great Arch.
Opposite: Harding placing Bat hooks high on the South Face of Half Dome.

eighteen-inch slot. At the end of this ordeal Warren was still eager to go on, but it was now my turn to plead the cause of retreat on the grounds of a bad cold. We made no further attempts on the south face that year.

Warren's work kept him out of the country for the next year. When he returned, he began designing his now legendary "Bat" equipment—the acronym stands for Basically Absurd Technology—for another go at the south face. Our living quarters would be Bat tents: single-point suspension, one-person, fully enclosed, semi-waterproof hammocks. Our progress over blank rock would be speeded by the use of Bat hooks, tiny steel hooks that could be wedged into holes only one-third the depth required for bolts. Even the name Warren Harding was no longer distinctive enough for the inventor of the Bat gadgets; Warren rechristened himself "Batso."

As we studied photo blow-ups of the face, the ascent began to take on an aura of fantasy. The dome itself resembled a giant bald head; its most obvious features were three closely spaced black spots that we named the Tri-clops Eye. Above this strange triple eye was a zone of darker rock that became known as the Gray Matter. Warren fantasized that the Tri-clops Eye was the entrance to a huge amphitheater in the center of the dome. When we reached it, we would be able to peer inside and see all the gods of the ancients seated around a table. Janus, the two-headed god of doorways, would be on hand to say, "Come in—we've been expecting you!"

In November 1968, after five days of climbing and fifty Bat hooks drilled into flawless rock, Warren and I reached the right-hand eye of the Tri-clops. Our imaginary amphitheater vanished in the face of reality: we found neither cave nor ledge—in fact, barely a dent in the armorplate. The reality proved exciting enough, however. As we set up our Bat tents for yet another night on the face, nature was changing the sets in preparation for a wild scene. Cirrus clouds raced by overhead, billowing cumulus hung over the High Sierra to the east, and a seething, sporadically moving mass of cloud oozed up from the floor of the canyon below. Darkness and the white mass overcame us simultaneously. At midnight we were awakened by raindrops; at four it began snowing, and by dawn everything was white.

Peering outside our Bat tents, we saw that our vertical wall was plastered with a thick layer of wet snow. As the day warmed, we witnessed a striking demonstration of how the Tri-clops were formed. They were focal points for drainage on the upper wall. Soon both of us were in the middle of a temporary waterfall and soaked to the skin. The hours came and went with painful slowness. Our Bat tents were indeed watertight: water seeped in where they touched the rock, but it didn't seep out. Our sleeping bags became thin bags of nylon with lumps of wet goose down coagulated near the bottom.

We punctured holes in the floor of the tents for drainage, shivered continuously, and prayed for sun. At noon we conferred via small walkie-talkies with our support party on the trail to the south of us and were advised that no major storm was forecast. Assuming our weather to be a local disturbance, we decided to wait it out, while our friends walked down to the valley in the rain.

Warren Harding peers out of a Bat tent in the Tri-clops Eye just before the big 1968 storm.

Small avalanches struck us as we hung motionless. Fingers and toes numbed, and our skin became as wrinkled as a prune. After another night and morning passed, the air grew colder and still the storm continued. Warren wanted to stay, but I wanted to descend. I didn't want to die without a fight, and the choices seemed absurdly clear: November snow, hypothermia, and frostbite versus a warm fire and a filet mignon dinner. Finally I yelled over the howling wind, "Warren, we have to go down!"

"We?" came the answer. "I've played that game before and I'm not moving anywhere."

I pouted for a while, and, considering the odds of freezing if I stayed, decided to descend alone. I figured that it would take about ten rappels with a doubled rope which I would have to pull down by one end after each descent in order to set up the following rappel. I said goodbye to Warren and promised him help as soon as I reached the Valley. Disappearing down the wall, I realized that I would need to swing across the face for a few feet in order to reach the next anchor point. Eighty feet below the Tri-clops, however, I discovered that I couldn't move out of the plumb line of the rope. The rock was coated with ice, and further testing showed that the rappel rope was frozen in place at the top and wouldn't pull down.

I was in a far more serious position than the one I had just left above in the Tri-clops Eye. Constant powder avalanches knocked me about and filled my supposedly water-proof clothing. I became infinitely cold, and my thoughts went from down to up, to the comparative safety of the bivouac. My mechanical ascenders wouldn't work on the icy rope; I tied special prusik knots so I could climb the rope. They held, but instead of sliding, they froze in place. My hands became immobile clubs, and I constantly fought blacking out as I neared the top. I yelled up to Warren to tie all our nylon loops together and lower them, but they reached only twenty feet. Dizziness overwhelmed me, and I didn't think I could make it. At long last I reached the loops and climbed the icy rope ladder to the Bat tents. They seemed much warmer—and Warren much smarter—than they had two hours earlier.

Hours later, a faint yell from the base of the face signaled a radio call. For the first time in his life, Warren Harding asked for assistance: "We're not doing very well. We're wet, cold, and a little numb. Get us off if you can!"

Our friends rushed down to the Valley and returned hours later with a terse message: "Helicopter . . . on . . . summit . . . two . . . hours." Then all was silent. Moisture had taken its toll on our cheap electronics.

Hours passed, and the sun set under a mantle of clouds. Suddenly, a helicopter flew by, then made several passes. Our hopes soared, then dropped to a new low as the sky once more grew dark and silent. We knew that the helicopter couldn't fly near the cliff at night, so we concentrated on just surviving the agonizing cold. Long after dark we were startled by a strange, squawking noise. Then a light shone down the cliff, illuminating a man with a headlamp, radio, and heavy clothing being lowered on the end of a rope. Unseen by us, the helicopter had been shuttling people and equipment to the summit of Half Dome. The man on the rope was Royal Robbins, descending like a guardian angel to bring us hot soup, dry parkas and gloves, and a lifeline to the summit. We started to warm

Galen near the top of the wildly overhanging Great Arch. Photo: Warren Harding

up as we climbed the eight-hundred-foot rope with Jumar ascenders, and by midnight we were on top in a spacious tent with dry clothes, warm drinks, and old friends.

Four months later, in March 1969, Warren and I recovered our unique and expensive equipment by climbing the tourist route on the northeast side of the dome and then rappelling down to the Tri-clops Eye. We planned to give the face another go later that spring, but melting snow from the heaviest Sierra winter on record followed by Warren's commitment to a construction project kept us away. Warren notified his boss that he planned to take time off in September to resume our climb, but fate took another nasty turn. On the afternoon of his last day on the job, Warren's thoughts were thousands of feet above the central California highway project. He walked squarely into the path of a fast-moving truck and his leg was crushed. For weeks the doctors didn't know if he would walk again, much less climb. But a series of operations reconnected ligaments and pinned shattered bones, and by December he was hobbling around on crutches and telling me: "May. We'll go back and do it this time."

Joe Faint had helped us recover our gear the previous winter, and he wanted to take part in the next attempt. On a sunny June day, the three of us hiked to the base. I knew

Helicopter on top of Half Dome during the 1968 rescue.

Warren was going to do fine when he limped past me with the heaviest pack. No sooner had we roped up for the first pitch, than the sky turned ominous. It was our fourth storm in four attempts, and Joe began talking about omens. After our first bivouac, the weather was still threatening, and he suddenly wanted nothing more to do with the climb. We descended but were caught in a downpour before we reached the base. "Those who fail to heed the lessons of history are doomed to repeat them," Joe told us with finality. (We learned the next day that he was offering all his climbing equipment for sale.)

Several days later, on a clear morning, Warren and I returned. True to form, it began to snow before we had climbed the four hundred feet of fixed rope back to our previous high point. With undiminished confidence—and plastic covers for our Bat tents—we resolved to wait out the weather. But as I stepped out of my tent to get some food from a haul bag, the sky lit up for a split second before the earth shook. The lightning gave me a strong jolt, sending me reeling against my anchor sling. Once I had recovered my wits, I figured out what had happened. When lightning strikes a cliff, electricity flows along cracks and flaws in the rock, and although we were on the least flawed piece of rock in America, it did have one: the nine-hundred-foot crack in the arch that we were hanging from. The storm continued for two days. We tried to climb anyway, but got soaked in a small waterfall that crossed our route. On day three we descended.

On the first day of our sixth attempt, in July, yet another rainstorm hit us. It stopped as we continued to climb, however, and on the third day we reached our familiar high point in the Tri-clops Eye. The plastic water bottles we had filled in the Merced River four years earlier still dangled from the anchor bolts; we added purifier to the water and drank heartily. The weather stayed blessedly clear for two more days, as we climbed up a two-hundred-foot blank headwall and into the thin cracks of the Gray Matter. On the third night's bivouac we hung our hammocks under a small overhang, not knowing whether we were 100 or 400 feet from the top.

Clouds moved across the sky all night long, and we awoke under total overcast at 5:30 a.m. I began a lead that consisted mainly of drilling and ended in blankness just before noon; then I broke out my Bat tent for the inevitable storm. I didn't want to think about the possibility that we might be forced down again, this close to the top. Raindrops fell as Warren donned his parka and started drilling up a black water streak that we had hoped might be a crack. The rock had a peculiar porcelain-like quality, as though it had been fired in a kiln, and was so hard that drilling took twice the normal time. For hour after hour the light drizzle threatened to worsen. I fed Warren all the rope, and he asked for more. Just as I gave him the last coil tied to my waist, he yelled, "Off belay! I'm up!"

As I climbed the rope to join Warren on the summit, a swift flew between us, unconcerned and unimpressed by our accomplishment. The fact that we had managed to falter our way through Half Dome's southern defenses had done little to change the formidable nature of the face. I remembered John Muir's words of exactly a century earlier, two years before a Scot named George Anderson drilled his way up the gentle slabs where cables now guide visitors: "The dome. . . would hardly be more 'conquered' or spoiled should man be added to her list of visitors. His louder screams and heavier scrambling would not stir a line of her countenance."

7

The Seventh Rifle

This essay first appeared in the 1972 issue of ASCENT, the Sierra Club's annual journal of eclectic mountain writings and photography. Rather than focus on a blow-by-blow description of yet another El Capitan-sized wall climb in a remote area, I emphasized the transitory nature of our human experience in the wilds of Canada in 1971, with comparisons to the not-so-distant past and a disturbing future that had already arrived in a more accessible part of the Bugaboo Range.

A quarter-century after these experiences, I returned on an assignment to cover helicopter hiking in the Bugaboos for an outdoor magazine. I enjoyed the comfort of the Bugaboo Lodge that I had denigrated in this essay and realized that none of the guests would be able to imagine what my first experience was like, exploring a wholly wild range a decade before the climb described here. When we landed helicopters directly beneath the west side of the Howser Towers and unloaded propane-powered barbecues for a final feast, it was driven home to me how much each generation loses as true wilderness recedes.

Dawn arrived, but no sunrise accompanied it. A veil of autumn snow filtered from the sky, settling on the limbs of trees and on the blankets of the men who slept in the clearing. One man was awake, building a fire. Next to him, camouflaged by the white sky and falling snow, lay the fresh skin and feet of a mountain goat; nearby were the dim shapes of ten live horses and three dead grizzly bears. Under the trees lay an assortment of equipment, including a theodolite, several rifles, an immense camera, and an ice axe.

The year was 1910, and the setting was the Bugaboo Mountains of British Columbia. As I watched this imaginary scene out of the past, the sleeping men arose and joined their comrades by the fire. They talked of surveying and picture-taking, and of animals and shots they had missed with their rifles. They spoke of shooting at grouse, squirrels, deer, a bear cub. I wanted to jump in among them and say, "Look here! Have some respect for those animals! They have as much right to be here as you. And killing all those grizzlies—they're becoming scarce, you know."

Tony Qamar on the west face of North Howser Tower, Bugaboo Mountains, British Columbia.

But this was sheer fancy, removed as I was by some sixty years and six thousand feet from that September morning scene. I was also pioneering, halfway up the 3,300-foot face of North Howser Tower. My eyes were focused on a spot in a forested canyon more than a mile below me, and my gaze had not wavered for a long time. I wondered if I was looking at the spot where those men, the first Bugaboo climbers, had camped over half a century before.

At my back was a virgin granite wall; below me was some of the wildest country I had ever seen. In the whole vast panorama I could see no trace of a trail, a road, or other evidence of man, yet the image of that 1910 survey party intruded on my impression of an untouched wilderness. The current of evolution had been interrupted, however slightly, by early visitors with the pioneer ethic and lots of ammunition. More disturbing still was the realization that had I been alive in 1910 and sitting around the campfire with six men, ten horses, dead goats, grizzlies, and grouse, I would not have questioned their ethics. There would have been a seventh rifle leaning against the tree.

I started as though waking from a dream, but I had not been sleeping. It took me a moment to notice that the evening wind had blown out the camp stove at my side, and slowly I became conscious of the other details of my surroundings. I was alone on a ledge, 1,500 feet above a glacier. Above me, my climbing partners, Chris Jones and Tony Qamar, were fixing a rope. The ledge was strewn with equipment: bright blue sleeping bags, red jackets, orange jackets, various colors of polyethylene rain gear, freeze-dried food, Jumar ascenders, a Bleuet stove cartridge, a bolt kit, and two ice axes. Except for the last item, how foreign it all would have seemed to Conrad Kain, the man by my daydream campfire.

The 1910 scene in the clearing I had recalled from a description in Kain's memoirs. The first mountaineer to explore the Bugaboo Range, he was also first to climb the highest of the Howser Towers, the peak whose west face we were now climbing. If Kain were alive today, he would be in his late eighties, about as old as my father. I could hardly believe that people of his generation, born in the age of muskets, before the advent of the automobile, were still alive in the age of the hydrogen bomb and space travel.

Our climb seemed to bridge that time span—it was technical in a limited sense, yet primitive—still wild, but only a long day's walk from civilization. We were carrying a bare minimum of equipment; if we succeeded, it would not be because we had carried all the "right" gear, as many advertisers would have one believe. On the contrary, it was the absence of items often considered essential that enabled us to move quickly in Alpine rather than Himalayan-style climbing in one push without moving up and down fixed ropes between established camps on the face.

It felt satisfying to be doing a big wall in this "ethical" style. But climbing ethics are rarely as lofty as they seem. Often they are merely the ethics of convenience. For instance, British climbers began using nuts for protection, not because they saved the rock from damage—which has become the modern rationale—but because local rock was well-suited to them. Americans began to remove pitons en route, not for montane esthetics, but because they were heavy and costly. A climb like the Howser Tower might require ten pitons on each of thirty rope leads. This would mean carrying 300 pitons that would weigh about 75 pounds and cost about $600. By recovering them as the last man came up, we were able to get by with a collection of only twenty pitons and a few nuts. On the low cliffs of England, or the less technically demanding climbs of the Alps, however, it made perfect sense for the first ascent party to leave its hardware in place. But now we were moving quickly and carrying as little gear as possible because heavy hauling is hard work; because the less time spent, the lower the odds of being caught by a storm, and because keeping my family in a motel in the nearest town was expensive.

Fixed ropes, placing bolts, and step-cutting in ice have all been called unethical by modern climbers. Doing without such techniques is indeed bolder, but it is also faster and less strenuous than the old-fashioned methods. Behind the mask of courage and style, the masters of modern techniques still follow the ethics of convenience.

Our three-man system moved us up the face efficiently, in much the same manner that the jerky, opposing motions inside an engine deliver a constant flow of power in one direction. Compared to the normal alternation of two climbers on a wall, our system allowed for only minimal rest time. After a lead was completed, the second climber jumared up immediately to take over the lead, while the third cleaned the hardware and tied on the loads to be hauled up. Pitch after pitch flashed by as we leapfrogged in this way over mixed terrain.

Chris kicked steps up a snow patch; I slithered over a wet overhang; Tony frisked past an awkward headwall. The holes in the knees of my 69¢ U.S. Air Force Tropical Blues gaped to the wind after a difficult jam crack. By lunch on the second day we couldn't count the pitches we had climbed in the morning. As we nibbled on salami and cheese, a bald eagle glided past and landed on a rock gendarme. Without acknowledging our presence, the great bird soared on, then turned in a circle over the glacier and flew between our towers. An earlier generation might have taken that as an omen; as we watched the bird disappear, I thought of how it was an animal counterpart of a B-52 on a combat mission.

I began to gauge our progress by carving imaginary notches on the ridge of the adjoining South Tower. Following the ridge downward with my eyes until it ended on a snowy shelf, I spotted the black boulder under which forty man-days of food had been cached by an earlier expedition that had been forced off the face by bad weather. Having obtained their permission before our climb, we had feasted on canned bacon, hotcakes, and Trappist Monk-brand jelly—another benefit of coming sixty years after Conrad Kain.

As the sun set under a cloud bank, we traversed the final, knife-edged ridge to the summit. We bivouacked just below the top and found the morning air alarmingly warm. As we descended via the easier east face route, the bergschrund groaned repeatedly, and moments after I reached the glacier and stood clear of the steep wall, a wet-snow avalanche erased my tracks behind me. Tony finished the last rappel and made new tracks rather more quickly.

After pulling out our camp at the base, we reached Boulder Camp, four miles from the roadhead, late in the afternoon. We experienced a strong dose of culture shock, for where generations of climbers had found only wildflowers and waterfalls, we were treated to the sight of two new huts erected by the Alpine Club of Canada—white plastic

Above: Chris Jones on easier ground high on North Howser Tower.

Below: Aerial view of the 3,300-foot west face of North Howser Tower.

hemispheres capped with red ventilators. These dwellings housed a gaggle of guides, cooks, and clients on the main floor, and the basements were occupied by noisy families of super ground squirrels. These rodents, termed "snafflehounds" because of their propensity for theft, had become a master race with a gene pool that changed far more rapidly than under natural conditions. The slow and unwary were shot with a guide's rifle as they free-climbed up the hardest boulders toward food or snaffle-prusiked up ropes toward suspended bags; in consequence, the survivors displayed considerably more speed, cunning, and wits than their primate cohabitants. To our dismay, we learned that the Alpine Club planned to move one of the huts to the west side of the Howser Towers, blasting a platform with dynamite if necessary. A newer, multi-story hut would be built in Boulder Camp.

On a previous trip I had stayed in antique cabins at the roadhead. We now found them gone. Nearby, the new Bugaboo Lodge graced a clearing below the toe of the glacier. The interior proved to be a tasteful blend of the Old World and the modern, yet I felt vaguely uneasy. I picked up a brochure bearing a picture of a helicopter hovering over the Bugaboos and the caption, "Conquer the High Country by Helicopter!" A sign innocently asked us to remove mountain boots before going upstairs, a ritual that defined our arrival in civilization.

My uneasiness gradually became fathomable. Had the Bugaboo Lodge been in town instead of near the foot of the glacier I would have welcomed its comforts with open arms. Now that the climb was over I had little desire to remain in the mountains. Kain had once stayed comfortable for months in the Bugaboo high country by carrying in enough equipment to live simply off the land. We had managed with far less gear while in the mountains, but always at hand was the prospect of a fast return to civilization. This was my "seventh rifle"—not actually leaning against a tree like Kain's but always part of my mental arsenal.

When Kain had returned from the Bugaboos six decades before, he hiked out thirty miles further to reach civilization and wrote in his diary: "It was pleasant to see a covered table once more and a good bed with sheets. But I could not sleep—it was too soft and comfortable."

8

A Winter Traverse of the White Mountains

The White Mountains rise to 14,246 feet above the Owens Valley of Eastern California, the deepest valley in America. They are best known for the Ancient Bristlecone Pine Forest, set aside in 1958 for the protection and study of the world's oldest known living things. During summer visits by road, I became intrigued by the views of the High Sierra through these venerable works of nature's art, individually sculpted by the elements into ever wilder forms over thousands of years.

In 1973, I expressed the idea of skiing the length of the range in winter to some hardy friends who lived directly below the range in Bishop. They said they had already tried such a traverse, but had been stormed off more than once. I joined up with them for a February 1974 attempt with sponsorship from the NATIONAL GEOGRAPHIC. We got the best equipment to survive the extreme winds for which the range is infamous, as well as permission to place a food cache in a high-altitude research station. The trip was so well planned and successful that the NATIONAL GEOGRAPHIC decided not to run the story because of its lack of life-threatening incidents, other than waiting out storms. For me, seeing the stark beauty and remoteness of the range in winter, with constant views of the snowy Sierra as if from an aircraft, rivals any mountain experience I've had in the greater ranges of the world.

The sound began as a low roar far up the canyon. Then it shrieked, groaned, and tore its way out of the sky as if a giant object were falling. Powerless, we braced ourselves for the inevitable shock. Out of the darkness it came: the headlong, invisible charge of the wind. Our tent leaned, twisted, stretched, and flapped, until it seemed no longer anchored to the ground. Then, suddenly, all was still again, except for the whisper of falling snow and the anxious, uneven breathing of the four men inside the tiny shelter.

For four days and five nights we sat out the biggest winter storm of 1974 in our camp at 10,000 feet in the White Mountains of California. Winds of more than 100 miles per hour, we learned later, had ripped the ice from the surface of Crowley Lake twenty miles to the west. During a lull near the end of the storm, we skied to a grove of lodgepole pines in search of wood for a warming and drying fire. We found a healthy tree more than two

Skiing toward Patriarch Grove on the crest of California's White Mountains.

feet in diameter that had been freshly broken—snapped off ten feet above the base. The broken piece, which must have weighed tons, had been carried thirty feet by the wind without leaving a single mark in the snow.

It was February 1974. The four of us were attempting the first winter traverse of the eighty-mile-long crest of the White Mountains. Paralleling the Sierra on the east side of the Owens Valley, these arid mountains have few trees, no lakes, very few fishing streams, and a Great Basin climate, with recorded temperatures reaching as low as –38° F. Pellisier Flat, an eight-mile long plateau at 13,000 feet, freezes every month of the year and has real Arctic tundra. The crest of the range averages over 12,000 feet. Miles of treeless highlands are exposed to relentless west winds. During the Pleistocene epoch, these winds blew so much snow to the lee side of the crest that glaciers formed in cirques above what is now the Nevada desert.

That same wind, not the steepness or the cold, was now our adversary. When we saw the storm coming on the fifth day of our trip, we descended toward timberline to about 10,000 feet. On the crest there was nowhere to hide from the relentless wind—no trees, caves, or natural windbreaks of any kind. At night our survival had depended totally on our four-man tent, which the manufacturer had personally assured us was the most wind-stable on the market. It was cozy inside, but from the outside, especially at night and with a light glowing from within, it seemed as fragile as a butterfly's wing. If the wind had ripped open a seam, we would have been rudely thrust into the Arctic night.

As desolate as these mountains seemed, we were not alone. Although humans had yet to traverse the range in winter, we found surprising evidence of mammals living at this unfriendly altitude. At 13,400 feet we had a rare encounter with a band of five desert bighorn sheep. At nearly 14,000 feet, tracks of coyotes and white-tailed jackrabbits made crazy, interlocking patterns in the snow. On a cache trip up a side canyon, one of us had seen a mountain lion at close range. And most surprising was a lone mustang standing on a bluff—at 10,000 feet in the middle of a blizzard.

Our foursome was a most unlikely group of adventurers: an ex-auto mechanic, two carpenters, and a sewer-line worker. Jay Jensen and George Miller, the two carpenters, lived in Bishop, California, a small town in the Owens Valley at the base of the White Mountains. Both had been introduced to wilderness adventures by Dave Sharp, the sewer-line worker, who had once been their high school teacher. Dave had an enviable winter job—making snow surveys on skis across roadless Sierra passes for the state of California. I was the ex-auto mechanic, and for me the Owens Valley had become a second home. For many years, while I still owned a business in the San Francisco Bay Area, I frequently drove a thousand miles in one weekend to spend time there. However different our backgrounds, we all shared a deep attachment to exploring these desert peaks.

This trip climaxed many earlier visits to the White Mountains. George, Jay, and three friends had previously attempted a winter traverse of the crest in 1973. By the fifth day of that trip, they had covered less than a third of the total distance. Some eighteen inches of new snow had fallen, and they decided to dig a snow cave rather than risk pitching a tent in high wind at 13,200 feet. As usual in the Whites, they found the windblown snow very shallow; they were compelled to dig into a hillside and to build the cave on two levels with

Above: Bristlecone forest in winter, Patriarch Grove.

Below: Dave Sharp checks out a tree freshly broken off and carried thirty feet without a track in the snow. Winds were over 100 mph while we waited out a five-day storm in a tent.

a low roof only two feet thick. At 3 a.m. Jay awoke with a sensation of being smothered. The roof was closer to his head than it had been; there was not enough light to see his hands in front of his eyes, and he began to feel panicky. The cave was starting to collapse. Quickly waking the others, he crawled outside into a 60 mph winds and blizzard conditions. Putting up a tent was out of the question; some of the group couldn't even find their boots. Those who could locate theirs frantically dug a small alcove near the door of the cave, then tried to protect the entrance with the unfolded tent. Spindrift blew steadily inside, and gradually, over a twenty-minute period, the old part of the cave collapsed. The tiny alcove began to fill with snow.

Blindly, they fumbled into boots, gloves, and skis, and took off toward lower elevations. Within a few feet of the cave, George set off a small avalanche but rode it out safely. A few hours later, on descending as far as a subsidiary ridgetop at 11,000 feet, they found clear weather; above them the crest was still in storm. The summits didn't come out of the clouds until fourteen days after they gave up.

The present trip had been planned more carefully. Realizing the seriousness of any equipment failure, we began with new, identical packs, gaiters, skis, bindings, and poles. The exception was George, who insisted on trying thinner, lighter skis. A month before the trip, we had spent three days skiing up a side canyon to place a food cache on the crest. A second cache was flown in to the only permanent residence on the crest of the Whites, the University of California Barcroft Research Laboratory. At 12,470 feet, this facility is the highest year-round dwelling in the United States, supplied for more than half the year only by helicopter. Normally the lab discourages visitors, but we had obtained special permission to leave the cache.

But even careful planning can't anticipate the weather, and when the storm finally ended in its fourth day, we weren't sure how to proceed. The day before the storm began, we had reached the first cache and picked up a six-day supply of food; we now had two days' worth left. Some of us thought we should return to the cache—a full day's round trip—and pick up an extra margin of food for the fifteen-mile journey over the top of White Mountain Peak to the Barcroft lab. George suggested abandoning the effort altogether in favor of taking a ski run into Nevada, and then hitchhiking to a hot spring for a long soak. At last, however, we decided to go for it with only our less-than-ample provisions.

The morning after the storm ended was perfectly clear. In sub-zero temperatures we broke trail through deep snow, and by noon were back on the crest, enjoying the sun and the novelty of a rare windless day. Eye-to-eye with the peaks of the High Sierra across the 11,000-foot chasm of Owens Valley, we seemed to be far above the Earth, skiing in the floating clouds.

To the north, 150 miles away, we could see Mount Rose fading into the horizon. To the south, we looked past Mount Whitney to where the declining skyline of the Sierra merged with desert haze. Late in the day, we arrived at a col at 13,400 feet. It was a strange place where some of the cornices, unlike those at our other camps, faced west instead of east. That evening we discovered why. Violent eddies of wind tried to rip the tent from its moorings, and we barely slept.

Bristlecone pine at sunrise with the High Sierra in the distance.

The next morning was still clear. After an hour's skiing we reached the north ridge of White Mountain Peak—a granite knife-edge plastered with rime ice, with a drop of thousands of feet on either side. Tying our skis to our packs, we inched along the ridge through high winds and blowing snow, arriving at the summit around lunchtime. At 14,246 feet, White Mountain Peak was the highest point of our trip. The snow on the summit pyramid was glazed and wind-packed, and I was very glad to have metal edges on my skis for the steep run down the back side. The first mile went very quickly, but we soon reached an unskiable plateau where thousands of small rocks poked through the shallow snow. Barcroft Lab was still four long miles away. Some of us walked and others kept their skis on, stepping carefully through the rocks, trying to avoid the frequent grating noises. Late in the day, totally out of food and with the sky promising another storm, we finally reached the lab.

Our eleventh night in the mountains was very different from the first ten. We ate steaks, took showers, and walked around in T-shirts, perfectly warm. Upstairs in the two-story Quonset hut, we found the nation's highest library and its highest pool table, both in the same room. The library contained some rare nineteenth-century books on mountaineering and exploration. Reading them there, with the bitter cold blowing against the walls, lent a special significance to the historic adventures. The big storm that had trapped us in our tent had also damaged the power lines to the lab. It was operating on emergency power from an ancient diesel generator. Mechanical failures were frequent; lights flickered, and the generator room took on the appearance of the hold of a leaking ship as hoses burst and workmen waded through a mixture of water and grease.

We spent two days waiting out the new storm: playing pool, reading, repairing ski bases, and watching the lab's resident mice and chickens. Its facilities were amazingly complete. Much high-altitude and space research has taken place in this tiny building which resembles an Antarctic outpost more than it does a California laboratory.

The next morning we were off again, stepping from the warmth of the lab onto snow that squeaked underfoot. For miles we followed treeless highlands, imperceptibly descending a thousand feet toward a gentle meeting with timberline. Not far from here a friend of mine had sat around a fire with a scientist named Edmund Schulman on a cool September evening in the 1950s. As the two men warmed their hands, Schulman pulled a brand from the fire and examined it closely. "1277 to 1283 A.D.," my friend recalls him saying. "This six-year ring pattern never repeats itself." When he had finished studying the flame-blackened ring pattern, he tossed the wood back into the fire. It burned long and hot and even.

Dave Sharp negotiates the wild north ridge of 14,246-foot White Mountain Peak.

Not long after that, Schulman became famous for his discovery that bristlecone pines are the oldest living things in the world. He never enjoyed his fame, however; he died before the publication of his most important work. History remembers Schulman as a practical scientist who proved with numbers and graphs that some bristlecones of the White Mountains are more than 4,000 years old. My friend remembers Schulman as a man who lived in the wilderness of logic, seeking patterns in what appeared random—a man whose thoughts often wandered along loosely structured, mystical pathways. Already ill with heart disease in his forties, Schulman could not fail to note the contrast between the bristlecones and his own tenuous claim on life.

Even in his wildest dreams, however, Schulman never imagined the far-reaching effects of his discovery: that the twisted trees of the White Mountains would bring about a revolution in the study of Old World prehistory. Archaeologists formerly had dated European artifacts by the carbon-14 method; but Schulman's tree-ring chronology disagreed with carbon-14 datings of the wood—sometimes by as much as a thousand years. When the debate was finally settled, the bristlecones had won. A new bristlecone-corrected carbon-14 dating system came into being, which proved that artifacts of European culture were actually older than their supposed Mediterranean progenitors. The theory of cultural diffusion, which held that European culture was derived from the earlier civilizations of Egypt and Mesopotamia, was no longer valid.

Schulman had visited the bristlecones when the snow was gone and the trees rose naked from rocky ground. We saw them in quite a different setting, approaching on skis through an open forest clothed in white. The Patriarch Grove resembled a giant stage occupied by a troupe of frozen dancers; each tree seemed involved in the same motion, caught in pirouette, limbs extended. The west wind had shaped them and coated them with fingers of ice. They seemed to point toward some distant force in the sky.

We camped on the edge of the grove, watching sunrise color ancient bristlecone limbs crimson while a full moon touched the horizon of the distant Sierra. It seemed a sacrilege even to hang our sleeping bags to dry on those trees. Each of us ran his hands over their wood, feeling the sensual warmth of a living thing that was already old in the winters of 1492 and 1776. Compared to these trees, we were a renewable resource.

That evening, sixteen days after we had begun the traverse, we reached Westgard Pass at the south end of the range. Our thoughts were still on the heights as we returned to a much younger world in the valley below.

9

Yosemite's Other Valley

In the late sixties, I came across a most interesting description in John Muir's classic book, THE YOSEMITE: *"The correspondence between Hetch Hetchy walls . . . and those of Yosemite . . . has excited every observer. . . . There is a counterpart of El Capitan that rises sheer and plain to a height of 1,800 feet."*

I had visited Hetch Hetchy years before with my family, but never with a climber's eye. When I made a scouting trip with Joe Faint in 1969, I could hardly believe that a scant fifteen air miles from Yosemite Valley was its smaller counterpart that had never heard the blow of a piton hammer. Over the next three years, I climbed all three of the valley's major walls, each with a different partner.

The tale of Hetch Hetchy Valley resembles a Greek tragedy, but with a place instead of a person at its center. In the beginning there was a perfect half-scale version of Yosemite Valley, discovered by white men a year before they first entered Yosemite itself. While the larger valley soon bathed in international renown, Hetch Hetchy was being prepared for a different kind of bath. It was to become a reservoir. The final scene featured a star-studded cast that included John Muir, Woodrow Wilson, Gifford Pinchot, the Sierra Club, and most of the population of San Francisco.

As in all tragedies, the entire cast made out rather poorly in the end. Between President Wilson's signing of the fateful Raker Act, which permitted the long-fought Hetch Hetchy Dam to be built, and the actual drowning of the valley, both Wilson and Muir had died. Pinchot, undeniably a brilliant and conscientious man, would become infamous in environmental history for his support of a dam within a national park. Although Muir and the Sierra Club lost the battle, the city of San Francisco ended up with only half a plum: through a strange contract, Hetch Hetchy power is sold to the Pacific Gas and Electric Company before it

Joe Faint high up on Wapama Rock, Hetch Hetchy Valley.

reaches the city, and PG&E then delivers it to the consumer—at a huge profit.

Once the dam's work was done, Hetch Hetchy entered a kind of limbo. The promised recreational facilities never appeared on its steep shoreline, and for most of this century it seemed that the valley's sole use—other than for water and power—was as a propaganda tool against future wilderness encroachments. Countless old Sierra Club Bulletins are sprinkled with references to the tragedy:

"What is Hetch Hetchy now? Just another damned artificial lake."

"Hetch Hetchy now isn't worth 35-mm Kodachrome film."

". . . nothing but a narrow body of monotonous water with an ugly shoreline surrounded by stark stone walls."

"Why should anyone go to Hetch Hetchy now?"

Thus admonished, conservationists shunned Hetch Hetchy. Even climbers ignored the place, generally supposing that access to its superb walls was not possible without a boat. Since boats are not allowed on the reservoir, and since swimming with a load of climbing equipment is rather difficult, the "stark stone walls" remained untouched as late as 1969.

In the spring of that year, Joe Faint and I made the first major rock climb in Hetch Hetchy: the 1,400-foot face of Wapama Rock, the counterpart of Yosemite's El Capitan both in appearance and geographical situation. The approach to the face was a surprisingly pleasant two-mile trail that meandered along a wide glacial bench directly below the cliffs. The bench itself seemed little affected by human travel, and the ugly shoreline was not visible unless one walked to the edge of the bench and peered down. Over glacier-scoured granite, through streams, meadows, and wildflowers, the trail delivered us to a point midway between two Yosemite-scale waterfalls. Two days later, we reached the summit of the rock, but the main event of the climb was not reaching the top; it was the change in our attitude toward Hetch Hetchy. We had started the climb with a feeling of who-cares-what-they've-done-to-the-valley-we're-just-going-to-climb-the-rocks; we finished it with a new sense of the meaning of wildness.

It began with a nightmare. We had bivouacked on a sidewalk-width ledge about halfway up the rock. Just before dawn I had been dreaming about sleeping on a ledge and slipping very close to the edge, but I wasn't worried because I was convinced that I was tied in. Then, still in the dream, I rolled over the edge, powerless to do anything but wait for the rope to stop me. It didn't, and I fell through the air for seconds or perhaps minutes. I awoke with a start to find myself in reality very near the edge but reassuringly tight against the anchor rope. I peered through the predawn haze at the imposing cliffs across the valley. Still befuddled, I thought for a moment that I was on a climb in Yosemite Valley. It was the look down that turned my ideas about Hetch Hetchy onto a different track.

There lay the valley floor. But I saw no roads, no buildings, no campfires or smoke; heard no horns, motors, or voices. Below me was only a "narrow body of monotonous water," whereas if I had been in Yosemite Valley, the same site would have been occupied by Curry Village, fifty motor homes, a dozen tour buses, and the Valley tram car—all the dubious benefits of national park status. As the amber glow of the morning sun came creeping down the wall, we ate breakfast on our tiny ledge—a far cry from Yosemite Lodge, with its comfort, hot food, and Early Los Angeles decor. I repeated my environmental catechism: Yosemite was made a national park, and the Valley was saved for posterity; Hetch Hetchy was ruined for all time. It had a hollow ring.

In the spring of 1970, I returned to Hetch Hetchy, eager to repeat the serenely beautiful experience of the previous year. Joe Faint and Chris Jones joined me in an attempt to climb Hetch Hetchy Dome, a longer and smoother face than Wapama Rock. A full day of hard climbing gained us a huge ledge below the unbroken seven-hundred-foot final monolith. Above the ledge the unforgiving glacier-burnished armor plate of the dome was punctuated by only a single system of vertical cracks.

In the morning we awoke to find gray masses of vapor moving past us with great speed. Below, the view of the reservoir flickered as we built a fire and discussed the merits of continuing the climb. Soon, falling snow brought about a prompt decision, and I suggested that the best escape would be to traverse eastward into a large gully. Although it dropped away toward the reservoir in a series of overhanging steps, the gully's upper half appeared to reach the rim of the valley without any obstructions. From the rim we could travel cross-country for several miles until we hit a dirt road leading to the dam.

An hour later we had completed a touchy roped traverse off the ledge and were walking up the gully through thick brush in a heavy snowfall. Several inches of snow covered the ground by the time we reached the rim of the valley, and visibility was less than a hundred feet. After crossing a raging stream, we crashed for hours through deadfall in a trailless forest, trying to convince ourselves that although we had no idea where we were at the moment, we definitely were not lost. Navigating by the moss on cedar trees, we attempted to follow a course parallel to the rim of the valley. We soon reached a place where the horizon was suddenly darker, and the wind seemed to be coming from below instead of in front of us. I threw a rock and counted to eight before it hit with a splash; at least we now knew the location of the reservoir. After an hour more of hiking, we reached the roadhead, bedraggled and ready to embrace civilization.

Chris and I returned the following weekend, while Joe went climbing in Yosemite Valley instead. The intervening week had done nothing to lessen the difficulties of the lower section, and once again it took us a full day to reach the ledge at the end of the eleventh pitch. The fifth pitch is worth singling out. It followed a crack for a full 150 feet of consistent 5.8 and 5.9 climbing with a 5.10 stretch at the finish. The lower half consists of a series of vertical lie-backs and hand-jams; the upper section is a continuous four-inch wide crack, up which I wriggled with all the elegance of a dog chasing a cat through a storm drain.

Chris, who was not feeling well, relinquished the next lead to me, and after what seemed like an eternity of exhausting direct-aid climbing, we finally reached the commodious ledge midway up the face. The spot offered so many amenities—room to

stretch our legs, a natural spring, firewood—that our night could hardly be called a bivouac. We barbecued steaks over a roaring fire and bedded down on soft ground.

In the middle of the night I was awakened suddenly; something was tugging at the down jacket under my head. I turned on the flashlight and saw a ringtail cat calmly eating my Juicy Fruit gum-wrapper, foil and all. Ringtails are supposed to be shy animals, yet this fellow sat munching on my rations with the gall of an alley cat. As we stared at each other, the light from my flashlight reflecting in his eyes, I wondered which one of us was the intruder. I could perceive no fear in his steady gaze, but rather the calm assurance of a creature well in control of the situation. I began to resent his self-possession and looked around for something to throw at my uninvited guest. When I glanced back, he was gone into the night.

Before sunrise, Chris informed me that he felt much worse and might not be able to continue the climb. That he chose in the end to go on showed an extraordinary amount of determination. Although Chris is not a strong free-climber, he has a long record of major ascents in mountain ranges all over the world, demonstrating that more complex factors are involved in making big climbs than merely the technical ability to lead the hardest pitches. I felt a heavy weight on my shoulders that clear, calm morning. Climbing with someone who is ill is as difficult as solo climbing, but has the extra element of responsibility for another's welfare. I watched anxiously as Chris winced at the light from the sun as he followed a pendulum several leads above the ledge.

The climbing was mostly direct-aid in a single crack, which gradually dwindled into a water streak. Before it ran out, we reached a slanting horizontal ramp. With a bolt for protection, I face-climbed across the crackless ramp, feeling quite proud of my route-finding ability until I arrived at the end, where an unexpected blank headwall led to a marginal crack. By the end of the lead, I had placed two Bat hooks, driven several shaky pitons, taken a short fall, skinned an elbow, and bruised an ego. Two bolts at the start of the next pitch gave me the confidence to free climb into a dihedral which led us to a ledge near the summit. Late in the afternoon, we unroped at last and began walking up the inclined slabs to the crest of the dome. I felt happy and relieved; Chris was quiet and miserable. He was to spend the next week in bed recovering.

The walk back to our car provided a sharp contrast to our earlier retreat. Spring had arrived, and the greenness of life was everywhere. Only an occasional spot of snow in the shade of a log reminded us of the intense storm only a week before. Wildflowers carpeted clearings in the forest, and rivulets cascaded down every cliff. Hetch Hetchy had been trodden by people for more than a century, but on that afternoon we felt as though we had discovered it for the first time.

Chris Jones and Joe Faint temporarily lost in the forest above the rim of Hetch Hetchy Valley during a snow storm.

10

The Moose's Tooth

On my first trip to Alaska, I made a serious attempt on a great, unclimbed face of the Moose's Tooth near Mount McKinley. Though we failed, I had a chance to climb with some of the best climbers of my generation and to see how well they handled adversity. Visiting such a wild, alpine face in a huge uninhabited area was a fantastic wilderness experience, regardless of whether I reached the summit. I never forgot that lesson, and in years to come returned to Alaska and ventured out to the Himalaya firmly convinced that so long as all returned home alive and well, any extended visit to the wilds was time well spent.

Talkeetna, Alaska. Fifty-three residents, two airstrips, hundreds of dogs, and two bush pilots who refused to speak to each other. At ten in the morning, the main street looked like a typical western town of the 1950s: two-lane road, dirt shoulders, neon yet to come. Outside the town bar sat two young men—one wearing Levi's, a sweatshirt, and a crewcut; the other in a Hell's Angel-style leather vest, cowboy hat, and gun belt. A wizened, almost blind Indian, leaning heavily on his cane, rattled the door of the closed tavern. Age, alcohol, and twenty hours of Alaskan daylight had fogged his awareness of time. The bar did not open for many hours.

Two young men carrying rifles walked in lockstep down the main street, as a dusty Winnebago creaked over chuckholes not ten feet away. The driver of the Winnebago stared straight ahead at the pavement, ignoring the young men, who returned the compliment. The motorhome rumbled on another hundred yards to a dead end, where it turned around and headed back and out of town without stopping. Through the large, dusty windshield the motionless head of the driver seemed to form the pupil of a cyclopean, myopic eye, apparently unable to focus on anything but the road before it.

The true focus of the town was not the main street, however, but the dirt airstrip that led from the door of the tavern straight toward the river. A man dressed entirely in buckskin stood at the town end of the strip, negotiating with a pilot to airlift him with his dog

Jim McCarthy and Yvon Chouinard on the morning after a hammock bivouac on the east face of the Moose's Tooth.

team to a remote lake. He wanted a one-way fare; he had no plans for coming out. A prospector with tomorrow in his eyes approached me with a chunk of rusty metamorphic rock. "Gold," he said with evangelical emphasis. "It assays at over $200 a ton, but I've got to fly it out. I'd be rich if there was a road."

On the other side of the airstrip a chattering group of Japanese men wearing double boots and bright parkas busily crammed an enormous pile of equipment into a new Dodge van. In the distance, far beyond the town, beyond the river, and beyond the spruce forests, the Alaska Range loomed above the horizon. A forty-minute plane ride would soon transport us into an ice-age scene. As if traveling through a time warp, we would suddenly enter a Yosemite Valley of the Pleistocene, but one with a larger landscape and much higher rock walls, one where glaciers more than forty-miles long plunged from alpine heights deep into wooded lowlands.

Our flight was delayed by a small oversight in logistics. Four of us—Jim McCarthy, Yvon Chouinard, Sandy Bill, and I—had come from different corners of the country to attempt the unclimbed 4,500-foot granite face of the Moose's Tooth. Jim McCarthy had organized the expedition in New York. Since Yvon Chouinard owned a company that manufactured the best climbing hardware available, Jim had asked him to supply the expedition's pitons, carabiners, and chocks. Unfortunately, Jim's phone message failed to reach Yvon, so we met in Talkeetna with no equipment. It seemed that our climb might be over before it could start until Cliff Hudson, our bush pilot, located an expedition that had just returned from another technical climb. When he asked if they would loan their gear to an expedition that included Chouinard himself, they looked at their Chouinard equipment and had a good laugh.

Jim McCarthy was the leader of our obstinate quest to climb an Alaskan big wall. Although many snow and ice climbs of great difficulty had been made in the Alaska Range, none of its fabulous sheer cliffs had ever been climbed. A year earlier, in 1971, Jim had reached the 1,800-foot level on the Moose's Tooth with Chris Bonington, Tom Frost, and Sandy Bill before a twenty-day storm drove the party back down. Only he and Sandy were returning. Sandy and Jim had also climbed together on the first ascent of the face of Lotus Flower Tower in Canada; they were well-matched for another go on the Moose's Tooth.

Chouinard, an incurable, grumbling romantic who had climbed a greater number of difficult Alpine routes than any other American of his time, seemed at the moment to be going through a phase in which direct-aid climbing and long routes failed to hold his interest. While the rest of us discussed the Alaskan weather, Yvon kept talking about the surf in Southern California, but we hoped that once on the wall he would make the same remarkable effort that had gotten him up "impossible" faces all over the world. Yvon also gave us pause by asserting that a fast, light party could climb the Moose's Tooth in four days or less. Jim's idea of how to climb such a face was more conventional, and I concurred; I was terrified by the unknowns of Alaskan conditions. I wanted to bring

A bush pilot flies beneath Mount McKinley past the east face of the Moose's Tooth.

hardhats, lot of wool, a fifteen-day supply of food, and waterproof hammocks. Chiefly, I wanted to stay alive at all costs.

The morning after the equipment impasse was settled, we flew up the Buckskin Glacier toward the Tooth. The toe of the glacier was covered with debris, but as we moved from temperate zones into the Arctic world, its surface became pure white, broken only by crevasses and an unexpected set of animal tracks that led tens of miles beyond the last timber. Cliff explained that they were wolverine tracks, but he could think of no reason why the animal would venture up the glacier—except that wolverines are obstinate creatures. He glanced at us and smiled.

The Cessna 185 landed in a glacial cul-de-sac directly underneath the great cliff. We set up a basecamp tent and spent the night listening to avalanches crash around us. The walls blocked out most of the sky in all directions; we had the impression that we were looking up from inside a well. We feared that without a view of the horizon, predicting the weather would be impossible.

The very next morning we began the climb on wet, decomposing rock. Forty feet up the first pitch a huge piece of ice was plastered to the cliff, as though an oversized, half-cooked pancake had been thrown against it. Beyond the ice patch, a single crack, aiming for the sky, split the monolith. We had climbed for twelve hours when it began to storm, and we set up our first bivouac on small ledges a thousand feet above the base. All of us used hammocks except Yvon, who decided to test his company's newest rain gear by bivouacking on a ledge less than a foot wide. The rain stopped just after dawn. Jim, Sandy, and I assembled together on a ledge about fifty feet above Yvon, who expounded excessively on the fact that he had stayed totally dry. I began free climbing an intricate traverse that Tom Frost had figured out the previous year. Jim, who was to follow, had contracted a mild case of dysentery from bad water in the Yukon. All night he had held back his bowels until they developed the urgency and capacity of a ready-mix truck caught in a traffic jam; as soon as I left the ledge, he defecated onto a tattered parka left behind by the previous year's party. When it came time to follow my lead Jim tied the parka in a knot and threw it off the wall. This unlovely package opened in mid-air, raining its contents on the hapless Yvon, who instantly regretted his decision to spend the night below us.

As Jim started climbing, he began to feel worse. His face took on a cadaverous hue, and he vomited uncontrollably. I expected him to voice doubt over his ability to make the final, unprotected traverse, but he said nothing. I held my breath as he began a long, difficult diagonal up wet, rotten rock. He never faltered; his body had practiced hard face climbing for so many years that he seemed to move by instinct. I never saw anyone move with such precision while feeling so poorly.

The quality of the rock continued to deteriorate as we climbed higher. On the first lead Yvon had used skyhooks on small flakes; by the fifteenth pitch I could remove any

Just after dawn, Jim McCarthy jumars quickly past a frozen snow patch plastered on the east face.

piton without a hammer and crumble the rock into gravel with my bare hands. Rockfall, too, became a serious problem. Missiles falling of their own accord from far above as well as rocks loosened by the leaders rained down on us. We all had brought hardhats except, as usual, Yvon, who claimed not to believe in them. After a particularly heavy barrage, however, he underwent a sudden religious conversion, and we began a ritual of reserving the three hardhats for the lower climbers. The unprotected leader was compelled to test his reflexes against the natural rockfall.

On the second evening we reached the first real bivouac spot on the wall, a sandy penthouse with accommodations for four. Although the ledge was wide, with enticing areas of level gravel that made perfect beds, that gravel could have come only from rockfall. If proof of the hazard were needed, two foam pads left behind during the previous attempt were almost completely covered by granite debris. I opted for another night in my hammock, in order to present as small a target as possible.

If our bivouac ledge was less than entirely safe, it had compensatory attractions. We were surrounded by bold beauty. In the distance was a perfect granite cirque capped with hanging ice. The monochromatic landscape of shades of gray was broken by a wreath of pink and green moss campion clinging to the face at the back of the ledge. It seemed magical that a single plant was able to survive in such harsh conditions. One pitch above the ledge we came upon a great hole in the granite; inside were fist-sized crystals of quartz, tourmaline, and albite. We gathered a few loose ones and stuffed them into our packs.

In the morning Sandy and Yvon began leading above our high point. Jim waited on the ledge, still feeling under the weather but determined not to retreat. Sandy led a section of excellent rock; then Yvon encountered the worst rock of the climb—so crumbling that he had to begin drilling expansion bolts next to a rotten crack that wouldn't hold pitons. I could sense Yvon's frustration. He had finally hit his alpine stride and was eager to complete the route, but the terrain wouldn't permit him to advance. We watched him rappel down without completing the lead and, shivering in an icy rain that had just begun, we held a council of war.

Sandy thought the route should be pushed and was against going down, saying that he'd climbed through worse conditions in the Alps. Jim wanted to descend because of his illness. Yvon wanted to descend because the rock was so poor that he could not recommend the climb to anyone; ergo, it was not worth pursuing. I was developing the same symptoms of nausea and diarrhea that Jim had. I was willing to stay if the majority went that way, but my heart was no longer in the climb. The issue was soon decided: we descended.

The twenty rappels down to the glacier lasted well into the night. When the ordeal finally was over, we gazed up at what we had thought would be the Mona Lisa of the alpine world. From this distance she looked beautiful, but we had touched her flesh and found gangrene. In the years that followed our attempts, several other parties tried the east face of the Moose's Tooth; each one convinced, as we were, that reality of the face must surpass the descriptions brought back by previous expeditions. None even reached our old high point. Perhaps they learned their lesson more quickly than we did. I went back to try the face a second time in May 1973, hoping that clear weather and freezing conditions would make the route feasible, but one flight past the face revealed it to be dangerously plastered with snow and hopelessly out of condition. I led the expedition to within six hundred feet of the summit by a route from the opposite side, only to be stopped by an overhanging wall of rock even more rotten than that on the east face.

"Granite," according to a British encyclopedia of mountaineering, "varies from place to place but is always sound to climb upon and a great favorite with climbers." We had learned that all things in the wilderness are relative; a granite face does not always offer superb climbing, any more than skill and training guarantee success. In a larger sense, though, our failure on the Moose's Tooth only enhanced the mysterious attraction of the place, and it firmed my resolve to return to the great walls of the Alaska Range.

Nine years after our attempt, the east face of the Moose's Tooth was finally climbed, but not by the granite wall that we had attempted. Jim Bridwell and Mugs Stump, two of the finest climbers of their generation, chose exactly the conditions we had rejected in 1973 to ascend a system of ice-plastered gullies and slabs to the right of the still-unclimbed main wall. Their four-day Alpine-style push in March ushered in a new era of extreme Alaskan climbs in winter conditions.

Yvon Chouinard contemplating whether or not to continue following a bivouac beneath a section of rotten rock halfway up the east face.

11

Free Climbing Keeler Needle

I was asked to write this essay for a non-climbing audience of armchair adventurers by the editors of MARIAH, *a slick 1970s magazine that soon bought out and merged with a struggling similar publication called* OUTSIDE. *The editors were wary of writings by real adventurers, who tended to understate exciting moments and assume knowledge over the heads of most readers. Since I had recently done a* NATIONAL GEOGRAPHIC *cover story that integrated an account of a cutting-edge rock climb with the nuts and bolts of how it's done and the environmental ethics of the rapidly-evolving sport,* MARIAH'S *editors asked me to do something similar about a new climb of my choice.*

I chose Keeler Needle in the Eastern Sierra for many reasons. Its 1,800-foot east face had yet to be free-climbed without using pitons for direct aid, and the extremely spectacular spire is part of the massif of the highest peak in the contiguous forty-eight states. Mentioning an unroped climb of the nearby 1931 classic route up the east face of 14,496-foot Mount Whitney would give readers a comparison of the difference between free climbing with ropes and free-solo climbing without them. Also, I could compare our summer attempt to free-climb the Needle with my first winter ascent of the same face a few years earlier—a chilly epic with multiple bivouacs in hammocks.

That climb, the second ascent of the face in 1972, included Warren Harding, who had made the first ascent twelve years earlier. No other ascents had been made in the intervening years

---

It was my lead. I climbed thirty feet to the base of a smooth bulge where I stepped up and reached for a sloping handhold. My hand groped through loose gravel on the unseen shelf. Only ten feet separated me from easier going above, and I tried the same move again and again. No one had ever climbed those ten feet, and I realized then that neither would I.

I had been trying to bypass an overhang, and I was torn between two choices: relinquish the lead to Chris Vandiver, a better free climber than me, or attempt another way. I refused to consider a possible third choice: using direct aid placed in the rock to get past the difficult section. Why? Because three of us were attempting to free climb a rock face on Keeler Needle that had never been climbed without resorting to direct aid. It was just a game with us, but we were trying to play by the rules.

Wild ledge high on the east face of Keeler Needle.

For decades, the sport of rock climbing had been split into two factions: free climbers specialized in short, hard routes; big wall climbers concentrated on long but technically easier routes. Wall climbs were traditionally approached with different equipment and ethics than shorter free climbs. In the past, climbers recognized the stylistic purity of the short climbs but considered free-climbing tactics impractical on the long walls.

Was it possible to break these conventions? We thought so. The overhanging east face of Washington Column in Yosemite had already been climbed entirely free and renamed Astroman. The Diamond, a big wall on 14,225-foot Longs Peak in Colorado, had also been free climbed recently for the first time. Chris Vandiver and I had done a free ascent of the west face of Mount Conness, the sheerest wall in the High Sierra, only two months before. After that ascent Chris had asked me if I thought Keeler would also"go free." I wasn't sure, having made the first winter ascent of the route with heavy equipment and liberal use of direct aid over three days in 1972. Chris's enthusiasm for the project proved infectious, not only to me but to Gordon Wiltsie, the talented High Sierra climber who in August 1976 became the third member of our mini-expedition.

Just two weeks earlier, we had retreated from the same obstacle that was stopping us now: the tightest spot on this section of the rock tower, a slightly lower satellite of 14,496-foot Mount Whitney in the High Sierra. I had tried a different way, an overhang normally climbed with pitons for direct aid. I thought at the time about bypassing the overhang to the left, but it was too late on a cold and windy day. My fingers grew numb, the rock was rotten in critical places, and I got scared. We descended and spent that night below the face, hoping for warm, clear weather in the morning.

Dawn brought an incredible display of alpenglow, turning Keeler Needle's granite to gold. Every crack and rib was highlighted in bold relief. For several minutes we watched in awe until the colors suddenly disappeared. A hole in the clouds had closed, and the landscape took on the dismal gray of the sky. Our hopes for the climb wavered with the sunrise and were extinguished completely when snowflakes began to fall a few minutes later. We had no desire to attempt difficult free climbing during a snowstorm.

All that morning, while our gear remained 150 feet up the face, we lay in our sleeping bags biding our time until the weather improved. Voices wafted out of the mist from the east face of Mount Whitney, the cliff next to the Needle. Two climbers we had passed on the trail were up there in the storm. Heavily laden with pitons, hard hats, down parkas, and bulky mountain boots, they could survive many days on the mountain if the need arose.

When the storm showed no sign of abating by noon, we decided to go home and return in better weather. Chris waited in camp while Gordon and I headed toward the Needle to retrieve our equipment. An hour later, as the two of us were descending with the gear, we talked about the nearby east face of Mount Whitney. Gordon said,"I'd like to climb it some day, I've never done it before."

"How about now?" I hinted.

"You're kidding!" he replied."It's 2:30 in the afternoon, and it's snowing."

"No," I said."I'm serious. If we climb unroped we can be up and down in just a few hours. We can handle the difficulties, even in this weather."

Just then we heard voices above: the other climbers were still on the route eight hours after they had started. Gordon looked worried, no doubt expecting to be benighted on the peak, but his adventurous spirit won out. "Okay," he assented, "let's try it." Chris declined to join us because he had recently climbed another route on the same face. As we began the climb, Gordon experienced mixed emotions; he enjoyed the freedom of climbing unencumbered, but missed the safety of the rope. Both of us compensated for the lack of security by increased alertness. We checked and rechecked potentially loose rocks and placed our fingers and toes with far more conscious care than when backed up by the umbilical cord of a rope.

Just below the summit we caught up with the other two climbers, who were outfitted like models in a mountaineering catalog. Seeing that we were unroped, they asked if we had climbed to the top of Whitney by the foot trail and then scrambled down for a look over the sheer face. When we answered no, they asked where and when we had started our climb. On learning that we had left the lake at the base of the climb only an hour and forty minutes before, they expressed amazement at the speed of our ascent. Actually, it was not so remarkable. The 1931 first ascent party—four men wearing tennis shoes—had climbed Whitney's east face in three hours and fifteen minutes, unroped much of the way. Their leader was Robert L. M. Underhill, a famous figure in North American climbing history, who introduced technical rock techniques to both the Grand Tetons and the Sierra. In his account of that ascent Underhill predicted," I believe a good climbing party that knew the route could ascend in something like half the time we required." By this standard, our ascent was three minutes slow.

Gordon was ecstatic when we reached the summit. We were able to relax; there was enough daylight left for us to descend to the road before dark. With no ropes or hardware to carry, the hike would be pleasant rather than laborious. In many ways, our spur-of-the-moment Whitney climb shared the same spirit as our plans for Keeler Needle. Although we would use ropes for safety on the Needle because of the greater difficulties involved, we would avoid engineering our way up the cliff. Our style would be more akin to that of Sierra climbers of the 1930s than to that of present day big wall climbers, and our accomplishment, if we succeeded, would mean more than just an isolated"first free ascent." This effort was part of a larger trend to merge the two disciplines of wall climbing and free climbing. For years each specialty had gone its own way, but we believed that the guiding principle of simplicity in mountaineering must eventually bring them together again.

Two weeks after our Whitney romp, Chris, Gordon, and I were back on Keeler Needle for another go. I climbed to the base of the overhang that had scared me on the first attempt and found that nothing had changed. The wall still swelled ominously overhead, and the single crack was filled with loose rock. My attitude, however, was different: I knew that I could not climb the only alternate route. After carefully planning my intended moves, I climbed six feet toward the overhang and came back down; then I repeated the sequence, wanting to memorize this section so I could save my strength for the more difficult area above.

After a long rest, I yelled down to Chris, "Okay, I'm going for it!" He fed out the safety rope as I climbed upward. I expected each move to stop me, to force me to try a different technique, or worse, to prove so difficult that I would fall—but a minute later the crux was over, and I was resting in a wide crack before the final, easier moves at the lip of the overhang.

Most good rock climbers could have climbed the overhang as I did, without resorting to direct aid. The hardest move was 5.10, a rating near the top of the scale of difficulty but today commonplace in most rock climbing areas. The main reason no one previously had free climbed that section of Keeler Needle was that no one had approached the route as an ordinary rock climb. The east face of Keeler Needle had always been considered a"big wall," a multi-day climb requiring direct aid. Moreover, the face was an alpine wall where most climbers used gloves and stiff, heavy boots because of cold weather and snow.

Although we hadn't started until noon, we easily climbed more than half the face before dark. The absence of heavier equipment speeded our progress and enhanced the quality of the climb in countless subtle ways. I remembered one continuously difficult crack where I had used several direct-aid pitons in winter and watched with pleasure as Chris climbed the same pitch with hardly a break in motion. His thin shoes jammed perfectly in the narrow crack where earlier my mountain boots had grated on the outside edges. In spots where I had hung from pitons to rest, Chris stood comfortably with one foot jammed in the crack and the other on a tiny edge outside. He would climb ten or fifteen feet, pause to place a nut in the crack, attach it to his rope with a carabiner for safety, then climb another section.

We reached a bivouac ledge at sunset and prepared for the night as we had each done many times before. We strung a rope across the ledge and attached it to several anchors in the rock, then each of us tied himself in. Darkness came quickly, but sleep eluded us for hours. We talked about climbs and friends we had in common; and when we tired of that, we gazed silently at the lights in the town of Lone Pine, fifteen air miles and 10,000 feet below our airy perch. We felt far removed from the world of hot sagebrush plains and civilization. Our own world was condensed into some nine hundred feet of granite, the distance between us and the summit.

In the cool, clear dawn, Chris, Gordon, and I sat huddled together, waiting for the sun's warmth to flow into us before we resumed climbing. After a cold breakfast, we packed all our gear into two medium-sized packs—quite a departure from most big wall climbs where equipment must be laboriously hauled in huge bags up the wall. I felt almost guilty that the climb had required so little effort thus far. Spared both the drudgery of hauling heavy loads and the tedious work of hammering out long rows of direct-aid pitons, we were free to absorb the great beauty of Keeler Needle's setting. We were limited only by the extent of our skills rather than by logistical complexities.

Our test of those skills came very soon. I led an easy pitch to the base of a long corner. The next lead was Chris's, whose talent as a free climber is almost overshadowed by his exceptional control in tight situations. Because his movements are consistently smooth, many people who have seen him climb have found it impossible to tell where the real difficulties lie. I had climbed with him often and knew the telltale signs.

Overleaf: Alpenglow at dawn on the east faces of Keeler Needle and Mount Whitney.
Opposite: Gordon Wiltsie jumars with a pack high on Keeler Needle.

Chris climbed the first forty feet of the corner with long, fluid motions, stopping occasionally to place a nut in the crack for safety. Reaching a spot where the crack was about six inches wide and overhanging, he found a row of expansion bolts on the wall next to the crack, marking where previous parties had clipped nylon ladders to the bolts for direct aid. Chris wriggled halfway into the crack, which was too narrow for his chest and too wide for a fist or knee-jam. At low elevations many climbers vigorously wriggle up such cracks, but to do so at 14,000 feet would almost certainly result in fatigue and a fall. Chris reduced his efforts to tiny movements that gained him only an inch at a time. His eyes brightened, and his expression grew intense as he used all his skill to keep from sliding out of the crack.

I watched him from the ledge below. Although his movements looked less spectacular than on many of the easier pitches we had already climbed, I knew that this impression was deceptive. Chris was making an incredible effort, but it was taking place inside—in the interaction of mind and body. Only he knew how closely he was approaching his limits.

Chris gained a large foothold and took a long rest, and when he resumed climbing, his movements once again were easy and graceful. Although the greatest difficulties were over, we weren't yet sure that the climb was in the bag. I couldn't remember every move from my last climb, but I did recall a long section of direct aid quite near the top. Throughout the rest of the morning the three of us alternated leads up the face, encountering only moderate difficulties. When we reached the place where I had used direct aid on my winter ascent, we saw an obvious bypass to the difficulties: a system of cracks that in winter had been plastered with snow and unusable. Now, however, Chris quickly traversed to the very prow of the Needle where an absurdly positioned ledge interrupted a curtain of granite that dropped in a single sweep. It looked like a window washer's scaffold on the side of a skyscraper.

The difficulties were nearly over; even in winter we had free climbed most of the route above. The final pitches went quickly, and shortly after noon we reached the summit. It was, as always, a satisfying moment, but far more satisfying was the knowledge that we had accomplished our goal of climbing the big wall without big wall techniques. We lingered only a few moments, then coiled our ropes, stuffed them into our packs, and descended a few hundred feet to a trail, where we merged unnoticed with the queue of weekend hikers heading for the summit of Mount Whitney.

From the summit we dropped down a snow gully named "The Mountaineer's Route" into the peak's afternoon shadow. Most shadows move as slowly as the hands of a clock, but Whitney's shadow chased us through the timberline paradise faster than we could scramble. It skimmed down cliff bands and boulders, slowing only for level sections of meadow and forest, until, like us, it traveled across the hot desert floor toward town.

Warren Harding on the 1972 first winter ascent of the face of Keeler Needle.
He also made the first ascent of the face in 1960.

12

Skiing the High Desert

After skiing the length of the White Mountains in 1974, I became intrigued with the idea of exploring the crests of other Great Basin ranges in winter. Snow and ice transforms these desert peaks from barren, rocky ridges into Alpine wonderlands where bristlecone pines are flagged with rime ice and horizons are so open and vast that we could see blue sky through the legs of wild mustangs running across the high plateaus.

Beneath Wheeler Peak, now in Great Basin National Park, I searched out the remnants of the world's oldest known living thing, a 4,900-year-old bristlecone cut down alive in 1964 with a chain saw to measure its age. A few scientists and forest rangers knew what had happened, but my account in a general article on bristlecones published ten years later in the SIERRA CLUB BULLETIN *(now* SIERRA *magazine) turned out to be the first public knowledge of the destruction. The day after publication, my phone rang off the hook from the full gamut of major media—*THE NEW YORK TIMES, NBC NEWS, THE NATIONAL ENQUIRER*—hot on the scent of yet another American tragedy.*

The Great Basin extends from the crest of California's Sierra Nevada to the Rocky Mountains; it was so named by explorer John C. Frémont because it has no drainage to the sea. All waters in this vast region eventually run into alkaline "sinks" in the desert. Astronauts have reported that from outer space the Great Basin looks like a brown field sprinkled with giant caterpillars crawling south. The caterpillars are desert mountain ranges, more than fifty of which reach over 9,000 feet in elevation. They are roughly parallel and separated from each other by flat, arid valleys. The view from the highest summits is a repeating sequence of distant ranges and valleys. It is like being in a giant room with mirrors on two facing walls: the images on both sides are similar and ever more distant.

Summer backpackers find these desert mountains hot, dry, and brown. Forests are sparse, lakes almost nonexistent, and fishing streams few and far between. Desert hikers usually head east or south of the Great Basin into the shaded, well-watered canyons of the Colorado River and its tributaries. In winter, however the Great Basin ranges become more like their alpine cousins. Their rounded crests become corniced ridges, and the sage

Bristlecone snag beneath 13,063-foot Wheeler Peak in Great Basin National Park, not far from the remains of WPN-114, once the oldest known living thing on earth.

blanket of the lower slopes disappears beneath snow. Temperatures often drop below zero; Jiggs, Nevada, below the Ruby Mountains, once recorded –55° F. The snow-covered desert ranges differ from the Rockies and the Sierra mainly in their long, open sections, exposed to the elements and unbroken by trees, cliffs, or shelter of any kind. It is this aspect that makes winter travel in the Great Basin a more serious undertaking than in the more alpine ranges of the United States.

After successfully traversing the crest of the White Mountains in 1974, I looked forward to another Great Basin ski adventure. A member of that trip, Dave Sharp, interested me in his home mountains, the Ruby Range, one of the largest in Nevada. Eventually, a total of eight people wanted to ski the hundred-mile crest, so we split into two separate parties of four. We planned to meet in the mountains and travel together where feasible.

Early in the winter we skied up two side canyons and placed caches of food and fuel. Then we learned that Dave would be unable to join us for the final traverse. In his place we asked Mike Farrell, an experienced skier and climber, to join us. My group also included Doug Robinson, the first person to continuously ski the entire length of the John Muir Trail along the Sierra Crest, and Dave Lomba, a recent convert from the downhill slopes. George Miller organized the other foursome, which was composed of friends from Bishop in eastern California.

In early March we returned to the Rubies and began skiing from Overland Pass at the south end of the range. On the first night we camped with George's group in the pinyon pine belt just above the open sagebrush at 6,000 feet. For several days thereafter, we plodded through snowstorms. Forests became mystical places where somber forms suddenly materialized from the mist like headlights out of a fog. The bristlecone pines seemed like pagan idols brooding over the inhabited valleys below. These contorted trees were fluted with rime ice that perfectly complemented their overall configuration—little wonder, since the same wind patterns that sculpted the ice had shaped the bristlecones over the course of thousands of years.

The previous winter, in another Great Basin range, Dave Lomba and I had tracked down the oldest living bristlecone ever discovered, a tree that had died in 1964—sacrificed to the cause of research. The story of its death had been hushed up; only by reading between the lines in scientific journals did it become apparent that a 4,900-year old tree with living branches had been felled and then sectioned with a chainsaw. At dawn on a March morning we found the tree's remains on a moraine at 10,750 feet below Wheeler Peak, the highest mountain wholly in Nevada.

Trees that have died natural deaths are often more beautiful than living ones, and I couldn't pass these ancient souls without being reminded of the words my mother had written when I was a child:

> *The grandeur of Death in Nature! To see a tree that has lived and covered itself with foliage finally die, and for the first time show the Strength and Line of its limbs. To raise them naked and unashamed from the earth to the sky and there, silhouetted, to create for the whole world Beauty as it never before has been conceived.*

Remains of Bristlecone #WPN-114, found to have been the world's oldest known living thing in 1964, after it was cut down to count its rings.

THE ex-OLDEST LIVING THING ON EARTH

WAS ancient WHEN CORTEZ CONQUERED MEXICO—

WAS BENT WITH YEARS WHEN CAESAR ENTERED GAUL—

WAS OLD BEYOND MEMORY WHEN MOSES DELIVERED THE LAW—

WAS TIME'S PATIENT WATCHMAN WHEN CHEOPS BUILT HIS PYRAMID—

WAS SLICED BY A CHAINSAW TO SEE HOW OLD IT WAS.

Requiescat in Pacem

POEM BY STEPHEN WHITNEY

I found death by the hand of man an entirely different matter. A stump protruded from a blanket of winter snow, and chunks of chainsawed wood lay all around like arms and legs on a battlefield. The Forest Service had granted geographer Donald Currey permission to cut down a tree in order to date Little Ice Age events. Currey used a special drill to remove a pencil-sized core from a tree more than 4,000 years old. He missed the center of the tree, so he tried again. The tool broke off. Rather than wait months for a replacement, he asked that the tree be sawed into sections. In his scientific report Currey offers no apology for the destruction of the earth's oldest known living resident, which he fondly calls WPN-114.

After Currey's "discovery," the Forest Service invited a team of dendrochronologists to search for a still older tree. But WPN-114 was an anomaly; no bristlecone in that region was discovered within 1,200 years of its age. Today the oldest living thing by default is the Methuselah Tree in the White Mountains; its exact location is kept a secret for fear that tourists will desecrate it or carry off souvenirs.

bristlecone rarely die in natural catastrophes. With the exception of an occasional lightning strike, they grow at too high an elevation, too far apart, for fire to kill them. A few have toppled after gradual erosion of the mountain surface around them exposed their roots. Large trunks with bark on them lie at the bottoms of the steepest canyons in the White Mountains, apparent avalanche victims of the colossal winter of 1969. But the bristlecone's only real threat is from modern man; and in the twenty-odd years since humans"discovered" the tree, they have wreaked more damage than the previous 2,000 years. The cool, clear wind that brightened Schulman's campfire in the 1950s now carries measurable air pollutants. Some of the oldest snags are gone, in the interest of science—and wood paneling. Others have found their way into campfires, wood stoves, and curio shops. Their very longevity makes them especially vulnerable to human impact. With growth rates often less than an inch in diameter per century, they cannot recover quickly from damage, as rabbits or eucalyptus can. Their survival—and ours as well—depends on slowing down the frantic scramble we call civilization.

In the Ruby Mountains we found bristlecones far more intact than those I had seen near roads in the White Mountains or near the sectioned tree on Wheeler Peak. Day after day in this harsh, untracked landscape we grew closer to the timeless world of the trees. One day of storm and drifting snow blended into the next. We forgot about sunlight. Our world was always gray and timeless. It was only winter, and there was only snow. Night arrived like a morning fog, softly and unannounced.

One morning a week into the trip, the storm was too heavy for traveling. By midday it abated, however, so all eight of us decided to ski down a bowl on the west side of Pearl Peak. It was a fantastic run: two to three feet of light powder lay on top of the many feet of settled snow. Unencumbered by our packs, we floated silently down through open bristlecone forests, lost in the splendor of a white world with no firm boundaries between earth, air, and sky.

Here was wilderness skiing at its finest—superb conditions, as good as the best of Alta or Aspen, in a paradise where no one had ever skied before. I thoroughly tired myself by making six 1,000-foot runs through the powder, each followed by an hour's climb back to the crest.

The next day we looked forward to a descent of nearly 3,500 feet from the top of Pearl Peak, but the view from the summit proved disappointing. The slopes were extremely steep, and the avalanche danger was too acute for skiing. We chose instead to climb down a long rock ridge, carrying our skis on our packs. As we descended, the snow lost its fine powder consistency, and minutes after we again put on our skis, Dave Lomba's binding pulled out of his ski, a mishap that had already occurred once before. Taping it temporarily to the ski, we continued down to an abandoned Basque sheepherder's cabin in an aspen grove by Smith Creek at 7,000 feet to make more permanent repairs. We fired up the old wood stove to keep the room warm enough for the epoxy to set.

The next morning we were back on the trail, half a day behind George's group. The canyon bottom was serene, in sharp contrast to the harsh world of the crest. Gone were the twisted pines, sandblasted by the wind-driven snow and sculpted by a west wind that was already blowing when men still lived in caves. Here the trees were hardwoods—aspen and mahogany—and the sun-molded spring snow gleamed like porcelain.

Two days later we climbed over the crest again in rare clear weather. On the other side a steep glacial cirque with open, high-angled slopes dropped to a frozen lake. In the hour it took to reach the lake, the weather had changed again. A storm seemed imminent. We found an old cabin built of roughly hewn logs at the edge of the lake, and although it had no windows and was totally dark with the door closed, it seemed a more desirable shelter than our flapping tent, especially if the weather worsened during the night. Making it habitable proved to be more of a project than we anticipated, since it was filled nearly to the roof with snow. We spent hours digging it out, then chinked the holes in the roof and walls with blocks of snow and prepared for the night.

Bristlecone forest on the summit ridge of Pearl Peak, Ruby Mountains.

Above: Mike Farrell skiing in a blizzard in the Ruby Mountains.

Below: Drying gear after a storm on the crest of the Rubys.

I awoke at midnight to the call of nature and ventured outside in 60 mph hour winds. The sky was cloudless, but the stars were dull, as though seen through a dusty window. By morning a real blizzard was in progress, and we quickly discovered how the cabin had filled with snow. Spindrift leaked rapidly through the timbers, covering us and all of our belongings. To add to our discomfort the temperature was well below zero; I spent the dark day inside my sleeping bag wearing all my clothes and my down parka. We wondered how far ahead the other foursome might be and where they were camped during the blizzard, but we needn't have worried—unbeknownst to us, they had given up on the tenth day of the trip.

I felt like a subject in a deprivation experiment. I'm the type that always has to be doing something, even if it's just scribbling or pacing the floor; but here there was absolutely nothing to do. For two days and three nights I couldn't read, write, or see the outside world. After two restless nights I realized how differently Doug Robinson experienced winter. He didn't think in terms of days of the week, hours of the day, or degrees of temperature. He was totally in tune with the wilderness of snow and sky: seeing without categorizing, traveling without scheduling, discovering without searching. He created another world for himself, one separate from ordinary reality. Only equipment tied him directly to the world he left behind.

Our stay in the cabin finally ended on the twelfth morning of the trip. It was windless, cold, and clear as we set off. Only ten minutes out, Dave ripped off his binding yet again. We spent an hour on a makeshift repair, hoping that we could continue along the crest for at least a few more days. But meanwhile the sky had clouded over, and strong winds created a ground blizzard. After a council of war, we decided to retreat.

The descent through a trailless, brushy canyon was an exhausting, all-day affair. Late in the afternoon we struck a dirt road and followed it to a modern ranch house. An old rancher came to the door and broke into loud guffaws of laughter; he had never seen anything like us before. Later we heard that his wife had spotted us walking up the road— colorful, muddy, and bedraggled—and when she had called her husband to the window, he had asked her in all seriousness, "Are them Indians?" We were treated to some gracious Western hospitality, and then the old rancher had his son drive us forty miles back to our car, where another surprise awaited us. The car had been burglarized of all our personal belongings, more than $1,000 worth of everything from handmade equipment to underwear and tire chains. "Must have been those city people," said the rancher's son.

The sheriffs office was in a town nearly a hundred miles away. "Must have been some locals in the valley. Probably Indians," we were told there.

Although we had lost some of our most treasured possessions and had failed to travel the full crest of the Rubies, these misfortunes could not break the spell the high desert had cast. On the way home, we were already planning to traverse another lonely crest the following winter. As we drove west for hundreds of miles along Highway 50, snowy ranges rose before us. Here, so close to civilization, was an unofficial wilderness that remained virtually unexplored in winter.

13

A Vertical Mile in the Alaska Range

At an American Alpine Club annual meeting in December 1973, David Roberts and I chatted about the future of big wall climbs in the Alaska Range. At the time, he was far better known as a climber than as a writer. Since then, his many books and articles for most every major magazine in America have gained him so much fame that few people know that he was also at the top of his field in his former passion.

The self-assured young Harvard grad sipping a glass of wine had been pushing the standards of the possible ever higher in Alaska. From a major new route up Mount McKinley, to the West Face of Mount Huntington, to exploratory climbs in the Brooks Range, David was an all-around mountaineer who seemed to have done it all in Alaska except for big rock walls. That's where I came in. Was I interested in joining him and his friend Ed Ward for a Yosemite-style wall climb in the Alaska Range? We agreed that the 5000-foot Southeast Face of Mount Dickey was probably the biggest continuous rock face in Alaska, and we made plans then and there to attempt it the following summer in a single, alpine-style push.

The three days we spent on the wall, climbing well into nights that never got fully dark, were in contrast to a later ascent of a route parallel to ours that took 28 days of siege climbing. David later wrote, "After I got home from the expedition, I had dreams about being stuck on Dickey for fifteen consecutive nights."

While I continue to do big wall climbs into my sixties, David saw technical rock climbing as a young man's sport, and in his own account of our climb described himself and Ed as "over the hill at 30 and 31," while I was "plugging creakily away at 34." He judged the route to be "technically the hardest I ever did" before easing away from high-level climbing.

Opposite: David Roberts leads clean granite on the lower part of the 4,500-foot Southeast Face of Mount Dickey.
Above: Galen belaying in a blizzard on the Southeast Face of Alaska's Mount Dickey, 1974. Photo: David Roberts

The interior of the Alaska Range is an alpine world few people realize exists on earth: ice, rock, snow, and sky, each element in oceanic, overpowering quantities. Unlike the Himalaya, "the abode of snow," the landscape is nearly monochromatic. There are no greens; yellows and reds appear only at sunrise or sunset. The scene is white, gray, and blue.

The giant rhythms of this land distort normal perceptions. Thoughts slow down like records played at too slow a speed. We humans have natural clocks, reset each day by sunrise and sunset, high noon, and stars. But June in the Alaska Range has twenty-hour days followed by brief, starless twilights. Near the solstice, weather permitting, the sun shines all day on the summit ramparts of Mount McKinley, whose 20,320-foot bulk intercepts light beams aimed at the Arctic Circle nearly two hundred miles north. McKinley's shadow scribes a daily arc over thousands of miles of primeval landscape.

Well-informed as we are about travel to the moon and planets, most of us know little of this ice-locked part of our own nation. In 1903, Frederick Cook followed the great shadow's arc around Mount McKinley in a 540-mile orbital expedition that has never been repeated Three years later he was the first person to travel up the Ruth Glacier (named after his daughter) en route to an attempted ascent of McKinley. He discovered the Great Gorge, where some of the greatest granite faces in this hemisphere tower over either side of the glacier. True to the giant rhythms of the area, distances and features are much greater than they appear.

Until 1974, not one face in the Great Gorge had been climbed. In the summer of that year I came to Alaska with Dave Roberts and Ed Ward to attempt the southeast face of Mount Dickey—the highest granite cliff in North America. The peak has a moderate snow and ice route up the back side, but drops a vertical mile to the Ruth Glacier plus an unknown distance below the surface of the ice. The three of us had been on a combined total of more than twenty expeditions to the North, but our first sight of Dickey from the air still took our breath away.

As we were flown into the gorge by the legendary bush pilot Don Sheldon, days of foot travel were compressed into minutes of flight. Sheldon edged his turbocharged Cessna 180 close to the wall for a look at our proposed route. Snow-covered ledges tiered like the windows of a high-rise building inspired both confidence, as resting places, and apprehension, as potential traps during a long storm. The area has received more than eighty feet of snowfall in a single season. Much of the snow on those ledges had only recently been salt water in the Gulf of Alaska, perhaps lapping the sides of a Japanese fishing boat or roaring up Cook Inlet with the tide. Although we were now a stone's throw from the ledges, they were actually a hard week's work away.

We landed at Sheldon's "Mountain House," a tiny cabin he had built on a rock promontory on the Ruth Glacier to accommodate his clients. It was the only building for fifty miles around. At 2 a.m. the next morning, we set off to climb Mount Dickey by the easy north side in order to cache a tent, food, and ice axes on the summit. At one point an invisible snow bridge collapsed, and I fell into a gaping hole. The rope snapped tight just as my skis struck a snow shelf inside the crevasse. Unhurt, I stared thirty feet overhead to the hole in the roof of the icy trap; by luck I had missed hitting hard ice nearby. Using Jumar ascenders, I escaped on a rope that Dave and Ed anchored above, and we continued

the climb. The weather gradually enclosed us as we approached the summit ridge. We cached our supplies and descended by the same route to a col, marking our route with willow wands tagged with red ribbons. We camped on the col that night, then continued around the mountain to a base camp at the foot of the southeast face, where we waited through several days of poor weather to begin our ascent of the wall.

There was only one natural campsite on the vast glacier, a Shangrila in the relentless, icy world. Base camp was secure and friendly—warm clothes, level glacier, no bugs, no rockfall, no avalanche danger, plenty of food, and books to read. Boulders and gravel lay strewn on the ice, the beginnings of a lateral moraine. A flat, ten-foot rock was our kitchen, and a stream flowed into a deep blue pool nearby.

Our strategy was completely different than it had been on the Moose's Tooth two years before. Instead of bringing vast amounts of equipment and food in order to survive storms en route, we planned to go light and rush the face when a break in the weather came. To get a slight head start we spent a preliminary day fixing four ropes on the lower part of the face. The rock was firm, and the weather was as balmy as summer in the Tetons. Dave later wrote, "If we got no higher than this . . . we'd have had one great day of climbing, the like of which whole expeditions starve themselves for in the Alaska Range." We planned to climb with only a three-day supply of rations—and no tent. We would have to move through the mountains' defenses for up to eighteen hours a day, quickly, decisively—a problem not unlike that of crossing a freeway on foot on a dark night. Better naked and fleet of foot than the deceptive safety of plodding caution.

After waiting out a short storm, we began the ascent beneath clearing skies on July 17 at 2 a.m. It was still early in the morning when we reached our previous high point at the top of the fixed ropes. The loads were the lightest I'd ever taken on a big climb, even back home in California. Relying on the snow, we carried little water. I had two wool sweaters and a rain parka—but no down jacket. We carried one tarp, one bivouac sack, one ice axe, and a single pair of crampons—token gestures if conditions became extreme.

On the huge, complex cliff we felt like rats in a vertical maze. Each lead was a pathway which had to connect with the next in order for us to get through. Because we moved separately and concentrated intensely, our inward experiences were rarely shared. Dave would slow down on an unpredicted section of rotten rock, but neither Ed nor I would really ever know how bad it was. We'd see it as we mechanically ascended the rope after him.

"Nice lead, Dave."

Aerial view of the Southeast face of Mount Dickey.

"Thanks."

Then I'd watch Ed lead higher, back on firm rocks moving confidently and using nuts and occasional pitons for safety. His hour of hard work, too, would rush by me in five minutes as I climbed the rope to take the lead above. Our progress was relatively rapid, about one hundred feet per hour. In other parts of the world this would work out to six nine-hour days of climbing to ascend the mile-high wall. Light gear, long days, and a little luck would put us on the summit in three days, in theory.

On the twentieth lead, about 2,000 feet above the glacier, our mechanical ritual was halted by a series of problems. The rock was rotten and frostriven. A section of the wall that had appeared relatively gently angled now proved desperately dangerous. Higher, a vertical headwall of crumbly rock was broken only by a single flaw, a wide chimney hundreds of feet high. It was my lead, and using a rope traverse, I entered the chimney and found firm rock inside. Its sides were slick with water, however, and its few ledges covered by snow. My progress was blocked by giant chockstones, one of which required 5.9 climbing. The chockstone thrust outward like an awning, dripping water on my head. Jamming hands in the wet crack that connected it to the wall, I worked my way to the outside edge, reaching blindly over its brow into gravel and snow. A fall seemed certain so I backed down to a resting spot and then tried again, this time driving a piton into the crack near the lip. This would at least protect me from a long fall, and I moved upward more confidently, frictioning my boots against the flaring walls of the chimney. They held, and I soon had a death grip on a blocky handhold. At the end of the lead I reached a ledge. The absolute clarity of my mini-battle with the chockstone soon diffused into dull anxiety about our progress.

Later that evening, Ed completed a difficult pitch in the ten-o'clock twilight, and we bivouacked on a comfortable ledge. We cooked dinner and talked optimistically about our progress: half the climb completed in a single day, with, of course, a head start of fixed lines. Soon we were dozing beneath the clear sky.

The sunrise poured through slots in thick clouds to spotlight summits with a strange orange phosphorescence. Yesterday we'd seen only occasional cirrus clouds moving from the south like a giant migration of geese, but today a storm was upon us. Valleys to the south were locked in cloud, and streamers of white mist crept up the Ruth Glacier, lapping at the base of our mountain. In the gloom of four-o'clock dawn we discussed whether to abandon the climb. Our decision to keep moving up was made out of psychological commitment, not logic. There was a world of difference between the first and second day's climbing. The vastness was suddenly gone, replaced by dank confinement. Gone were the ice highways twisting through distant gorges. The sky was depthless gray, as was the air below our feet; clouds below me made the rope disappear.

At noon we reached an amphitheater surrounded by overhanging rotten walls and again found the rock bad—so bad I could chop steps in it with my alpine hammer. The only way out was to climb the skyline to the right. Dave led to a ledge beneath a steep headwall. On the next lead, he mistook my call for "slack" to be a warning of "rock!" and instead of feeding the rope, he pinned me for life's longest seconds on rotten rock high

After Galen fell into a crevasse on Mount Dickey and was held by the rope,
he asked Dave Roberts to peer into the gaping hole for a photograph.

above a dubious safety anchor before he finally understood my yell. We had no confidence that either pitons or nuts could safely anchor the rope in such poor rock.

Imagine a floor covered with marbles. Make the pile of marbles bottomless, glue them together in some weak fashion, tilt the angle to sixty degrees, and you have a rough approximation of the difficulties. Even in chopped steps my feet felt insecure. It took me more than two hours to climb a hundred feet up terrain that I knew I couldn't climb down. Finally I reached a ledge—a triumph but also a trap, for the cliff above was vertical and blank.

I had the dull feeling that we'd done something irreversibly wrong, but Ed had a perpetual smile on his face; I feared he didn't understand the gravity of our situation. But Dave's notes on the climb contained a similar appraisal of me:

"Would Galen . . . keep that blithe cheerful countenance to the end?"

I began to understand why politicians smile.

Ed was still smiling as I lowered him around a blind corner to search out a route in the invisible gloom. His voice, now more cheerful than his face, warmed our hearts.

"Perfect rock. It goes!"

Throughout the climb we could find no reason why the rock was good in some places and bad in others. We knew that the bad rock was shattered by exposure to the elements, but the good rock was the same quartz monzonite; good and bad were often found side by side on similar exposures. The good rock was climbable even when it was overhanging; the bad rock was virtually impossible as it approached the vertical.

We were lucky to have escaped the amphitheater before the storm began. A few hours' delay and the rock would have been plastered with snow. We climbed all afternoon on fine rock, wondering when the storm would begin and hoping that its slowness was not an indication of its size. By early evening it had begun raining, and we stopped on a giant ledge about a thousand feet below the summit.

The rain turned to snow, and a strong wind came up. An Alaskan blizzard was upon us. Dave covered himself with the tarp and slept in a small nook; Ed crawled into the bivy sack and remained exposed on the ledge. Blanketed with snow and curled in fetal position, he looked, Dave said, "like a victim's body discovered by rescuers." I wriggled into a natural coffin under a boulder. Protected from the wind, but exposed to blowing snow, I spent the night so cramped that had the rock shifted half an inch I would not have gotten out. Sleep came slowly, and my thoughts drifted.

If we were successful, would our climb be considered just another gymnastic feat? Would failure, whether by a hairbreadth or a calamity, make us look foolish to have even attempted the climb? We asked no rescue, and none was expected. How different our situation might be if, as in Switzerland, a téléphérique went up Mount Dickey and a rescue crew was even now lowering a cable. How many men, how many planes, how many changes would it take to destroy our remote experience in this alpine sanctuary?

Mount Dickey, unlike most of the McKinley massif, was not in a national park. It was currently unprotected, but was included in a large southern extension proposed for Mount McKinley (now Denali) National Park. On an earlier expedition I had seen no threat of

Dave Roberts climbs rock coated with rime ice in a blizzard near the summit of Mount Dickey.

development to the lands that constituted the southern extension, and I doubted the need for official protection. I suspected that the minimal development that always comes in a national park's wake might be more damaging to the region than leaving it alone.

I've since changed my mind; I had drawn a romantic comparison between this land and Yosemite National Park. I had seen the Ruth Gorge as Yosemite had been in the Pleistocene epoch. Its ice hasn't melted, most of its peaks are unnamed, and it is rarely visited. In sharp contrast are the stores, golf course, jail, and bank of Yosemite proper. A national park in this part of Alaska had seemed grossly premature, but it now seems obvious that development throughout post-pipeline Alaska is imminent. The time for parkland is now. [The proposed extension became part of Denali National Parks and Preserve in 1980.]

The existing Denali National Park is not plagued by the excess development so common in parks of the lower forty-eight. Its harsh climate and remoteness protect it, but a large share of the credit must go to its early superintendents. Three of the first four were men who had climbed Mount McKinley. Unlike most modern park managers, who acquire their jobs by administrative musical chairs, they had a hard-won, intimate appreciation for the land. Today, most important park decisions come from Washington, but Harry Karstens, Denali's first superintendent, was in a unique position. Not only had he led the first ascent of Mount McKinley, but he had also shared in the very birth of the idea of making a national park when he wintered north of the mountain with naturalist, Charles Sheldon, a decade before the park was created.

If John Muir could see Yosemite today, he would certainly question the idea of national parks. Denali National Park, however, is a monument to the national park idea and the goals of Sheldon and Karstens as they sat around campfires in the mountain's great shadow. The only indoor accommodations are at the park boundary. Fewer than one hundred campsites—and no other accommodations—exist along the eighty-seven mile dirt road that crosses the park. Except for those with campsite registrations, all visitors must ride tour buses or walk through the park; private vehicles are banned. In contrast to the lifeless ice and rock of the Ruth Gorge, the park road traverses green, rolling tundra and spruce forests. Control of mechanized transportation keeps North America's finest wildlife viewing area much the way Sheldon saw it in 1906. During a single day in the park I saw moose, caribou, eagle, gyrfalcon, ptarmigan, porcupine, beaver, grizzly, Dall sheep, wolf, and, most remarkable of all, a lynx stalking a snowshoe hare forty feet away from me. To have this—and the Great Gorge—in a single national park would give Denali the finest cross section of wilderness in any park in the world.

The morning after our bivouac in the storm, I peered out at a white world from high on Mount Dickey. A blizzard filled the air with snow, and rime ice clung to the rock above. It looked like photographs I'd seen of the north face of the Eiger in storm. I was wet but warm in my fiberfill bag and suggested that we try to wait out the storm where we were. Both Dave and Ed wanted to head for the summit. I was worried about technical climbing with icy ropes, but descending 4,000 feet in a storm was out of the question, and we had no inkling of how long it would last. Conditions could get much worse before they got better. Because we were running low on food, we agreed to continue climbing.

Using our only crampons and ice axe, Dave took the lead, and we soon came to a sudden juncture with dark, stratified, metamorphic rock held in place by ice and snow. Above, the angle of the face averaged sixty degrees, and the surface was about half rock and half snow, although much of what looked like snow turned out to be ice. We regretted not having more ice axes and crampons but, on the other hand, they might have slowed us down on the two previous days of rock climbing.

How totally different from our beginning on dry rock and a sunny day! It was as though we had switched to a different mountain on a different continent. We climbed roped together in a claustrophobic world of blowing snow, with visibility often less than one hundred feet. Our rate of progress slowed to a vertical crawl. Even Ed dropped his ever-present smile to say, "I don't like this. It seems real dangerous."

Dave, on the other hand, exuded confidence as his clawed feet led the way over icy black rock. He smiled and made quick decisions, seemingly totally in control of the situation. He was carrying a detailed aerial photo by Bradford Washburn of the face, now crumpled like a handkerchief, and occasionally he stopped to correlate features. As we moved higher we found progressively less rock and more snow, and finally we came to a place where everything above was white. Dave announced that we were close to the top. Estimating the angle would ease off in fifty feet or so, he climbed directly up steep ice and soon became a dark shadow in the snowy tempest. After climbing 150 feet without seeing an end to the ice, he retreated.

Ice from Dave's footsteps crashed down on our hard hats. Our smiles had entirely vanished by now; we were cold and disillusioned in the blowing storm, perhaps even lost. We began traversing hundreds of feet to the south, searching for a weakness in the continuous ice wall. We wanted rock outcrops for belays and piton protection, but rock was the exception and snow the rule. Our diagonal traverse angled upward, and Dave occasionally stopped to belay us individually over steep sections. I slogged through deep snow and climbed over a small cornice onto unexpected level ground. Dave shook hands with me, saying he thought we were on top. But where? We were in a white out.

Ed soon joined us. At first we didn't agree on which direction to head on the broad summit plateau, but we decided to walk blindly south. Suddenly, through the storm, a tall flagpole appeared with a large, red flag blowing in the wind. I stared at it in disbelief. Who could have put such a thing near the summit of Mount Dickey? It hadn't been there a week before. We must not be in the right place.

It took only a few seconds for these thoughts to race through my mind, and as I took another step, my perspective error became obvious. It was one of our four-foot-tall willow wands with a small red ribbon, glowing from the shadowless murk of a white-out.

As we continued across the plateau, new wands appeared like tail lights out of fog until we came to our tiny cache. Two ice axes for the descent; one two-man tent, crowded for three, but luxurious compared with our previous nights' accommodations; and two days worth of freeze-dried food. These meager things were a pot of gold, and we were soon resting in the tent: tired, cold, satisfied.

14

The Cirque of the Unclimbables

If North America has a Patagonia, it is in a remote corner of the Northwest Territories of Canada where an isolated glacial cirque of granite walls fringed with snow and ice erupts from unbelievably green meadows. The hidden cirque in the heart of a roadless area had been visited by less than twenty-five people when I first saw it in 1972 on the climbing expedition described in this essay.

Since then, I returned in 1973 to make several new climbs, and again in 1992 on the first free climb of the 2,000-foot face of Proboscis with Paul Piana and Todd Skinner, who also made the first free climb of El Capitan up the Salathe Wall in 1988. Though I found the cirque to be no longer as pristine and wild as on my first visit, its unique character remains unchanged. My memories of time spent there are among life's fondest, and I would love to conjure up an excuse to climb and photograph there again, despite the fact that many climbers from around the world have discovered the place and sanitation has become enough of a problem to warrant construction of the region's first permanent structure: a latrine.

In the summer of 1972, my friend Jim McCarthy and I flew in his small Cessna toward his favorite spot on earth—the Cirque of the Unclimbables, an isolated group of granite peaks in the Logan Mountains of Canada's Northwest Territories. Located in a completely roadless area larger than California, the cirque is so remote that at the time of our visit fewer than twenty-five people had ever set foot there, although it is more spectacularly beautiful than any place I have seen in the national parks of North America.

Jim and I had just returned from an unsuccessful attempt on the Moose's Tooth in Alaska, and he assured me that the Logan Mountains, although at the same latitude, had far better weather than the Alaska Range. He had initially visited the area a few years earlier, making the first ascent of Lotus Flower Tower in several warm twenty-hour days. After a wretched spell of Alaskan rain and snow, we were ready for such a sunny paradise.

Our flight in Jim's Cessna over the vast, unpopulated reaches of the North provided a classic contrast between timeless nature and timebound man. The little plane was fully equipped for instrument flying. Often we slipped into the translucent void of a

A helicopter passes by Lotus Flower Tower in the Cirque of the Unclimbables.

cloud bank, and I would watch Jim scan the panel and recreate in his mind the dynamic perspective of his craft moving across the landscape. Gradually I began to realize the limits of the various devices. When a call to an airport gave us a new barometer reading, Jim dialed it into the altimeter. The needle moved up. The plane did not. It was theoretically possible to read 2,000 feet of ground clearance on a gauge a split second before slamming into the side of a mountain. The magnetic compass wigged and wagged as we passed near ore bodies. Nothing was absolute, I thought to myself, except time. Every thirty-six seconds, a new digit snapped into the hundredth's place on the gauge that registered hours.

But how absolute is the human conception of time? As we flew north across Canada, the dwindling number of settlements below us made it seem as if we were returning to a time long past in the United States. Calgary, a potential Canadian Los Angeles, quickly sprawled into a checkerboard of farms. The fields were dotted with small patches of forest, the only remnants of what was once an unbroken expanse of woodlands and lakes. Gradually the farms grew fewer until they became islands in a sea of lakes and forest. In the Yukon, signs of man became still less frequent. Regardless of the regular ratcheting of the hour gauge, we were traveling backward, not forward, in time.

We landed the plane on the dirt airstrip of a small mining town. On a hillside above a long valley was the open pit. Ten-ton Euclid trucks howled back and forth on the Z-shaped road from the pit to the groaning and clanking processing mill in town. Pipes gushed black water into siltation ponds. Abandoned cars, empty oil drums, bits of lumber, and sewage formed a wreath around the town; tungsten and people were the only things carried out. A portly woman in her forties came riding down the hill on a motorcycle. We met her later in the mess hall and learned that she was the cook for the single men living in the dormitories. She offered us food and coffee, and I commented on both the quality and quantity. "The boys get lots of good food and high pay," she replied. "They have to. A person needs that and more up here or else he'll go crazy. In the winter it sometimes goes seventy below, and the days are only four hours long. Most everyone has snowmobiles. In the summer people play baseball, go hiking, swimming—I ride a motorcycle, you know. A person has to have something else besides working. Why one fellow, he worked lots of overtime and did nothing but work, eat, and sleep. We warned him, but he wouldn't listen. They carried him out of here in a strait jacket."

An hour later we were in a jet helicopter, crossing icefields and snowy ridges on our way to the heart of the mountain range. Blue lakes lay below peaks in glacier-carved bowls. Far below the hanging alpine valley were the trenches of the main rivers. The long hours of summer sun had melted the surface of the permafrost, changing level valley floors into impassable brush-tangled bogs that formed moats around the granite cathedrals in the center of the range.

The helicopter deposited us and our pile of gear in an alpine meadow and flew off. We planned a multi-day ascent of nearby Parrot Beak Peak and brought food for five days; the helicopter was to return on the fifth. Granite towers thousands of feet high loomed over the small meadow where we pitched our tent.

Above: August snow storm in the Cirque of the Unclimbables. The tent is pitched in the same spot as below, when the run-off from rapidly melting snow flooded the meadow.

Below: Survival by the frontier ethic in 1972: Jim McCarthy celebrates victory after trenching a pristine mountain meadow to prevent his tent from flooding.

That evening I took a long walk into the next valley. From the air, the vegetation had appeared uniformly green, but on closer inspection, the verdant grasses and mosses proved to be merely the dominant color in a melange of hues. The north sides of the rocks were splotched with colorful lichens; the south sides carpeted with thick mats of yellow moss. Streams were gray, not blue, because they were laden with glacial silt. Wildflowers grew in profusion on the meadowed benches. Rivulets snaked through the meadows and dipped off into the distance. I felt like an intruder as my footsteps squashed down the living mat.

I walked through a meadow decorated with tremendous squared boulders. One gigantic rock was split in three parts and through a narrow crack I could watch clouds swirling around the tops of towers. It gave me the unmistakable impression of being in a natural Stonehenge. Timberline was at only 4,000 feet, and this meadow was far above the last trees. I saw marmots, finches, ptarmigans, and plenty of signs of mountain goats. I was surprised to find a dwarfed spruce growing behind a boulder in less than two inches of caribou moss. Although it had more than twenty sets of limbs, it was no more than eight inches tall. I would have taken for granted the most stately spruce, but this one small tree caught my attention and made me wonder how long it could last.

Morning dawned gray and cloudy. Jim and I agreed to delay our multi-day ascent and instead chose to climb a shorter but fine-looking buttress on the highest peak in the region, Mount Sir James McBrien. After three hours of unroped scrambling, we reached the beginning of technical climbing. A few hundred feet higher we came to a steep headwall. It was my turn to lead. Climbing here required a more cautious attitude than in a more accessible region; in case of injury or sickness, one might wait a long time to be evacuated. My feet began to twitch involuntarily, and I placed three pitons within arm's reach to protect one move over a difficult 5.10 ceiling.

Reaching the summit early in the evening, we saw a storm advancing from the other side of the peak. The complex descent on the easiest side of the peak involved traversing narrow ledges and kicking steps down snow-filled couloirs. Lower down we found fresh goat tracks and followed them onto a well-worn trail across grassy ledges. As we rounded a corner, I spotted a family of five goats ascending a nearby ridge. It was ten o'clock that night before we reached our tent in the rain.

It was still raining the next morning, and it continued for three more days without stopping. Around noon on the third day, Jim discovered that our beautiful meadow was fast becoming a lake. Although we had chosen the highest piece of ground, it was only six inches above the overall level; the water was rising fast and we were already on an island. Within five minutes we were furiously digging trenches with ice axes, defending our little portable environment against an onslaught of silt-laden water—the same waters which had created the meadow from a trap basin in the glacial moraine. It didn't work; the water was coming from every direction, faster than we could drain it with our crude tools. We paused to take stock of the situation and then spotted the main source of the water—a large stream pouring down the hillside just above the meadow. We concentrated our efforts there, building dams and trenching until we had altered the course of the stream to avoid the meadow completely.

Creek beneath the north face of Mount Harrison Smith, Cirque of the Unclimbables, 1973.

It would be nice to be able to say that we considered all the alternatives and chose one that was both practical and environmentally sound. However, I can't recall either of us suggesting that we simply move up onto the rocks and huddle under a tarp. How ironic that we who talked of preserving this place were busy trenching and damming at the first threat of getting wet. We even felt proud of our efforts. I finally understood how Floyd Dominy must have felt when he dedicated Glen Canyon Dam. All the same, I was horrified at my thoughts. Just a week earlier, flying over endless miles of woodland, I had experienced similar feelings when I found myself thinking, "Why are they cutting all that beautiful timber in California when they could be logging up here and nobody would miss it?" I quenched the thought immediately but recognized that for a moment I had experienced the frontier ethic of the North.

There was nothing to do now but wait in the tent. I teased Jim about his weather prophecy. He said the rain would quit soon, but I noticed him toying with his dismantled survival rifle and began to consider the serious possibility that we might be trapped here long enough to need it.

It was snowing the next morning when we awoke. As the clouds parted for a brief glimpse of the cliffs, the scene was wild beyond description. Towers plastered in white loomed somberly out of the mist. A foot of snow lay on our meadow, and the goat paths on the mossy ledges were buried. Falling snowflakes dampened the acoustics of the cirque; except for the roar of an occasional avalanche, all was still.

The sixth day passed. Our food supply was very low, and we talked about what we could do if the helicopter never came. It might take us weeks to hike the fifty miles of brush and marshes between our cirque and the mine town. Suddenly I was no longer in a comfortable living room thumbing through a picture book of wilderness images. Here, in trouble, the value of civilization came clear. The embarrassing pride we felt over damming the stream, my flash of faulty logic about logging the North, and our present helplessness all began to fit together. I needed the tools of civilization. What did I have that I could do without? My mountain boots? My food? My sleeping bag? Without the umbilical cord to civilization that these things represented, I would be in bad shape. Back home, I had been lulled into false confidence in my own survival abilities by the nearness of civilization. I could reach habitation in two days of hiking from the most remote area in California.

In strict terms, much of what passes for a "wilderness experience" is counterfeit. Once in a while, someone really does make a break for a short time—often it is accidental, termed "exposure," and results in a visit to a hospital. The "ruggedness" of a wilderness experience is not merely the physical effort involved, but the chance that the conditions of nature will exceed the capabilities of the equipment we bring with us. In other words, we risk being thrown into a true wilderness situation, one that modern people carefully avoid by special equipment, clothing, and rations.

Jim and I trenched the meadow to protect an element of the technological world we had brought into the backcountry. Mountain tents may do considerably less damage than many other kinds of portable environments, such as recreational vehicles, but

A 1973 attempt on the north face of Mount Harrison Smith failed due to constant rain and mossy cracks. Afterward, the climbers watched the mountain goat on page 16 ascend the lower part of the cliff in a few bounds.

even the most adaptable self-contained travelers—wilderness backpackers—leave their marks. Footsteps gradually wear footpaths; campfires gradually develop into permanent campsites, and the pursuit of the unknown sooner or later becomes a section in a guidebook. Even though backpackers are equipped to deal with a far wider set of circumstances than are recreational vehicles, when the limits of their adaptability are exceeded they must either suffer or change the land to suit their needs, as we had chosen to do by trenching and damming.

In the natural world, an animal must adapt to its environment or perish. Civilization implies adapting the environment to human needs; much of the appeal of wilderness is that it can return people to the primeval situation to which humans are adapted. Keeping equipment down to a few simple items is one step toward this goal, but many people become more concerned with the means than the ends. Equipment is counted and compared like batting averages. The differences between various brands of equipment are far down the list of things that the modern, urban person needs to know in order to understand and enjoy the wilderness.

I peered outside the tent into a mist-shrouded dreamland of meadows, streams, and granite towers. A heavy rain was washing the snow from the meadow, but it was still snowing on the summits. The scene was magnificent, but I longed to be back in the mining town, though a week earlier I had scoffed at its prefabs, snowmobiles, and life styles. Once again the ethic of the North had caught up with me; it is hard to consider the intrinsic value of wilderness while it is a real adversary. In the United States, we are beginning to realize that our wildlands are finite, but in the Northwest Territories, an earlier spirit prevails. The people of the North are not wrong, any more than Americans were wrong to drive cars without smog devices in 1935, or to shoot buffalo when there were millions of them. Modern pioneers are living in a different age. Their daydreams are still of the future, and their frontier heroes have modern equipment. Today's Abraham Lincoln lives in a log cabin with central heating and a freezer full of moose. Today's Snowshoe Thompson has treads and makes rather more noise. And today's Davy Crockett—I met him in person, in Alaska—dynamites coyotes from his airplane. "Thirty-dollar bounty and you get to keep the pelt, you know."

My mental ramblings might not solve the problems of the developing North, but they did lead me toward an increased awareness of how thoroughly we are trapped in our own time—I in mine, and the pioneers of this land in theirs. They must live through the same mistakes made by earlier pioneers before they can realize what they have lost. As for me, I still had to think in terms of basic survival. There was a helicopter buzzing in the back of my consciousness, and I hoped it would soon appear in reality.

The eighth morning dawned gray. Rain was intermittent, and fog hung low in the distant river valleys. Clouds still veiled the summits of the peaks. I put on my wet boots and stepped outside. Every watercourse was full. I grabbed my pack and a camera and announced that I was going for a walk. I'd gone only a hundred yards when the humming of the water was drowned out by a gradually increasing noise; I barely beat the helicopter to the tent. Suddenly time was of the highest value. Minutes ticked by at hundreds of dollars per hour as the helicopter waited for us to dismantle our camp. Darting around the meadow, we must have resembled the frantic, choppy characters in an early silent film. The pilot seemed puzzled that we took the time to bag up garbage and tie it into the baskets.

As we rose into the air, we had a view of the lower meadow completely submerged in water. We were witnessing the forces of its creation still at work today. But the silt-laden water was prevented by our earthworks from reaching the meadow where we had camped. We had been thoroughly conditioned to pick up garbage, even at great cost; but we had not thought of tearing down the dams during our expensive rush to return to civilization. Unconsciously, we had placed a dollar value on nature's chosen course for a mountain stream. I looked back at the sheer 2,000-foot face of Proboscis, as impressive as Yosemite's Half Dome, following the clean granite with my eyes until it abruptly merged with jumbled red rock. A contact-metamorphic zone: what every prospector seeks when hunting copper, lead, and gold. The list could continue—tungsten, molybdenum, silver, zinc—but the meaning was the same. Call it progress, manifest destiny, the ethic of the North—time could all too easily catch up to these mountains.

When I returned home I wrote about our visit without using a single place name. I wanted to emphasize the nature of the experience rather than the place itself, and I feared that the area might be damaged by overuse if my article attracted too many visitors. Through word of mouth and mountaineering journals, the Cirque has since become well known to climbers all over the world, and the experience is no longer the same. There is garbage in the meadows and the solitude is gone. What I choose to remember is the feeling of moving backward through time, back to the kind of experience enjoyed by the early explorers of the Grand Canyon, of Yellowstone, the Grand Tetons, or Yosemite; back to the time before these scenic wonders became islands of wild country surrounded by cities, roads, and farms. Finding this experience in North America in the 1970s was the journey's greatest reward.

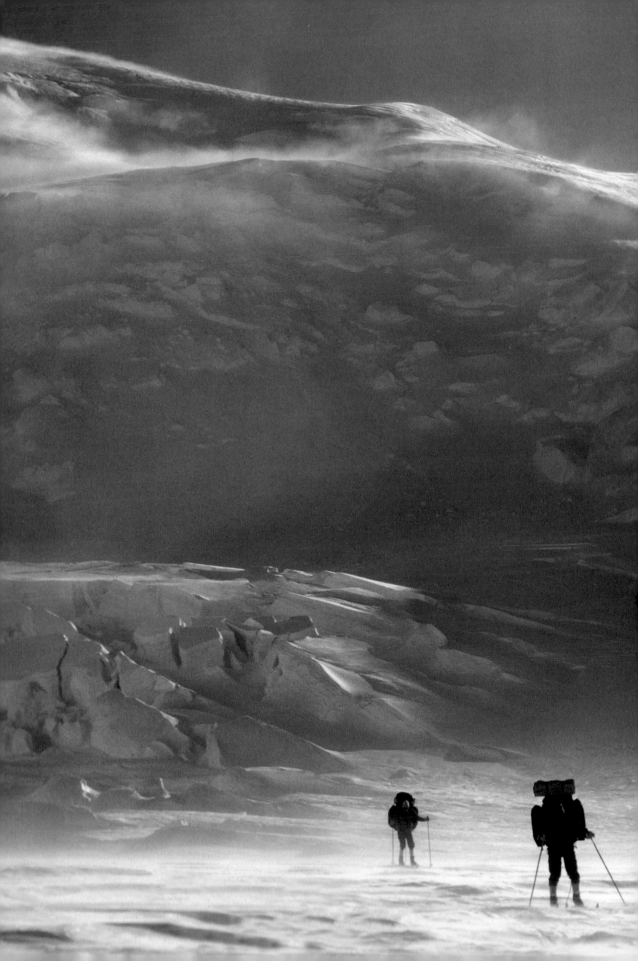

15

Around Mount McKinley on Skis

When Olympic cross-country skier Ned Gillette invited me to circle Mount McKinley within the limits of its glacial systems, I pitched the idea to NATIONAL GEOGRAPHIC and was given a personal assignment for both text and photos. After we succeeded in April 1978 and I started writing the essay that appears here, Ned asked me if he could write the story, since he was the leader of our four-man team and the trip had been his idea. I conceded after getting written permission from GEOGRAPHIC to publish my own full account in the 1979 AMERICAN ALPINE JOURNAL, tailored especially for members of the American Alpine Club who were quite knowledgeable about climbing and exploration.

When the journal was published for a few thousand mountaineers, I was quite surprised to field an upset phone call from a GEOGRAPHIC editor who said I had done something very wrong: NATIONAL GEOGRAPHIC never gives permission for another article to be published before their own. I cited my permission letter for the 1979 journal and asked why Ned's article had yet to be published, more than a year after our trip. I was told only that there had been some delays.

I was surprised when the NATIONAL GEOGRAPHIC story in the July 1979 issue had both text and photos under Ned's byline, but I did not learn the rest of the story until decades later. In 1997, a retired GEOGRAPHIC writer who was interviewing me for a book project happened to mention that he had previously written a story about one of my adventures. I could not imagine which one. I usually write my own texts and have a clear memory of all the other writers I've worked with. He explained that it was the McKinley ski story, and that he had done other ghost writing for adventurers and public figures whose bylines were used in the magazine.

In 1998, Ned was shot and killed by village locals in a wild part of Pakistan before I had a chance to talk to him about how much of the story might be in his own words. Both the other team members, Alan Bard and Doug Weins, had also suffered tragic accidental deaths in the mountains. Thus I can't reread this account without feeling many pangs in my heart as the only living survivor.

Skiers in a ground blizzard on the Peters Glacier.

In 1906, the explorer Frederick Cook reported that his fast, light expedition had made the first ascent of Mount McKinley in only eight days. Cook's climb was soon discredited, however, and the rest of his life unfolded as if the hoax had been branded on his forehead. His claim to have reached the North Pole in 1909 was disbelieved mainly on the basis of the Mount McKinley episode, while Admiral Peary's polar jaunt, reported to the world at the same time and with even less documentation, was accepted as authentic. (The consensus of present-day authorities is that neither explorer actually reached the Pole, although both spent considerable time very far north.) McKinley figured yet again in Cook's life, when the climbing hoax was mentioned in a judge's verdict convicting him of selling useless land in Wyoming as oil property during the Teapot Dome scandal. Cook spent more than a decade in federal prison; his confiscated lands, in which his life savings had been invested, eventually produced more oil than he had ever promised prospective buyers. On his deathbed, he was pardoned by FDR.

Like other explorers, Cook named many of his geographical discoveries, but his names for the most part have disappeared from modern maps, and his actual achievements are all but forgotten. One of his more unusual adventures was a land circumnavigation of Mount McKinley in 1903. Up to that time, the approaches to the highest point in North America were unknown, and Cook spent four months making a 540-mile orbit along rivers, through forests, across passes and glaciers. For three-quarters of a century to come, no one else circled the mountain on the ground.

When I circled McKinley in a small plane in 1972, I was amazed by the interconnecting pattern of five major glaciers, each one longer than any in the Nepal Himalaya. They flow down the peak's flanks and abruptly turn to form a ring of ice ninety miles in circumference and shaped like the outline of a cottonwood leaf. McKinley's great circle of moving ice, entirely above timberline, is unique among the 20,000 foot peaks of the world. The great circle would have become a popular ski-mountaineering route years ago were it not for one problem: the mountain's three major buttresses trisect the route at elevations of 10,000 to 12,000 feet. This makes the difficulties involved in circling the mountain even greater than those of climbing it. In the last two decades, several groups attempted the circle, but were forced to retreat by frostbite or technical difficulties. My own eagerness to ski such a great natural route was tempered by the realization that packs might weigh one hundred pounds, a broken ski could be devastating, and certain icefalls might prove impassable.

In 1978, I was invited to join the Mount McKinley Great Circle Expedition. Ned Gillette, an Olympic cross-country skier in 1968, had full financing from some Norwegian ski companies to attempt an "orbit" far tighter than Cook's. It would be the first within the limits of the peak's glacial systems and would follow the precise route I had studied from the air. Had the choice been mine, I would have brought sturdy downhill skis with mountaineering bindings, but Ned wanted to prove the strength of the light touring skis and the narrow fifty-millimeter racing bindings that he used on packed tracks. He had already used "skinny skis" to cross Ellesmere Island, the Canadian land mass nearest the North Pole. Our foursome consisted of myself plus Ned, Alan Bard, and

Doug Weins, all of whom had skied Ellesmere in 1977. We had the climbing experience necessary to cross the three icy ridges that separate the glaciers.

We estimated that the Great Circle would take about three weeks and require two food

caches. On April 7, bush pilot Cliff Hudson landed us on the Kahiltna Glacier, just outside the boundary of Mount McKinley (now Denali) National Park. Each of us was in shape for cross-country skiing and for carrying big loads (our packs weighed ninety pounds) but not for both together. We skied off with all the grace of newborn calves, and instead of linked figure-eights, our tracks down the first easy slope resembled a child's by-the-numbers sketch, each circled number corresponding to a crater in the snow.

Three days and one storm later, we reached our first obstacle, Kahiltna Pass on the West Buttress. It was −12° F as we started up what appeared to be a forty-degree snowslope; we quickly discovered that a thin frost layer lightly covered blue ice underneath. I led a full rope length on front points without finding a belay. With our second and last rope tied on, I reached a snow-covered crevasse about two feet wide. I couldn't place a secure screw in the rotten ice, and my axe sank too easily into the powdery snow outside the crevasse. I dug my way inside and sat on a snowbridge directly over the rope; if the screw and axe pulled out, I planned to become a human anchor by jumping in.

When we reached the crest of the Alaska Range, we could see endless white plains to the north beyond peaks coated in a winter armor of blue ice. Below us, the Peters Glacier stretched smoothly into the distance. To gain the head of the glacier, we descended several thousand feet of steep snow. The surface of the glacier was a frozen ocean of icy waves and swells. A ground blizzard driven by high winds added a mystical haze to the landscape.

We found little time to contemplate the great beauty of the scene, however, for without metal ski edges, we fell down repeatedly. Alan took an especially bad header and dislocated his shoulder. He stood up in pain, popped the joint back in with his own tug, and held his arm helplessly against his chest. We set up camp immediately, wondering if two of us would have to make at least a week's journey out to summon a rescue.

In the morning Alan was able to continue, but on foot instead of on skis. Luckily, we were now on a section of hard windslab rather than the powder snow of earlier days. That afternoon Alan decided to try skiing, timidly on gentle slopes. He was afraid of losing control on the downhill runs, but the conditions made this impossible. The surface of the entire lower glacier was underlain with depth hoar—bottomless sugar snow formed in cold, dry conditions—and for the next two days we were held to a pace of two miles in ten hours. Typically, we alternated from knee-deep snow to sudden holes of thigh-deep crystals that rolled underfoot like ball bearings. This resulted in frequent falls, always onto

Alan Bard skiing up the Kahiltna Glacier on the first day.

*Above: Ned Gillette skiing near
camp beneath the Moose's Tooth.*

*Below: Ned links turns in
fresh powder on cross-country
skis carrying a 90-pound pack.*

one's back, followed by the tiring struggle to get up again. I was reminded of a cartoon that showed a backpacker lying on his back by a trail, his arms and legs flailing, and one observer commenting to another: "I hear they die if you don't turn them over."

From the wretched Peters Glacier, we headed up Gunsight Pass and onto the Muldrow Glacier. The depth hoar was gone, and we had easy sailing for several days as we turned up the Traleika Glacier toward the East Buttress of McKinley. We were through the easy half of our circle, and by this time our individual roles in the expedition had become clear. Ned was our leader. His job was to make decisions when there was a difference of opinion on how to proceed, but we always wanted to do the same things; so instead he busied himself with watching his carefully planned dream unfold. I was our logistics officer, responsible for such key decisions as which way to aim the tent door each night. Each morning, with the consistency of the rising sun, a brisk wind blew from the exact direction the door was aimed. Alan Bard was to have been our humorist, but since everyone joked, he contributed his laughter to the general supply. Doug Weins, the lightest member of the party, quickly earned the title of chief crevasse locator. Regardless of whether he was first or last on the rope at any given time, he faithfully punched his body through the snow to discover dangerous holes for us. As it happened, he had the greatest fear of crevasses.

The East Buttress was the next major problem to overcome, and we spent six hours ascending it over 2,500 feet of steep ice and snow. The route down the Ruth Glacier side was even more continuously steep, so we decided to bivouac on top rather than risk getting caught on the headwall, which averaged seventy degrees for a thousand feet. We pitched our tent on the narrow ridge crest as clouds swirled around us blocking our view. Just before sunset they lifted to reveal one of the most beautiful landscapes on earth. From an elevation of nearly 11,000 feet we looked directly across the glacier at the granite and ice of the Moose's Tooth, Mount Dickey, and Mount Huntington. The moon rose into a clear sky that turned pink, then lilac, and finally the indigo blue of an Alaskan spring night.

The next morning we made the first rappel down the headwall. It was underlain with water ice, and placing anchors was a major problem. After we left our only two ice screws behind as rappel anchors, we relied entirely on fixing the rope around bollards shoveled out of the snow cover or chopped laboriously into the ice. When the afternoon sun hit the slope, we became concerned about avalanche danger. As we neared the base and the angle lessened, Ned unroped and rushed out of reach of potential slides. Alan and I followed. Walking in our tracks, Doug dropped into a bergschrund and disappeared from sight except for the tips of his skis. It was just blind luck that the bergschrund was nearly full of snow. Doug was able to climb out without our help. When all four of us finally stood clear of the headwall, we jumped up and down in joyful relief. (On returning from the expedition, we learned that we had been the first to cross the East Buttress. A British party in 1962 had crested the ridge, only to retreat after looking down the other side.)

The next day began in trepidation and ended with joyful surprises. At first we felt closed in by the peaks and icefalls that separated our arm of the Ruth Glacier from the main trunk, but after some anxious searching, a skiable route opened in front of us.

Nearing the great Don Sheldon Amphitheater we crossed outside the national park boundary, [into the unprotected public lands then under consideration as a southern extension of the park].

Around midday as we lunched on the open glacier, two loud noises interrupted our solitude. The first was a great avalanche, falling 4,000 feet and rolling half a mile across the flats before it stopped uncomfortably close to us. The second was even louder and nearer: an airplane buzzed us at fifteen feet. Now that we had entered an area where low flights and air drops were permitted, Cliff Hudson was checking our progress before leaving our final cache next to Don Sheldon's Mountain House. As the plane passed overhead, we were bombarded by falling objects marked with yellow streamers. The others rushed for cans of beer, and I found a letter from my lady in California. When I opened it, a wildflower fell out into my hand.

In the midst of this sterile landscape, the tiny flower affected me powerfully. Like animals on the hunt, mountaineers must rely almost entirely on immediate sensations. The wildflower in my hand freed my thoughts from the present and set them on a track of wild speculation; I began to see both the surrounding scene and my companions through the veil of time. I wondered if the same species of flower had once grown during an ancient interglacial period in the place where I now stood. Here in the Ruth Gorge was a glimpse of how the Sierra and the Rockies must have looked during the height of the Pleistocene glaciations.

Some of the same sort of cooperative behavior that primitive man had developed for hunting and defense was evident in our group. Modern equipment couldn't hide what we left behind us each morning; a depression in the snow surrounded by tracks and droppings, not unlike the bedding area of any large mammal. Traveling this glacial world forced us to recognize our primeval heritage. I recalled John Muir's feeling of "an unexplainable mysticism" while in the presence of glaciers, and the more explicit theory of the modern biologist Valerius Geist, who discounts Africa as the major source of recent human evolution and believes that the coming of the ice in more northerly latitudes was the major factor that forced our ancestors to cooperate in groups and develop their brains.

Holding a flower on an ocean of ice, I wondered if the joy I felt in the cold, inhospitable world might be rooted in my genes. Perhaps our venture, away from our homes and loved ones over primeval valleys of ice, somehow replicated an archetypal way of human life. A sense of unfathomable nearness pulsed through me and the world seemed to be closing in around me. Then I looked toward the Gateway to the Great Gorge. Imagined images from times I never knew were intertwined with explicit memories of my earlier visits to the gorge, and then the moment was gone. I was back in the present.

Continuing on across the Ruth Glacier, we reached the Mountain House, where we spent a blissful night in the comfort of the cabin, followed by a rest day. Our second and final cache lay buried near the house in two cartons. I tore rapaciously into the first box, but Alan suggested waiting before we opened the second. On Alan's suggestion, Ned and I went off together on an afternoon ski tour to the mouth of the Gorge. We returned to a cabin brightly decorated for a surprise party. Alan and Doug had packed the second box in Ned's Vermont basement and had included all the trimmings for Ned's thirty-third

birthday. Balloons, crepe streamers, and party favors hung from the ceiling. To the strains of "Happy Birthday," Ned was presented with an endless array of things-you-always-wanted-on-a-glacier: party hats, whistles, a toy telephone, a plastic gun that spun tops into the air, popcorn, a cake with candles, and a tall bottle of whiskey. Just then a group of younger climbers on their first remote expedition happened on the scene; they couldn't have looked more surprised had they been invited into a spaceship. The party continued well into the night.

A day of waiting out a storm, plus two easy days up the west fork of the Ruth Glacier, brought us to a cul-de-sac underneath Ruth Gap, the lowest point between the Ruth and Kahiltna Glaciers. Festooned with overhanging ice, this low point had wisely not been called a pass. To the best of our knowledge it had never been crossed, and it still hasn't. We opted for a longer, less steep route that crested the South Buttress of McKinley at 12,000 feet. Luckily we had acquired two more ice screws from a Mount Huntington expedition; these aided our passage up a section of 60-degree blue ice. That day ended in the middle of a broken icefall on the Kahiltna side of the buttress. Two long over-hanging rappels were necessary to connect a route through the giant seracs. One ended hanging over space. I had to swing back and forth in order to sink an axe in the far wall of a deep crevasse.

On our nineteenth day we found an easy path through the steep lower icefall onto the east fork of the Kahiltna Glacier. When we joined the main glacier we spotted some ski tracks that were nearly imperceptible until the light hit the snow at just the right angle. It took us a while to realize that these tracks were our own. We had closed the "Great Circle."

Our expedition lacked the great geographical climax of a summit. Like polar explorers, we stood in a snowy expanse where one spot looked like the next. Our goal was to come back to a starting point, not to reach the heights and turn around. By itself, the patch of snow where we stood was insignificant; what counted was how we had come to reach it. As Ned simply put it: "We have reached completion."

A moonlit night at Don Sheldon's Mountain House on Ruth Glacier,
the only permanent structure in thousands of square miles on wildlands.

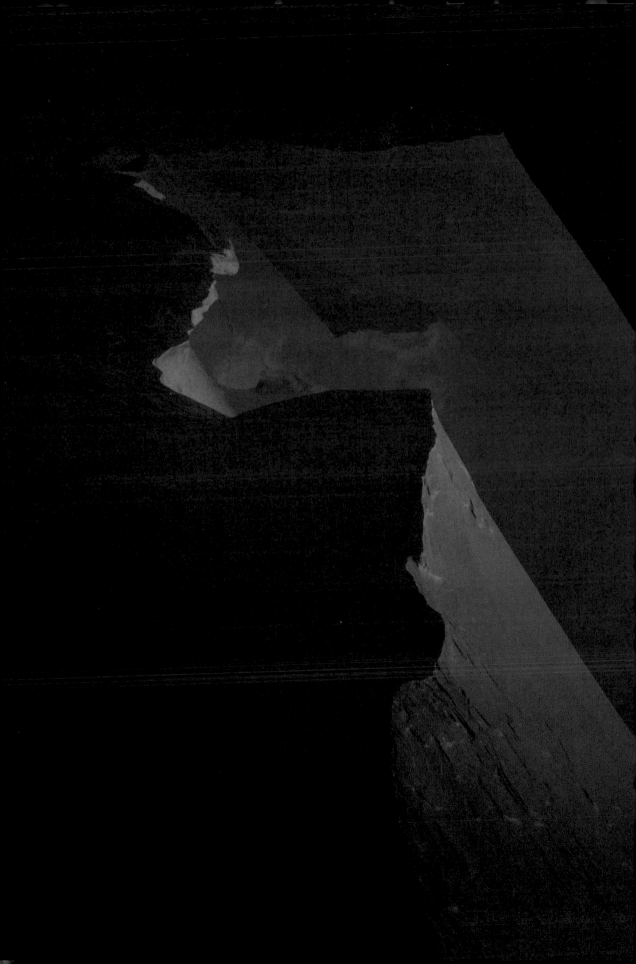

16

A One-Day Ascent of Mount McKinley

The idea of climbing McKinley in a day came to me while guiding a three-week ascent of the peak in 1976. I had to descend to help evacuate a sick client from 14,000 to the 7,000-foot landing area on the Kahiltna Glacier, and I was surprised how few hours it took me to return with just a day pack instead of the usual load of enough food and gear to wait out long storms on the mountain.

The fastest previous climb had taken three days, with one member requiring a rescue, but I believed a one-day ascent was not only possible, but also more satisfying with just a light pack and the minimum of climbing and cold weather gear. I planned to acclimatize with a partner for more than a week at 14,000 feet in California, then fly to Alaska and set off in the night from 10,000 feet between Mount McKinley and Mount Foraker. When Ned Gillette invited me to circle McKinley at altitudes up to 13,000 feet, I saw a great opportunity to try the day climb at the end of the ski trip.

We succeeded on our second attempt and had our bush pilot fly us directly to Anchorage to catch a flight to Europe to make a scheduled meeting with future expedition sponsors. Weeks later, we learned that our climb had been discredited in the Alaskan media. The super-intendent of Denali Park told a reporter we couldn't have done the climb in a day, as did Bradford Washburn, the world's expert on the mountain. A year later, when the NATIONAL GEOGRAPHIC called to ask if I had a summit photo to verify a brief mention of our climb in Ned's story on our ski trip, I said that my tiny Minox camera had frozen up and I had no photos high on the peak. When they said they were going to delete mention of it, I suggested they contact a British climber we had met just below the top. When they reached him by phone in London, he told them how he and his partner had passed us on the final stretch hours after we had walked by their tent in the night, stopped out of sight a few feet from the top, started their stove, and announced, "Would you like a cup of tea?" when we showed up. He sent them a photo of us sipping tea by the summit.

Had we not met the Britishers, our ascent would have gone down in the literature as doubtful, if at all. The foundation of mountaineering is trust. Since this experience I am far more inclined to take the claims of climbers who say they completed a wild ascent without documentation at face value, unless solid evidence exists to the contrary—as in Cook's faked photographs of the supposed first ascent of McKinley.

Midnight sun on corniced ridge at 16,500 feet on Mount McKinley's West Buttress.

When we became partners for two unique Alaskan adventures, Ned Gillette and I hardly knew each other. Chance had brought us together in Vermont when Ned had driven forty miles on a winter night to attend my lecture on high-altitude climbing. As we talked after the lecture, we both felt an unusually strong bond of understanding and trust. Ned invited me to join his ski expedition to circle Mount McKinley (described in the preceding chapter); I in turn asked him to join me immediately afterwards in an attempt to climb McKinley in a single day from its western base at 10,000 feet. Although we had no way of foreseeing it then, our mutual trust was to undergo an extreme test.

After the ski orbit went like clockwork, Ned and I camped at the base of McKinley's West Buttress, waiting for a clear day. When it came, we were off at 2:30 a.m. in the April twilight of the Alaska Range. By 5 a.m. we had reached Windy Corner at 13,400 feet where the temperature was –20° F. Instead of the soft snow I had found on a previous climb, we encountered windblown snow and patches of blue ice. Just as we stopped to switch from skis to crampons, Ned's ski edges suddenly slid, and he plummeted toward a cliff, sixty feet away. Ned and I were roped together with our ice axes cleverly lashed to our packs, well out of reach. In the seconds before the rope pulled tight, I jammed the tip of a ski pole into the ice in a futile attempt at a self-arrest; then a tremendous jerk at my waist launched me toward Ned's falling form. I saw myself headed for a last, long ride in space—a vision as ghastly as Slim Pickens riding down the bomb in the final scene of "Dr. Strangelove."

A mere arm's length from the cliff, I stopped face first against Ned's steel ski edges. Our individual actions, unknown to each other, had cooperated to save our lives. My self-arrest had failed, but not before it slowed Ned for a split second, enabling him to grab a fixed rope left by an earlier expedition as he fell head first on his back. Adrenalin gave his gloved hand a death grip on the quarter-inch polypropylene. Had he not stopped with his skis in the air, I would have fallen past him and pulled us both off the cliff.

My hand went to my face, and my fingers felt a gaping hole where I once had a mouth. My front teeth were missing, and my lower lip was split, spread to my chin like blinders on a horse's face. With the gentle confidence that had gained my trust in Vermont, Ned said, "Don't move until we figure this out; I'm holding us with a rope in my hand behind my back."

Late that same day, a plastic surgeon in Anchorage put my face back together. We had managed our own rescue by climbing and skiing twelve miles down the peak and its glaciers to a landing area for bush pilots. Once, Ned slipped into a crevasse behind me, and I pulled so hard that he popped up like toast out of a toaster.

While my injuries healed, Ned and I spent hours on the telephone between Vermont and California discussing whether we could have made the climb if the fall had not occurred. We didn't wait long to find out. A month after the accident, we returned to Mount McKinley for another try.

Normal expeditions take a month to climb the peak. What made us think we could do it so quickly? Although we were more fit than most men in their mid-thirties, we were no more so than the thousands of men, women, and children who can run twenty-six mile marathons in less than three hours. Although I run five to twelve miles of hills every day, my efforts to move my fireplug-shaped body twenty-six miles at a time never bettered three hours. To climb McKinley in one day, I estimated that we would need to expend the effort of four marathons back to back—sixteen to twenty hours on the move. The comparison with running cannot be taken further. The runner has the security of knowing he can quit by simply walking off the course; the climber must find security elsewhere. Big expeditions rely on portable environments, survival equipment, and manpower. For two men with day packs on the coldest 20,000-foot peak on earth, security must come from within, from self-knowledge. Learning to combine extreme mental and physical stresses is a major reward of climbing mountains. Ned and I felt that we had the necessary blend of stamina, altitude experience, climbing skills, will power, and knowledge of the surroundings to try McKinley with no more equipment than could fit into a day pack.

Conventional expeditions move at a snail's pace because, like that animal, they carry their homes on their backs. Encumbered with hundreds of pounds per person of food, fuel, and Arctic survival gear, these groups follow the tradition established by the 1913 first ascent of Mount McKinley.

The story of the first ascent is relatively uneventful, with the exception of an astonishing sight the climbers saw from the top: a flagpole on the summit ridge of the north peak, which is nine hundred feet lower. Three years earlier, in 1910, an Alaskan sourdough named Tom Lloyd mushed his dog team into Fairbanks, claiming that he had led his party of four from 10,000 feet to the summit of McKinley in a single day and had planted a fourteen-foot spruce flagpole on top. After an initial flurry of interest, the story was classed with legends of lost gold mines and Sasquatch sightings, but the verification of the pole by the 1913 party confirmed the tall tale as partial reality. It turned out that Lloyd had exaggerated his personal role. Weighing well over 200 pounds, he was not particularly fit, and, in fact, had never ventured over 11,000 feet. His three companions, however, had indeed gone for the summit from a camp at 10,800 feet. Charley McGonagall, reputed to be the strongest man in the North, tired of carrying the pole and quit at 18,000 feet. Billy Taylor and Pete Anderson then took the pole and reached the top of the north peak—an amazing 8,500-foot climb in one day. They had spent three previous weeks shoveling and stomping a path to 16,000 feet before finally going for the top, and in this way they had inadvertently acclimatized themselves to levels well above their high camp. Their claim that they would have reached the true summit, had they known it to be higher, is entirely plausible.

If Taylor and Anderson had been credited with the true first ascent, subsequent McKinley climbs—and perhaps the entire history of American expeditionary climbing abroad—might have been based on their bold style. As it was, the Sourdough's saga became a Paul Bunyan tale repeated around campfires but not in real life. For sixty-eight years, no one attempted another one-day climb from a comparable altitude. Meanwhile, more than a thousand people had reached McKinley's summit using traditional heavy expeditions and high camps.

The Sourdough climb was the unwitting forerunner of the most modern style of high-altitude climbing, a sport that had moved up a blind alley for most of the century.

Giant military-style expeditions hastened their own obsolescence by proving that any mountain on earth could be climbed—given enough time, equipment, money, and porter carries. The new challenge is to do great peaks in "alpine style," without fixed ropes, camps, high porters, or oxygen apparatus. An unsupported climber simply can't carry enough food and fuel to sustain himself for more than a few days on a big mountain; true alpine-style ascents must be done very fast, or not at all.

As of 1979, four of the dozen highest peaks in the world had been climbed in three days or less by fast, light expeditions. Although Mount McKinley is far lower in measured elevation than any of those, it is actually greater in vertical relief from timberline to summit. And its weather—the biggest unknown factor in any alpine-style ascent—is notoriously bad.

For two days after we had come up from sea level, Ned and I sat in the clouds at 10,000 feet, waiting for a perfect twenty-four hours of clear, still air on a peak that has the worst year-round climate of any non-polar spot on earth.

At noon on the third day the clouds lifted; the upper mountain gleamed against blue sky. Our day had arrived rather soon, for we had counted on at least five days of acclimatization at 10,000 feet before dashing up to 20,000 feet. The forecast was for forty hours of rare calm, followed by a storm; if we let it pass, we might not get another clear spell before our ten-day supply of food and fuel ran out. On the other hand, climbing too soon could be dangerous. Our one-day time frame was far from arbitrary. The extra weight of food and fuel needed for two days would probably push the climb into a third day. Pulmonary and cerebral edema, two forms of the often fatal "climber's bends" brought on by fatigue and sudden altitude gain, almost never start until twenty-four hours after stress. Descent is a sure cure in all but the most advanced cases. To get out of the clutches of extreme altitude in a single day was sound preventive medicine. But could we move that fast without acclimatization?

We tried to postpone a decision and sleep a few hours but anxiety kept us wide awake. At 9 p.m. on June 9, we shouldered day packs, stepped into our skis, and struck off. We made fast time, and the sun was just setting as we reached our old 13,400-foot high point at 11:00 p.m. The icy traverse where we had fallen was now covered with firm snow, but without exchanging a word we cached our skis for the descent and strapped crampons onto our boots. (Ned had devised a boot combination for us utilizing oversized "Habeler Superlight" summer mountaineering boots with thin foam inners from downhill ski boots, giving us more warmth than normal double boots at a fraction of the weight.) The four-hour Alaskan night held no threat of darkness, and we continued on.

At six in the morning, we took our first long rest at the standard high camp at 17,300 feet. Just below, Ned had vomited from the altitude and fatigue and was unsure about continuing, but I was eager to keep going. I started our tiny stove next to an igloo, waking two climbers who had been sleeping inside. One of them complained in a strong British accent. Hot drinks, cheese, and the warmth of the sun's first rays gave Ned the strength to continue, and we left before the other climbers emerged from the igloo. We climbed for two more hours to Denali Pass at 18,200 feet, where we paused on the crest of the Alaska Range under a sky of unbroken indigo in absolutely still air.

Ned Gillette just above the clouds on the first one-day ascent of Mount McKinley.

It was a day even better than our wildest dreams, but Ned was still feeling poorly and quietly announced that he wanted to quit. My heart sank. "We'll never have another chance like this," I told him. "Only 2,000 feet and we're there, and it's still early morning." He assented, and we moved on, marching like wound-down toy soldiers.

At 19,000 feet, two small figures approached from below as we lay sprawled in the snow resting, all dignity abandoned. The two men stopped and eyed the obviously unfit and out-of-place climbers at their feet, and one of them remarked, "Anyone who needs a rope up here doesn't belong on this mountain!" The British accent identified him as one of the men whose sleep we had interrupted at 17,300 feet. When we introduced ourselves, their attitude became friendlier.

The Britisher, Nigel Gifford, had been on expeditions to Everest and Nuptse and was planning to look me up as a climbing partner in California. His companion, John Purdue, was a Canadian. Nigel's comment about the rope had made Ned and I realize that we could do without the extra weight, so we left both rope and packs lying in the snow when we again set off. All four of us started out together, but because of Nigel and John's rest and acclimatization, Ned and I quickly were left behind. I soon began to feel like a zombie, while Ned's nausea disappeared. Our roles were being reversed and Ned was now the stronger, but our cooperative efforts kept us going.

As we neared 20,000 feet, we watched Nigel and John reach the summit, turn around, and start back down. When they stopped only a hundred feet below the top and didn't move for a long time, we wondered if something was wrong. We reached them half an hour later and found them sitting on a platform they had stamped into the steep slope, with their stove humming reassuringly in the still air. With the air of a proper British gentleman, Nigel inquired, "Would you like a cup of tea?"

We sipped and chatted for half an hour before continuing on a few minutes to the top. We were rewarded with a splendid view of the entire "Great Circle" of glaciers we had recently skied for the first time. Our climb had taken nineteen hours all told—nine for the 7,300 feet to 17,300 and another nine, after a forty-five-minute rest, to make the last 3,000 feet. The vertical distance we had covered was very nearly that from Mount Everest's base camp to its summit. The effort had required most of our strength, and as we started down, we moved like people with nerve injuries learning to walk—minds focused, but bodies responding with only a glimmer of their normal ability. Ned occasionally had to help me over even slight rises in the terrain, and we inevitably fell asleep during brief rests, even on steep slopes. Whoever remained conscious longer would jerk the other awake with the rope.

Just before we reached the 17,300-foot camp, I checked my breathing, as I had at least once an hour since we had been above 17,000 feet. Slight gurgles in my chest indicated the beginnings of pulmonary edema; the symptoms had appeared twenty-three hours after my first exposure to increased altitude and stress—almost precisely as predicted by the experts.

The National Park Service has spent tens of thousands of taxpayers' dollars helicoptering edema victims off McKinley's upper slopes, and they advise climbers not to go too high too quickly. Statistics do show that slower parties run less risk of edema, but fail to take into account the simple logic that fast, mobile parties have a far greater chance to reverse the course of the illness by prompt descent. Most rescues come after a climber has stayed in a high camp for a period of days—usually in bad weather, further delaying air rescue. We had no radio to summon a rescue and felt absolutely no need to call out, as we planned to descend quickly. When we reached high camp, we found Gifford and Purdue camped there with a large guided expedition. We were equipped to bivouac, but we gladly accepted their offer to join them for the short, four-hour night. Because the expedition had a radio, we decided not to mention the mild edema symptoms for fear of initiating an unnecessary rescue.

In the morning we climbed down to Windy Corner, where our skis were cached, and finished the descent with a splendid 3,500-foot downhill run through icefalls and snow bowls. By the time we crawled into our tent at Kahiltna Pass, my edema had subsided. Ned and I sat watching storm clouds creep up the forty-six mile length of the Kahiltna Glacier toward the mountain and talking about our experience. It was our first real opportunity to relax and reflect; the pace of the climb had been too intense, and we had been far too busy monitoring the weather, our progress, and our bodies.

We agreed that we owed our success on this venture—and our lives on the first attempt—to our cooperative actions, our mutual trust, and our common will. This knowledge was its own reward, and we found satisfaction in having met the mountain on its own terms—penetrating its defenses with a few classic tools. It had not been our goal to start a speed competition on the mountain; we knew that our time would be bettered some day by people who had acclimatized longer and trained harder. We hoped that others would adopt the heritage of the Sourdoughs, seeking simple ways of dealing with nature, rather than striving to overcome a mountain by a long siege. It was for this kind of experience that Ned and I had formed our partnership. Before we went to sleep, we talked of doing other fast and light expeditions in the ultimate range, the Himalaya.

17

Man and Beast in the Karakoram

On my very first Himalayan expedition in 1975, I had a chance meeting with one of the world's top zoologists, whose spartan travels were in sharp contrast to our K2 extravaganza with 650 porters. The time we spent together broadened my horizons about environmental problems in seemingly remote parts of the world. I came away with a keen interest in Himalayan wildlife and a resolve never again to climb with a large expedition, which I maintained through twenty-five more Himalayan journeys in years to come. Many of the campsites we used in 1975 soon became devastated by the passage of hundreds of expeditions with thousands of porters.

At the time, I was in favor of a proposed K2 National Park, but my new friend decided against supporting it after surveying less wildlife and less threat to the environment than around the newly constructed Karakoram Highway to Khunjerab Pass at 16,000 feet through Marco Polo sheep habitat. Mainly through his efforts, Khunjerab National Park was created later in 1975. Two decades later, my wish came true when the entire region surrounding K2 and its major glaciers became a large Central Karakoram National Park shortly before I made my ninth journey to the Karakoram. I was gratified to find that ibex, mountain sheep, and snow leopards are still to be found on the heights and valleys of the range.

Some of the Earth's most splendid mountain scenery is in the Baltoro Glacier region of the Karakoram Range in northern Pakistan. Seven of the world's seventeen highest peaks encircle the Concordia Amphitheater, where glaciers pause before joining into a single stream for a thirty-mile plunge down a granite canyon that makes Yosemite seem like a city park. Although the single peak of Mount Everest is taller, this region—a thousand miles to the northwest—has the world's highest mean elevation. Another feature that sets it apart from most mountain areas of exceptional beauty is that it has no legal protection whatsoever.

We Americans have a long history of isolationism, and although it has dwindled from our politics, it still haunts our environmental thinking. Many of us are lulled into a false confidence that certain areas will remain pristine because of their geographical remoteness. I thought so until I trekked over two hundred miles round-trip to K2, the 28,250-foot culmination of the Karakoram Himalaya.

The expression of a recently captured snow leopard seems to evoke George Schaller's comment that "when the last snow leopard disappears from the icy crags, an intangible aura of mystery will vanish, too."

I had dreamed of visiting the Karakoram ever since I began mountain climbing in my teens. Over campfires in the High Sierra, I found others who shared the same image: a light, self-contained expedition and one which would not pursue high summits that required oxygen and hundreds of native porters. A phone call erased that image in an instant. I was offered a place on the 1975 American K2 Expedition. The choice was clear-cut: to go or stay home.

In April 1975, ten of us sat in an ancient high-ceilinged hotel room in Rawalpindi, Pakistan. We were waiting for a daily-scheduled flight to Skardu in Pakistan-held Kashmir, the embarkation point for the Karakoram. We had begun to realize why PIA airline was locally called "Perhaps I Arrive," or "Please Inform Allah." The cloud-shy pilots fly only in perfect weather, so the flight was delayed by storms for eleven days. Stacked in the corner of the large room were dozens of five-gallon tins of rancid butter, purchased for our six hundred porters at a cost of over $700. We were discussing the $2,000 cost of our government-required porter insurance when someone knocked at the door.

A tall slender man dressed in American clothes entered the room. We had never seen him before. He asked if our expedition had someone named Dr. Schaller. We replied that Rob Schaller was our expedition doctor. He said, "My name is Dr. Schaller, too. I've been getting phone calls from a young lady I do not know in the United States. She's on the phone right now, in the hotel lobby." Robert T. Schaller, a marathon runner, shot out the door as if he had heard a starter's pistol. The new Dr. Schaller turned to leave. Something clicked in my head, but I thought, no, it couldn't be; this person is too young to have done all that. The man I'm thinking of must be seventy.

Leif Patterson, a step ahead of me, asked the new Dr. Schaller if he was by chance the zoologist, George B. Schaller, who had written *The Year of the Gorilla* and *The Serengeti Lion*. Modestly, he answered "Yes," then departed nearly as quickly as his namesake.

Curiosity got the best of me. I visited George Schaller in his hotel room that evening and learned that he planned to follow our same route, walking two hundred miles round trip up the Baltoro Glacier nearly to the base of K2. Because our expedition might disturb what he had come to study, he had planned to go ahead of us, but had also been held back by the flight.

Looking about the empty room I asked him where all his provisions were. He would be traveling over glaciers at high altitude far beyond the highest village. He pointed to a small box on the floor that contained about twenty pounds of nuts and meats. Only one porter and a Pakistani friend would accompany him. His object was to survey large mammals in the K2 region and assess the need for a national park as proposed by the government. K2 is possibly the most remote high mountain on earth, not visible from any inhabited spot. Why would such a place need the protection a national park could offer? Schaller wasn't sure that it did, but he realized that time was running out for the once-remote mountains. More

Above: George Schaller and Pervez Khan in the Skardu Valley.
Opposite: Crescent moon behind the ridge of an unnamed Karakoram peak near K2.

people had visited the Himalaya in the last decade than in all preceding history.

K2 and the Baltoro Glacier region missed this onslaught because the area was closed for political reasons from 1961 to 1974. Through no intent or forethought—most probably because of the lack of it—the government of Pakistan held the region back in time, saving it from clashes with modern culture. Now, a year after the floodgates were opened in 1974, nineteen expeditions had permission to travel the same route toward the Baltoro. While they would certainly bring back new aesthetic and topographic information, they would do little to illuminate other concerns more basic to establishing a park. How much pristine flora and fauna are left to save? Does human habitation in the valleys make the concept of a park untenable? Who would benefit? Who would lose? Schaller's tiny expedition had a better chance of answering these questions than all the others combined, but as I talked to him in his hotel room, I wondered if we each might have our special brand of blinders. I would be marching straight toward K2 in a caravan of six hundred, as insulated from the true environment as a politician touring a ghetto in a limousine, while Schaller would walk the narrow path of science, rendering unfathomable splendor into a jargon of numbers and words.

I couldn't have been more wrong. At first, Schaller's world seemed closed to me. He answered questions like a computer; just what I expected from a dedicated scientist. Then he began to quiz me:

"What route are you trying on K2?"

"The West Ridge. It's unclimbed, you know."

"Oh. That's on the other side of the mountain from the Italian route. You must be going up the Godwin-Austen Glacier, then up the Savoia very near the Chinese border."

"Exactly. Our route lies directly on the border. How do you know so much about the mountain? You're supposed to be a zoologist, not a climber."

"I've read a lot about the expeditions. I used to climb some myself."

Now in his early forties, Schaller's interests seemed as diverse as a child's. He had a healthy sense of wonder; he yearned to travel into Tibet, but had been turned down by the Chinese. He had studied the relationships between predators and prey in India, especially the tiger and the deer, and had made three prior visits to the Karakoram and the Hindu Kush on the Afghan side of the border, once taking the only photographs of snow leopards ever made in the wild. Eating *chapatties* in a native village was far less foreign to him than reclining in a comfortable chair in academia.

What separated Schaller from most adventurers was his keen intellect. He assumed nothing unless he confirmed the facts for himself, thus avoiding the common plight of building a false pyramid of logic on top of someone else's misconception. At the same

Above: Siberian ibex above the Baltoro Glacier.
Opposite: Barefoot Ballti in a dust storm, Skardu Valley.

time, he would not quickly dismiss a statement just because it was not backed by a verified fact. Instead he would tuck it into his mind: a new avenue to investigate if the chance arose. He professed what was heresy to many wildlife managers: "It is sometimes necessary for radical protective measures to precede, rather than follow, scientific studies and surveys."

Pakistan was a classic example. Wildlife research was at least forty years behind North America. Local universities were not ecologically oriented, and Schaller believed that wildlife officials worked almost in an intellectual vacuum. "I met no one who knew details of the wildlife research program in neighboring Iran," he mused. "I work mainly with large mammals not just because they are my specialty, but also because their status and condition normally indicate the concern with which a country treats its natural resources. In Pakistan, a great number of animals are on the threshold of extinction."

The night before I met Schaller, I had dined with a Pakistani who seemed most knowledgeable about local wildlife. When I asked about the Abominable Snowman, he laughed in open contempt. Schaller fielded the same question entirely differently:

"I don't know whether such a creature exists, but if it does it will be found in the forested regions between Nepal and Bhutan rather than in the arid Karakoram. I've studied photographs of the tracks and there are characteristics that have not yet been explained to my satisfaction. Some of them may be melted-out tracks of smaller animals, or of bears, but others have subtle things in common with gorilla tracks; things that no one could fake unless they had spent years studying primates. I'm not saying that the Abominable Snowman is a gorilla, quite to the contrary, but the latent similarities intrigue me. I would not be that surprised if an undiscovered large primate exists in very low numbers."

A few days later, Schaller joined us on a chartered flight to Skardu. We crossed the moist Western Himalaya near Nanga Parbat, then watched the terrain plunge downward for 23,000 feet into the canyon of the Indus River, the largest land escarpment on earth. Beyond, the Karakoram swelled in an endless sea of white caps rising from arid valleys into the clouds. In the distance, K2 rose high above the others, a perfect pyramid hoisted on the shoulders of giants.

Only ten of our twelve tons of gear were on the flight, so we waited an extra week for another plane. Meanwhile, Schaller went about his survey, inviting me to join him one day. We rode with Pakistani wildlife managers to a nearby valley that was reported to have ibex—large wild goats that inhabit mountains in Europe, North Africa, and Asia. Not far beyond the end of the jeep road, the officials stopped to go fishing. Schaller and I continued, hiring a native boy to help us spot wildlife. When Schaller drank from a stream, balanced on his toes and palms, I noticed that his posture was exactly like one of the big cats he had studied so long, a hint that he was somewhat more than a passive observer.

My image of lush mountain valleys dimmed after he told me that this valley, Shagarthang, was characteristic of the Karakoram. Insulated from the monsoon by the Western Himalaya, it was practically treeless, except for planted orchards, shade trees, and a few scattered junipers. The main wild growth was sagebrush and *ephedra*, similar to species found in the high deserts of the American West. Cultivation extended beyond 10,000 feet, and livestock grazed much higher, usurping almost all the available wildlife habitat. In summer, ibex could graze steep meadows up to 18,000 feet, but their population was limited by the need to descend into lower valleys in winter, where they were often shot if they didn't starve. Even with these problems, the ibex were doing better than many other species.

The snow leopard, one of the rarest of big cats, has the Achilles heel of eating its dinner slowly. With prey greatly depleted, they often resort to domestic sheep and goats. Many, while savoring their last supper, are killed by villagers. Others are shot for their valuable furs. There may be more skins for sale in city bazaars than live animals left in the mountains. Schaller estimated that only two hundred fifty survived in all of Pakistan.

He told me that existing government controls were a series of paradoxes. There were large forest departments, but few forests. There were strict laws against killing large mammals in the Karakoram, but almost no enforcement. One of the Skardu officials openly traveled with a rifle and had recently shot nine ibex and eight mountain sheep.

The day ended without seeing a single large mammal other than domestic yaks, sheep, and goats, but for Schaller it was not a failure. He questioned villagers carefully and gained considerable information on wildlife in the valley. To test them, he had thrown a few curves about species that were not present. If they passed the quiz, he placed some credence in their reports.

While we waited for our remaining equipment, Schaller began the long trek up the Braldu River toward the Baltoro. Weeks later, we met him near the glacier's snout. Excitedly, I told him about photographing a band of ibex from a few hundred feet away. He asked me for exact details, then told me that I had seen a species of urial mountain sheep locally called *shapu*; ibex have bigger horns and a grander appearance. Like a trophy hunter, I was disappointed. It was some consolation that urial were rarer. Fewer than 1,000 existed in all of Pakistan. Related to the Rocky Mountain bighorn sheep, they are built more like an antelope, and they avoid danger by speed rather than climbing cliffs.

Schaller told me of his own disappointment. According to the Pakistan Forest Department there were 4,500 ibex, 2,500 shapu, and 450 musk deer in the 1,600 square kilometers of proposed park. His survey of the heart of the same region indicated only about 100 each of ibex and urial with no sign of musk deer. He thought the department's figures were up to ten times too high. The low prey population supported very few predators. He found only old, faint signs of snow leopards and wolves plus the fresh tracks of one brown bear and several foxes. He never saw most of the high peaks because it had stormed every day. It was his opinion that the Baltoro Glacier was the ugliest in the world, and he seriously questioned whether much would be gained by creating a national park. Access was too difficult for most visitors, and wildlife could more easily be protected by stationing a game warden in the highest village. The urial needed special attention to survive, but this could be done without park status.

As he shouldered his pack to leave, he said, "If you want to try your hand at photographing ibex, there's a large herd above Liliwa, next to the glacier. They're very hard to approach."

Walking across the Baltoro I agreed with him. Completely covered with dark heaps of loose rock, it was certainly the ugliest glacier I had ever seen. The weather was still stormy, and I saw little of the mountains. Passing all that beauty hiding in the mist was as frustrating as being blindfolded on a tour of the Louvre.

I reached Liliwa camp long before the porters, and there, thousands of feet above, were ibex walking across steep snow. I climbed to within a few hundred yards of the animals at nearly 15,000 feet and counted fifteen. They were definitely aware of my presence. I tried not to exceed their toleration of closeness. When I moved a few feet nearer, they would group to retreat, but when I stayed back and pretended to ignore them, they would return to feeding on dead grasses buried under shallow snows. I watched them for several hours.

I knew avalanches were a major cause of ibex deaths, but was amazed how much their behavior resembled that of trained mountaineers and cross-country skiers. They crossed steep snow one at a time and moved vertically rather than horizontally in areas of great danger, so that their paths did not bisect the slopes. Even their daily activity cycle had adapted: they rested on ledges during the warm, dangerous hours of the afternoon. I plotted a way to get a closer look by forcing them toward a steep rock wall that could be climbed by a snow ramp leading back toward me. If they took the bait, they would climb to a ridge profiled against the sky nearly twice as close as their normal tolerance. I would try to get photos with a 500mm lens.

One by one the ibex climbed the ramp to a rock outcrop. There they regrouped and started for the next outcrop, females in the lead, youngsters in the middle, and males bringing up the rear. The first ibex reached the crest of the ridge, looked down at me, then disappeared around the corner. Each animal took its turn while I shot a roll of film in a minute or two. Here were animal counterparts of human mountaineers. Their ancestors had forsaken a more predictable but mundane existence in the valleys for an active alpine life filled with dangers. I felt a strong kinship, and as evening neared I regretted having to descend to the noisy camp.

The next morning, not far from camp, the large tracks of a snow leopard paralleled our route. They were only hours old, and though I never saw the animal, I felt something of its presence from the prints in the snow. They symbolized a bond with times not long ago when men, too, walked barefoot on the ice. I thought of the special attraction that recently glaciated valleys held for me, and realized that my emotions were dependent on finding bonds with things in my past. It was like returning to a forgotten street of my youth. Where things were changed and old buildings gone, there would be a dull ache, but it would take only a familiar tree or a crack in a sidewalk to make happiness flow into my life. In the Karakoram, much of that happiness came from meeting adversity and observing how it had shaped things. Was it my imagination, or did I see hidden similarities between the arc of a side glacier, the curl of an ibex horn, and the twisting grain of a juniper trunk, all hewn by the same wind, cold, and snow that were now acting on my own body? I knew Schaller had felt comparable emotions when he wrote, "The mountains will remain magnificent even without wildlife, but when the last snow leopard disappears from the icy crags, an intangible aura of mystery will vanish too."

This is the essence of what must be preserved by national parks: unstructured wildness where people can imagine their own destinies.

Schaller and I returned home with perceptions of the Karakoram enhanced by our own special interests. I was disappointed not to have climbed K2 and his wildlife Shangrila had not proved to be a reality. His memories were dominated by glimpses of mammals moving against a misty backdrop of mountains. Mine were of cold and sterile peaks in which wildlife decorated the foreground. These were not opposite viewpoints, but rather subtle shifts of the same basic impressions.

In a similar way, we differed on the park proposal. Schaller recognized that scenic grandeur alone would qualify the K2 region for park status, but his biological orientation made him question whether this was the place for a park. He believed that other areas of the Karakoram might be more suitable "as last refuges for animals and plants, as repositories of genetic stock in the event that some day the species may be needed to revitalize this plundered land."

I still hold to the belief that national parks should be shrines celebrating the grandest works of nature. The view from the Concordia Amphitheater exceeds anything in McKinley, Yosemite, or Grand Canyon parks. Nothing I have ever seen compares with one spring night spent at Concordia, when the cloud curtain rose after a storm and the moon shone on a vast, circular stage of incredible peaks.

Unfortunately, another extreme is also present within the proposed park boundaries. Unlike Schaller, I found no scarcity of large mammals. One species, my own, dominated all the others. Nineteen groups composed of up to 600 individuals far exceeded the meager resources of the lower valleys. Unlike other wildlife, these feral creatures had an apparent defect in their social mechanisms that lowered the carrying capacity of their habitat by concentrating them in the same places, which became quickly denuded of vegetation. Traveling with the largest group, I once observed the result of a three-day layover in one locale. The earth, the water, and the smell of the air were polluted by more than a thousand fresh piles of excrement. This barren, brown battlefield was but a wafting on the first breeze of a human tornado yet to come. The Pakistani government forbids airdrops or airlifts, thus ensuring that mass human impact will continue to increase. For the journey to the base of K2, porters must carry their own food for ten days beyond the highest village. By government regulation, they are allotted two pounds of food per day and a maximum of a fifty-five pound load. In perfect weather, with no porter strikes such as we experienced and with only half rations for the return, more porters would have to be hired to carry food than to carry expedition loads.

The problems of preservation in wildlands that have native residents are extremely complex. They cannot be solved within the normal concept of a national park. Either that concept must be modified into an overall plan to fit the K2 region, or proper measures must be undertaken individually, which seems unlikely at best. One thing seems certain: remoteness alone will no longer do the job. What is at stake is not just another frontier, but one of our planet's final strongholds.

18

Topping the Trango

The concept of climbing big Himalayan rock faces without big expeditions was quite new when my small team set out to attempt the unclimbed Great Trango Tower in 1977. Just two years earlier, I had been a member of a massive expedition with 650 porters and a $250,000 budget that failed to climb K2. Returning to do an alpine-style climb in the same area of the Karakoram Himalaya of Pakistan was an entirely different and far more positive experience. Climbing without fixed ropes or camps for a cost of less than $1000 each with a few friends and no porters beyond base camp was more like an extended version of the High Sierra rock climbs that had become second nature for me. Since then, I've made seven more journeys into the Karakorum, a range with the most consistently spectacular mountains on Earth.

On the way to K2 in 1953, Bob Craig saw the Trango Towers from the Baltoro Glacier. "These are hardly mountains," he later wrote, "they are fantasies of the imagination . . . blocks of rock, often capped with ice, rise vertically for 8,000 feet, for all the world like mammoth skyscrapers."

Even after this call to arms, the Trangos went untouched for another two decades. Mountaineers recognized that the world's greatest granite peaks were in the K2 region, but they were prevented from attempting them because of Indo-Pakistani politics. Meanwhile, the sport of mountaineering evolved more within those years than during the entire preceding century. During the years of the Karakoram closure, the distinctive mark of expedition mountaineering began to shift away from simply achieving altitude toward style. Joe Brown, the best British rock climber of his generation, made first ascents of Kangchenjunga and Mustagh Tower in the mid-fifties, but instead of turning his sights toward other big peaks, Brown put the Trango Towers at the top of his list.

In 1974 the Karakoram reopened, and Dennis Hennek organized an American expedition to the Trangos. I was invited, but opted to go to K2 instead when permission for the Trangos went to Brown's six-man expedition. As the huge K2 effort floundered on the

Reaching the summit of Great Trango Tower on the 1977 first ascent with Broad Peak, Gasherbrum IV, and Hidden Peak all topping 26,000 feet in the distance.

approach march, due to bad weather and porter strikes, I longed for the simple joy of a small expedition to the Trango Towers with a few friends. I had no clear mountain views until midway along the Baltoro Glacier. There I awoke to the sounds of a Beethoven concerto on a tape deck as the sun's first light struck the Towers. Like a branding iron held against the sky, they rose from a common base into distinctive forms of naturally pink granite that held a crimson glow.

The first tower was a castle roofed with ice, flanked by an exquisite, flawless spire culminating in a bird's beak. Then came the Great Trango Tower, a matriarch in flowing robes, at once sheer and portly. Beyond, and partly veiled in cloud, was Nameless Tower, the goal of Brown's expedition: a youthful, slim pinnacle that stayed relentlessly vertical during its final half-mile thrust. Nameless, a non-name, suggested a feature too eternal to be defined by mere mortals.

Not one of this array of summits had been reached, but their time was growing near. Returning from K2 on the flight from Skardu to Rawalpindi I sat with Joe Brown's expedition, going home after a failure on the Trangos. Six hundred feet from the 20,500-foot summit, Martin Boysen had jammed his knee in a crack. After hours of agony, his buddies brought up bivouac gear so that he could hang all night in some comfort. That inspired him toward a more drastic measure. He used a knife to cut away his thick pants from his knee, piece by piece. His knee came out bleeding and battered; the expedition, already far behind schedule, retreated.

By 1977, when we received permission to return to the Karakoram, a number of the region's granite peaks had been climbed, including Nameless Tower, but the Great Trango Tower remained virgin. My photographs of it showed a superb natural line ascending the southwest face in a bold "Z." I hoped our six-man expedition could climb it alpine-style, without fixed ropes or relaying of loads. To do an unclimbed Trango Tower with simplicity and speed seemed to us the ultimate joy in Himalayan adventure.

On the morning of July 19, 1977, I headed up a 3,500-foot couloir with a sixty-pound pack as fast as I could go. One trip up the gully: that was all; one trip that the six of us planned never to repeat again; one trip with everything we needed for an alpine-style climb. The couloir led to a col separating the Great Trango from the first tower, and it acted as an avalanche funnel for the massive south faces of both peaks. I felt like a snail on a city sidewalk, carrying my home on my back in the presence of forces that could squash me without warning.

We were rushing the couloir when the odds were with us in the cool of the morning. For five days we had camped under the Trangos, watching the face and the weather. On every one of them gargantuan slides of rock and snow had swept the couloir. When the sun struck the upper face, the safety catch would unfreeze on untold tons of poised rock and snow, ready to explode without warning down the gunbarrel we were ascending. Four of us reached the 17,000-foot col within minutes of one another, taking less than

Overleaf: Sunrise on Great Trango and Nameless Towers.

four hours to move 3,500 vertical feet with heavy loads at altitude—a sustained physical output equivalent to running a marathon. We four were equals, the best-matched foursome I'd ever climbed with. But we wouldn't have been on the Trango Towers were it not for the other two climbers, still in the dangerous couloir long past noon.

Dennis Hennek was a carpenter, John Roskelley a geologist, Kim Schmitz an unemployed ski bum, and I a free lance photographer and writer. Between us, we didn't even have the funds to cover our air tickets. Below us were doctors Jim Morrissey and Lou Buscaglia. Jim had led the 1973 American Dhaulagiri Expedition and had future plans for K2 in 1979 (which were cancelled after my 1975 K2 team reorganized for a successful ascent in 1978). He wanted to see K2 firsthand, so both he and his friend Lou paid more than their fair share of costs to make our expedition a reality.

We busied ourselves making a tent platform while waiting apprehensively for the two doctors. None of us felt selfless enough to go back into the danger zone and help them with their loads.

At two in the afternoon, the four of us saw our worst fear realized. A tremendous avalanche roared 6,000 feet down the face of the Great Trango, missed our protected col, and swept the couloir clean. We yelled down. No answer. A fresh tongue of sickening white snow curved out of sight, trackless and as empty as our hearts.

No one discussed descending. We intuitively followed the "Aleister Crowley rescue principle." After a 1905 Kangchenjunga expedition, Crowley had been ostracized by the British climbing establishment because he continued afternoon tea when his companions were buried by an avalanche. He reasoned that he had warned them not to be on that slope after midday; if they were in trouble, he wasn't about to risk his life for those already dead. And they did die.

Our situation differed because Jim and Lou had done nothing wrong except follow our mutual desire to climb the tower. The couloir's danger was a proven fact, and we four had proceeded every man for himself. Jim was the only one of us acting selflessly; he had stayed back to help his slower friend. What were we to do?

The obstacles that we had overcome to reach the Trango now seemed futile. I remembered dashing through Rawalpindi trying to replace items lost in transit by Lufthansa. And our worry when all communications were severed due to a military coup that deposed President Bhutto. And Mohammed Hussain, our chief porter, who missed a jeep because our liaison officer gave him the wrong departure time; then walked sixty miles without food or sleep to catch us in less than a day; Mohammed, who had carried frostbitten George Bell a hundred miles from K2 on his back in 1953; Mohammed who had carried our stricken K2 high porter, Akbar, along the Godwin-Austen Glacier as a 50-year-old man in 1975; Mohammed, who now waited at a camp below the couloir with concern etched into his features.

Above: Kim Schmitz leading the perfect granite of Great Trango Tower in mountain boots. In the distance, the Grand Cathedral and the Baltoro Glacier.

Below: John Roskelley carries a live goat across a swinging bridge made of twisted willow twigs.

I remembered double-staging in two days what were normally four days of travel, offering porters extra benefits. When they asked for fresh meat to eat on the Baltoro Glacier, I had made a proposition: we would buy the biggest goat in the high village and march it on a leash for two days. If we got to the four-day campsite, the porters would eat the goat; if not, the climbers would feast instead. At the end of a long day, we came to a wide torrent spanned by a rope bridge in an advanced state of decay. Many of the porters refused to cross with their loads. Their leaders solemnly announced that the goat couldn't be carried and would have to be eaten on the spot. We argued to no avail until suddenly the porters stopped and stared in awe as John carried the goat across the bridge on his own back! The next evening we camped in sight of the Trango Towers while the porters dined on goat.

We had made the fastest expedition approach march to the Baltoro Glacier in history, but what did that mean now? We had been powered by a constant state of optimistic expectation during those miraculous seven days from Rawalpindi to base camp. Today, dread was taking its place.

The afternoon lingered in suspended animation. The spell broke toward evening when we heard voices in the couloir. I felt as if the world's largest pack had been lifted from my shoulders. The doctors had heard the slide coming and had scrambled up the sidewall of the couloir moments before it swept past.

I realized that safety, health, and happiness were far more important than any summit. I wondered if the doctors should continue. Fatigued and blistered, Lou made his own decision to wait at the col until we came down from the climb. Jim wanted to go with us and offered to descend if necessary. I never figured out how this might have been accomplished. On the other hand, how could we deny a place on the team to a healthy member who had made it all possible? Jim trusted us and knew what he was getting into. He was a fit, experienced mountaineer who lacked our years spent on big rock walls. I realized that it took more courage for him to follow us up the Trango without our background than it did for us to lead the way using techniques that were as second nature to us as driving a car.

Before dawn, after a still and clear night, we said goodbye to Lou and shouldered packs that looked disturbingly small yet felt disturbingly heavy. Kim and I took lighter loads than the others because we were leaders for the day. We would alternate pitches and fix ropes for the others. They would follow on Jumar ascenders, pull out the ropes, and bring them to us so that we could continue leading.

Sunrise caught us near the base of a steep rockband where Kim was leading an ice-filled 5.8 crack in the best alpine granite we had ever seen. He moved with slow grace and confidence, belying the effort he was expending to lieback a crack in double boots at 18,000 feet. We were in ecstasy: the weather, the rock, the surroundings, and the companionship were all as fine as we could ever desire. When I reached the middle of a headwall, we looked at each other and giggled with delight.

When it was my lead, I had the choice of beginning a long headwall that would take all day, or veering left to a steep snow-and-ice ramp. The headwall would be safe for now, but it had a potential long-range threat. How long could we expect the weather to hold? I knew from 1975 that our fine rock could disappear under a crust of ice during a serious summer storm. The snow ramp offered speed, but it led past the chute that had supplied yesterday's monster avalanche. I gambled on getting beyond the chute before the morning thaw.

For a tense two hours we pitted our speed against the rising sun. Then we reached the safety of a ridgecrest and ate lunch. The source of the avalanches was now above us, a long ice field covered with a thin layer of snow. We chose an area that had already slid and headed up what appeared to be a five-hundred-foot beeline to a giant ledge. The distance proved to be 1,500 feet and the ledge was nonexistent. We found a narrow, corniced crest overhanging a 6,000-foot drop to the Dunge Glacier. It was separated from the main wall by a wide gap. There was no other bivouac site, so we dug a tiny platform into the cornice. Just under the snow was blue ice that took hours to chop away. We had no tent, so we tied ourselves to a safety rope anchored to ice screws and scrunched close together on ensolite pads.

Dinner was a great disappointment. We discovered that much of our food had been accidentally left at the col. The single stove refused to work properly, and it took an hour to warm a pot of water. After a meager meal we counted what was left for two more days of climbing: three packets of hot chocolate, six tea bags, one packet of soup, a half-pound of cheese, and two bacon bars. No one complained. Although the lack of food was due in part to an oversight, we had always planned to go as light as possible high on the peak. No one expected much in comforts, so no one was disturbed to have a bit less. Had we decided on normal expeditionary tactics, thousands of feet of rope would have been fixed and two tents would have been dug into the cornice. We would have had at least two stoves, several days of extra food, and possibly a radio to talk to base. And we would have taken the very essence of mountaineering, something primitive and uncivilized, and channeled it into a highly evolved situation totally dependent on civilized goods and long-range plans.

On the Trango Tower our civilized trappings were at a minimum. A few classic tools and supplies; that was all. We felt connected to the mountain rather than to a rope-and-camp system attached to the mountain. And although we were isolated from the world, we felt perfectly in control of our destinies.

We awoke at our 19,000-foot bivouac while stars were still shining and the snowy landscape was locked in the phosphorescent blue of night. As we packed our loads for the summit push, we were treated to a special high-altitude light show. Shadows of the Karakoram giants were cast into the stratosphere against the purple pre-dawn gloaming. Before sun hit the peaks we rappelled down to the ice field, leaving our bivouac gear on the platform. A traverse across the top of the ice field brought us left of the cleft that had separated our bivouac from the main wall. We chose a deep rock chimney filled with ice, where I hung for long hours from a piton as Dennis and John led upward. Wearing crampons to climb thin ice over rock, it took seven hours to make only 600 feet. In the middle of the afternoon, we reached an ice ramp that led to the summit ridge, where an awesome cornice blocked the route. I worried about time; in order to return to the bivouac by dark, we would soon have to turn around whether we had made the top or not.

Dennis gained the summit ridge by an easy notch hidden at the edge of the cornice. Soon all five of us were walking along the narrow crest toward the highest point. We were surrounded by giant peaks in late afternoon light, all in familiar positions save one. Nameless Tower, marked on most maps as the highest of the Trangos, was already below us before the final rise to the summit. Apparently surveyors had measured the highest point of the Great Trango visible from the foot of the Baltoro Glacier, a rock spire several hundred feet lower than the snow dome that was the true summit. We were making the first ascent of the highest Trango.

On top we hugged each other with supreme joy. The air was absolutely still, and we stripped off jackets and gloves. Glaciers and peaks extended out from us in all directions, and for a few minutes we felt as if we were in the center of the universe, perched on a cloud. We might have rolled in the snow and burst out laughing with complete emotional release, were it not for the prospect of the descent, always in our minds.

After half an hour on top we started down: rappels, interminable rappels, set up by two, descended by five, retrieved by two, then reset by the first two. Darkness caught us on the ice field traverse after we had to leave behind one of our ropes on a jammed rappel. We fixed our remaining three ropes to ice screws, kept going in the blackness, and got to the platform at ten o'clock with just a few feet to spare.

By the next afternoon, we were free of the couloir. Only then did we feel full satisfaction and freedom to celebrate. Mohammed Hussain greeted us with open arms at base camp. We reveled in level ground, flowers, wash water, and most of all, in food. The best thing about lightweight adventuring is that it makes you realize how very fine the smaller things of life really are. From a duffel we pulled out goodies that we had been saving and prepared a victory dinner of shrimp cocktail, hot tea, mashed potatoes with butter and chives, fried beef patties, rose cabernet, cognac, and blueberry pie.

Only twenty-four days after we had begun, we returned to Rawalpindi, still in ecstasy over a tiny expedition that lacked all the inescapable ballyhoo of big mountain sagas.

19

Skiing the Karakoram High Route

Even though we didn't reach any summits, traversing the uninhabited Karakoram Himalaya in winter was the most difficult adventure of my life. Crossing between glaciers at altitudes up to 22,000 feet on Nordic skis with up to 120-pound loads was far more committing than attempting a single mountain, no matter how tall or difficult. For six weeks we traveled 285 miles across northern Pakistan most of the way from India to Afghanistan. Our route followed four of the world's longest glaciers outside the subpolar regions through terrain with the highest mean elevation on the planet. We traversed the Siachen, Baltoro, Biafo, and Hispar Glaciers past 26,000-foot snow peaks, such as K2, Broad Peak, and the Gasherbrums, and even more spectacular rock peaks, such as the Ogre, the Latoks, and the Trango Towers.

The idea for the trip came to me during a reconnaissance flight around K2 in a Pakistan Air Force C130 Hercules in 1975. I was captivated by a dog-leg series of glaciers that bisect the range, and it took several years of meetings with Pakistani officials to convince them to allow an unsupported winter expedition into an area closed to trekking or climbing because it was disputed with India. Four years later, Indian troops occupied the Siachen Glacier, beginning the highest war in history, the subject of Chapter 22. As of this writing, the war continues and no one else has been able to repeat our route.

My expedition dreams have almost always failed, not in the field on some windswept ridge where the elements proved too strong for human powers, but around a campfire in the Sierra or the desert where an idea flickered out with the embers. The pattern has been nearly always the same. Random talk of mountains and people becomes specific. An image of a light, self-contained expedition to the Himalaya forms. Just good friends and good climbing. Big efforts with oxygen and lots of porters are out. The magnet is that time on the mountain, working together toward a meaningful goal, isolated from the rest of humanity and any need to depend upon it for success or enjoyment.

Dan Asay at over 21,000 feet above Conway Saddle on the first traverse of the Karakoram Himalaya.

The magnet has an opposite, equally forceful pole. All Himalayan climbing expeditions include a lot of time in the mountains that is not one's own. The shorter and more efficient the climb itself, the greater the proportion of time spent in the lowlands dealing and living with a basically unwanted caravan of men and supplies. Where air drops, vehicle access, or pack animals can be utilized, it is still possible to climb without coming face to face with one's own hedonism, but in the Himalaya, where each hour of mountain pleasure can be equated with days of toil by hired hands, the dream around a campfire is never fulfilled. When the embers go out, they leave a subtle division of minds. On the one hand are those who will not compromise their ideals. They stay to pursue simpler goals in accessible ranges. On the other hand are those like myself, who have sold their dreams short for a little instant gratification and experience.

One solution to this conflict is so simple it sounds absurd. If the root of the problem is all that gear needed to climb a mountain, why climb a mountain at all? With this non-objective firmly in mind, I organized the 1980 American Karakoram Traverse Expedition. Our goal was to traverse the highest range on earth, the Karakoram Himalaya, across northern Pakistan from the Indian border three-fourths of the way to Afghanistan. We would follow the greatest of all the world's high routes, an aesthetic line over four of the largest glaciers outside the subpolar latitudes. This pathway of ice doglegs from glacier to glacier, yet in an overall way follows a remarkable east/west trend through the very heart of the range. From the high perspective of satellite photos taken in summer, the blue glaciers rest on a tawny landscape like long beads of turquoise strung on a loose necklace. In the winter and spring, however, all is hidden under snow.

After the shortest days of winter were past, but long before the snow melted from the highlands, our four-man expedition would set out on Nordic skis with small sleds. We hoped to become the first expedition to move through the heart of the Karakoram Himalaya under its own power, and thus capture something of our elusive dreams.

On March 27 we began our 285-mile traverse from the village of Khapalu at the confluence of the Shyok and Saltoro rivers. Ten porters were hired to take us to the snow-line, from where we would strike out on our own, with just one food cache in the village of Askole, a short distance off our route between the Baltoro and Biafo glaciers. Otherwise, we would travel entirely above human habitation. Each man would have 120 pounds. We could find no way to go lighter. Besides food and survival gear for weeks of sub-zero living, we needed considerable fuel to melt snow for water, climbing gear to

Above: Galen totes 120 pounds: 60 on his back, 60 on the sled. Photo: Ned Gillette
Opposite: Skiing at 20,000 feet on the upper Siachen Glacier.

*Above: Aerial view of the
Biafo Glacier with the Ogre
and the three Latok peaks from
left to right in the center.*

*Below: Skiing toward Mustagh Tower
on the Upper Baltoro Glacier.*

traverse the south face of Sia Kangri at 22,500 feet between the Siachen and Baltoro basins, durable ski equipment, and ropes for protection against crevasse falls.

Our foursome consisted of Dan Asay, Ned Gillette, Kim Schmitz, and myself. We set off up the Bilafond Glacier, feeling very alone as the porters retreated. Here, just a few miles from the Indian border, we planned to cross the 18,000-foot Bilafond La and follow the Lolofond Glacier to its juncture with the Siachen. It had proved politically impossible to begin in India on the snout of the Siachen itself.

The conditions were extremely gratifying. No one had been on these great glaciers in winter and we had been given every conceivable prediction. One geographer told Ned to expect unconsolidated powder several feet deep at high altitude. What we found was a steady, firm surface. It was too cold to form a crust, yet windblown enough to allow the leader to break trail almost as fast as the others could follow.

Cold was our enemy on the Siachen. The basin of over four hundred square miles of gently sloping ice was a perfect trap for temperature inversions. In the populated Saltoro Valley the temperature never dropped below 20° F at 11,000 feet, but at 16,000 on the Siachen we found ourselves trying to pass a −25° F night with light sleeping bags rated above zero.

For me, the greatest hardship to this point was not the huge loads or the icy winds, but the simple act of rushing out of the tent with full bowels on that coldest dawn. My hasty motions dislodged hoar frost from every panel of the dome tent, dusting Kim and me with a thick layer of ice. For the first time in decades, I thought about the old crystal paperweight that used to sit on my father's desk. When I was a child, I turned it over in my hands and watched artificial snow fall on the hapless figure inside. I used to imagine how small, cold, and insignificant that little man felt in a world beyond his control. On the Siachen, surrounded by bleak and foreign peaks, I became that little man.

Our travel up the glacier was ritualistic rather than eventful. We gained about a thousand feet each day, spending only about five daylight hours out of twelve actually skiing. Two hours were used to break camp, and two more to set it up. Frequent rest stops ate up another three hours. Our effort was not much greater than it would have been with lighter loads. We just moved far slower with sixty pounds on our backs, fifty on a children's roll-up vinyl sled, and ten more in a reversed fanny pack.

On the afternoon of April 12, we reached the Siachen's end. Though our maps had warned us of what was coming, we were surprised to watch our gentle plateau disappear into a Grand Canyon-sized chasm. A vertical mile below us was the head of the Kondus Glacier, and just a mile and a half across from us was Conway Saddle, hanging into space like the abutment of a collapsed bridge.

Here was the gap that had stopped the Workmans and other turn-of-the-century explorers from traversing between the Baltoro and Siachen basins. Not until 1979 was a crossing finally made, and then by a fully equipped Japanese expedition with 116 porters that had just made an ascent of Sia Kangri.

We planned to follow their route, traversing the south face of Sia Kangri between 20,500 and 22,500 feet. The fact that the Japanese had made their traverse with full equipment and portage in summer did little for my confidence that we could follow the same route on Nordic skis in winter conditions. Ned was convinced that we would find easier going than on our Nordic circumambulation of Mount McKinley, and his hunch proved right.

It took three days and several rappels to make the mile-and-a-half traverse, but the true story was in what it didn't take. We never switched to our crampons, and we never encountered hard ice except going down on rappel. The route just opened up in front of us as we went. Each portentous obstacle had a reasonable alternative, hidden from view until the last moment.

Both Kim and I had been to the Baltoro region on two previous expeditions. We began to see familiar landmarks in the distance. Mustagh Tower loomed into the golden light of dawn from the same intimidating perspective made famous by Vittorio Sella's 1909 telephoto. At one point, we saw the Trango Towers profiled through Conway Saddle on the last morning of our traverse. Then came the Gasherbrums, I, II, III, and IV, filling the western sky. We had hoped for a view of K2 or Broad Peak, but they remained hidden behind the greatest row of lesser peaks on earth (all four Gasherbrums being among the seventeen highest mountains).

The last day to Conway Saddle was a seemingly endless traverse through seracs and cliffs. Just before sunset only one final barrier separated us from the rim of the Baltoro basin (and imagined security for the remainder of our journey). A short overhang dropped onto a steep snow slope that soon plunged into the mile-deep chasm. I was lowered—pack, skis, and all—from two ice screws. The sled tugged at my waist, and I spent long minutes thrashing my way on my knees to a spot where I could stomp out a platform. Dan followed in nearly as awkward fashion. Kim and Ned planned to lower their packs and sleds, then climb down. It was a great plan, but almost a tragic end to the trip. Ned's pack with all his personal survival gear and a stove came unclipped from the rope. I ran for it, stumbled, and missed. Below me, the pack began a straight shot for the Kondus, interrupted at the last moment by Dan's flying tackle. He made a tremendous end run across the slope and, without a moment's hesitation, jumped on the seventy-pound bundle armored with crampons like a lineman for the Steelers.

The next day we made a steep but straightforward descent to the Abruzzi Glacier. Dan and Ned turned around to see yet another wild bundle hurdling out of control. Kim's sled shot by at tremendous speed, followed immediately by roaring laughter. Kim, tired of being passed by his sled and tripped by its cords, had purposely let it fly into a smooth basin where it came to a gradual stop. That night we camped opposite the icefall of the South Gasherbrum Glacier, a place made forever mystical by the poetic musings of Fosco Maraini in his classic book, *Karakoram: The Ascent of Gasherbrum IV*.

Karakoram pundits had warned us that the upper Baltoro and Abruzzi glaciers were riddled with huge crevasses, making travel difficult, circuitous, and dangerous. Early in the year we found precisely the opposite conditions. A veritable highway about two hundred feet wide followed the arcs of the moraines as far as we could see. On either side of this perfect ski path was jumbled ice and rock. After double-poling gently mile after mile, we touched our first rock and drank our first running water in eleven days.

The weather had been good to us. After a few mild storms on the Siachen we enjoyed a week of mostly clear skies for our high traverse. As we headed down the Baltoro, skies blackened and temperatures soared far higher than they should have for the loss of elevation. We had experienced five straight nights below –20° F, and now we began a longer string of nights over 20° F above, a phenomenal shift of forty degrees. Heat, not cold, became our greatest adversary. By nine each morning the hard snow was collapsing under our skis, and with loads still over a hundred pounds, we sank into baseless depth hoar of the worst order.

On the morning of April 18th, I awoke just a few miles above Concordia, where the Baltoro and Godwin-Austen glaciers join in a great amphitheater in full view of K2. The clouds were lowering quickly, and I asked the others' permission to pack up and leave early. By five a.m. I was gliding easily on the hard surface, remembering a day five years before when I had also been alone on the moraines of Concordia. In 1975 after an attempt on K2, a mail runner had handed me a bulky envelope from my mother in California. It contained my 90-year-old father's ashes. He had died while I was on the mountain, and I left the group that day to release his remains to the winds over a moraine of pure marble. The letter from my mother had compared the tranquillity of his face in death to a fine marble bust, and I felt fortunate to find the same material in its raw state.

The 1980 morning was bleak and gray. My spirits were low until I rounded a corner and saw K2 for the first time on this trip, rising over a great block of white marble. Tears ran down my cheeks, and I sat down to absorb the simultaneous emotions triggered by memories of my father and the mountain. For an hour the mountain showed its top above the clouds. Just before the others arrived, it disappeared, never to be seen for the remainder of our journey.

Below Concordia our natural path ended. Rivers of melt water sealed us off from the most inviting corridors of travel. The landscape looked as if God's own construction company had torn it up and left it unfinished. Moraines marched infinitely in every direction, presenting jagged rocks toward the sun and a marginal snow layer in the shade. It was a skier's Hell.

Day after day we got up at 3:30 a.m., thrashed partly on skis, partly on foot with giant loads, ate from our quickly-eroding supplies, and slowed from a peak speed of four miles an hour on the Upper Baltoro to an agonizing four miles a day.

One morning, after eating a gourmet breakfast of soup concocted from the last spoonfuls of instant potatoes, I moaned to Kim, "How are we going to get through this?" He turned to me with a confident air, and said, "I think I have the answer."

Kim was our medical officer. Although not a doctor, he had a strongly developed historical sense of medication for mountaineering. He knew of a drug that had been developed precisely for this purpose by native people who found it necessary to carry tremendous loads at high elevations with low caloric intakes. Small amounts of this extract from a South American leaf were at one time a main ingredient in the most successful multinational soft drink until the potential for abuse made it illegal. Propitiously, Kim had been able to purchase an ounce of this material on the Afghan border at the Khyber Pass to add to our medical kit.

Kim and I were tentmates. We decided that our medical experiment needed a valid control group. Ned and Dan, unlike us, were not complainers. They were members of the stiff-upper-lip school who never swore when their sleds passed them, nor beat their sleds into submission when they attacked one's feet or became tangled in one's skis. We had been moving at relatively equal rates, and we thought it fitting that the non-complainers should continue unaware.

At noon that day we waited an hour and a half for them. In the evening we waited yet another hour. Sleep, of course, also had to be induced by drugs, but the entire process was repeated successfully day after day until we arrived in Askole about twenty-five pounds lighter than when we began.

After three days of gorging and resting, we set out on the last leg of our journey. Dan decided to stay behind, partly because of sore knees and partly from a desire to help the efficiency of our travel. Three of us could cut our weight by using one tent, one rope, and one stove. Without the climbing gear or extreme clothing needed for the first leg, we were able to start with a more reasonable ninety-five pounds each.

We hired nine Askole porters to carry for three days until we could ski on the Biafo Glacier. Our sirdar was Haji Ali, who had carried my father's ashes up the Baltoro as a mail runner in 1975. He was an old hunter with a keen eye for wildlife, and we were amazed at the profuse evidence of large mammals living above the inhabited valleys. On my first trip to the Karakoram, George Schaller and I had found the Baltoro region sadly depleted of wildlife. Inexplicably, the Biafo was another story. Nearly every side canyon beyond Mango Brangsa at 12,200 feet had ibex tracks in the snow. I sighted more than fifty animals in one day. A major recession of the ice had left level, moist moats on either side of the glacier, and these were pocked with the footprints of brown bear, snow leopard, fox, and ibex. Farther up the glacier a lammergeier landed within two hundred feet of us, only to soar with its nine-foot wing spread toward the granite faces bordering the glacier.

Here, lining the sides of the upper Biafo, was the greatest display of granite spires in the entire Karakoram, marching up the glacier like organ pipes in an ordered procession. Enough major climbs to last several generations were spread around us, untouched and unnamed. The Bilafond and Saltoro valleys also had considerably more large granite faces than the fabled Baltoro, but for aesthetics the Biafo won, hands down.

An icefall at the top of the Hispar La was a nonevent, buried so completely in snow that we encountered no crevasse problems. A snowstorm forced us to camp directly on top of the 16,900-foot pass. When it cleared we were treated to a superb view of the Ogre rising above a cloud bank in the moonlight. The fresh snow gave us sixteen miles of downhill powder skiing the next day. Too soon we were back on mixed ground again as the snow cover gradually ran out. Just eight-and-a-half days after leaving Askole, we walked into the village of Hispar. Two more days of hiking and a short jeep ride brought us to Hunza and the end of our journey.

It would be nice to conclude with an image of ski mountaineers gamboling through the green fields of fabled Hunza, overcome with the sensual flow of returning to the living world. To do so would intimate that we found the dream of the campfires of my youth. What we found at the end of six weeks of the most intense physical activity of our lives was sensory and social deprivation. At our first dinner in a hotel, I said, not really believing it myself, "Isn't it wonderful to return to hot water and cold beer?"

Kim held a thousand-yard stare and answered, "The special things I miss are not what we're finding here, but what we've left behind in the dusty villages and campsites in the snow." Somehow, we had lost much of our capacity to enjoy not only the wonderful excesses of civilized life, but also the clean, simple emotions of love and beauty that color all heights of experience. Never on a mere peak-climbing expedition had any of us undergone such a shift. Among us were those who found the mountains of the Karakoram undistinguished and our partners little more worthy of intimacy than passengers on an elevator. I believe that we experienced to a lesser degree the same sort of mental and physical trauma that left most survivors of Auschwitz unable to laugh or love for a long time. Dan summed up all our immediate feelings when he told a newspaper reporter, "The trip was hardly enjoyable; it was an accomplishment."

For three years after the expedition, I strongly felt its effects. I no longer dreamed of that ideal expedition, "isolated from the rest of humanity and any need to depend upon it." I learned the reality, the trade-offs, and the strange mental filtration that eventually turned it into the favorite mountain adventure of my life.

Ned Gillette celebrates the end of the 285-mile ski traverse in the old Kingdom of Nagar near Hunza.

20

Cholatse: Last Virgin of the Khumbu

After I had signed on with Mountain Travel to guide a 1982 photographic safari through Nepal, I learned that a coveted permit for the last unclimbed peak in the Everest region had just been given to my friend, Al Read, who managed Mountain Travel trips in Kathmandu. He had put my name on his application four years earlier, and now only two members on that list were in a position to go. Read would be too busy managing a banner trekking season to join us, but both myself and Peter Hackett, who operated a high altitude medical clinic in the Everest area, would already be in Nepal that spring with our airfares covered. Peter was fresh from a successful climb of Everest from the south, and I had recently been to the North Col from the Tibetan side.

Between us, we invited three more climbers and arranged for me to join the expedition in base camp, instead of returning to Kathmandu with my photo trek. The result was one of the most satisfying first ascents I've ever made, done for less than the cost of a normal Everest base camp trek.

In April 1982, while the first Russian expedition was climbing Mount Everest from Nepal with a cast of nearly a thousand climbers and porters, five of us attempted Cholatse, the last named, unclimbed peak in the Everest region. We felt almost smugly certain of success. Our team was strong and our motives were fitting and proper. We had avoided pre-climb publicity, funded cash costs entirely out of members' pockets, planned not to use porters above base camp, and brought the latest equipment, courtesy of several manufacturers. The mountain—however hard it might prove to be—was only 21,130 feet. Furthermore, all five members had previously seen Cholatse and believed it could be rushed up and down in two to three days with good weather.

We were unanimous in underestimating the mountain. The white coating that appeared to be snow on our chosen Southwest Arete turned out to be brittle ice for thousands of feet. To complicate matters, unseasonable pre-monsoon storms brought wind and snow every afternoon.

John Roskelley front-points up the Southwest Arete of Cholatse.

Before the climb I led a two-week photography trek in the same region, passing countless yak caravans loaded with bright-colored duffels, trekkers in even more vivid hues, and Sherpas decked out in the latest boots, jackets, and specialty items that were only just hitting stores in the United States. It was hard to keep in mind that just thirty-two years earlier, no Westerner had ever visited the Khumbu homeland of the Sherpas. In that short span, the Khumbu had become the Mecca of the Himalaya, visited by far more people than any other region so close to a great peak. More than 8,000 trekkers and climbers from around the world came in 1982, mostly bound for a close view of Mount Everest. The finely shaped lower peaks—Ama Dablam, Thamserku, Kantega—had been climbed legally or illegally by the middle 1960s. Why Cholatse had gone untouched was something of a mystery. It was a bit too hard to climb illegally without attracting attention, but no one knew for certain why it had been kept off the permitted list.

Cholatse, sometimes spelled Tsolatse or given the Tibetan name, Jobo Lhaptshan, became the "last virgin of the Khumbu" not by way of virtue, but by paternal restrictions begun by the Ministry of Tourism when the mountains of Nepal first opened in 1950. Cholatse's continued closure was more a quirk of bureaucracy than the result of a clear rationale. It was not worth a large peak fee, and it was hidden up the Gokyo Valley, lacking the obvious appeal of mountains closer to the classic route to Everest Base Camp. Another consideration was that some Sherpas considered Cholatse a very sacred mountain, one of five goddesses surrounding Everest. Others said the peak had no special significance. The head lama of the famous Thyangboche Monastery told me simply, "All mountains are sacred."

Four years earlier, Al Read, director of Mountain Travel Nepal, had asked me to join a prospective Cholatse climb. He kept after the government until they finally gave him a permit at the end of 1981. As late as six weeks before departure, the expedition had no funding, no equipment, and just two certain climbers: Peter Hackett and myself. Read had a busy trekking season, and he decided to "godfather" the expedition rather than actively climb himself. He had also invited Bill O'Connor, a British mountaineer with considerable Himalayan experience. Peter and I decided on a minimum of four climbers for an alpine-style attempt on what appeared to be a safe but steep ridge. We invited Vern Clevenger and John Roskelley to round out the team.

We met in Kathmandu and sent our gear ahead with porters, saving some of the cost of flying it to the high airstrip at Lukla. The others took off on a two-week acclimatizing trek while I was with my photography group. On the morning of April 15, I left them just before their flight from Lukla and took off toward Cholatse with one strong porter. We covered five normal trekking days in one, reaching a point half an hour below our base camp at dusk in clouds so thick that we couldn't find our way up the remaining trailless hill. The next morning, I arrived to spot the other four heading out of base camp for the peak. I stayed back to rest while they spent the day establishing a route through a long

Following a tentless bivouac near the summit of Cholatse, John Roskelley peeks out of his sleeping bag at dawn.

icefall to a col at 18,600 feet where an advanced camp could be placed. A fixed line was placed on the final six-hundred-foot headwall to help haul loads on the final push. They returned to base camp late in the day.

For the next four days it stormed; not all the time but just enough to quell our enthusiasm. The morning of April 20 was clear. We regained the col with food for two more days, and fixed three ropes on the hard ice above. In the afternoon it snowed yet again.

The next morning was clear, but Hackett was too sick to climb. A world expert in mountain medicine, he was quite sure that his ailment was short-lived and not due to altitude. We faced a triangle of awful decisions: wait a day or two and not have enough food to attempt the climb; leave a sick man alone, a man whose desire for Cholatse and whose efforts on behalf of the expedition exceeded any of our own; or make multiple trips through the icefall, which, due to hanging glaciers above, Hackett felt was as dangerous as the Khumbu Icefall on Everest. We trusted his judgment. Just six months before he had gone through that icefall on his way to the top of Everest.

After considerable discussion, Hackett volunteered to stay at the col camp until we returned from the attempt. To fail on a lower peak after so recent a success on Everest was hard to swallow. He said goodbye, then crawled into his bag as we jumared slowly up the ropes above the col.

Losing Hackett was just the beginning of the day's problems. On previous light expeditions where we had brought our own timeworn gear, I had rarely witnessed an equipment failure. Using new gear donated by manufacturer's was a different matter. Vern's crampons sheared a front screw. A new "superwide" strap tore off my crampon at the rivet. John's "Lifetime" ice tool broke off clean at the adze. By noon, my new "Explorer's" digital watch was in pieces, and I had hacked big chunks of foam out of the new Alveolite inners of my plastic boots to try to make them fit something larger than a ballet dancer's heel. To top things off we came to the only feasible campsite far too early in the day. At just 19,000 feet it seemed much too low for a round trip to the top the next day.

In the afternoon, Clevenger and O'Connor cut a tent platform out of hard ice while Roskelley and I fixed our four climbing ropes on the steep ridge above. On the last lead, I stopped to place two ice screws for protection across a traverse of an 80° bulge. After Roskelley followed, he said, "Any one of us can climb anything on this mountain, but we're going to have to get up this fast, or we're not going to make it. I'm the fastest, and I can lead most of this without protection if it's okay with everybody."

It was. One day's food remained after two days of climbing. We were up at 3:30 a.m., the tents were left in place, and Roskelley led off. Pitch after pitch of steep ice went by without the placing of a single point of protection. "Ready," Roskelley would say with two ice tools stuck in the wall. I would pay out rope continuously for ten minutes as he climbed with thirty pounds on his back until the rope ran out. Then he would place ice screws for a belay, and I would follow. Clevenger and O'Connor would follow later, pulling out the ropes and screws for use above.

Overleaf: Three of the world's five highest peaks, from left to right—Everest, Lhotse, and Makalu— pierce the twilight sky beneath a full moon from left to right. Cholatse rises into the pink glow at far right.

Fifteen rope lengths of steep ice—2,250 feet—brought us to the summit plateau by noon. We cached some gear and headed on with O'Connor in the lead. When a massive crevasse blocked the route, Roskelley did an end run up yet another ice pitch. There we found not the summit, but a hidden three-hundred-foot ice headwall. After twelve long hours of climbing, Roskelley and Clevenger reached the top in a full blizzard with their hair on end from electricity in the air. A pre-monsoon thunderstorm had drifted in from India. O'Connor and I joined them on the summit minutes later, and we all beat a hasty retreat.

It was too late to attempt a descent to the high camp, so we stomped out a platform at the top of the ridge and camped without a tent or bivy sacks in a mild snowstorm. Lightning flashed in the southern sky over India as we heated water for one freeze-dried dinner between us. The others were testing Quallofil bags that would hold their loft when wet. Mine had torn a seam before the climb, so I had brought a down bag instead. Knowing that it would collapse like a wet sock as soon as my body heat melted the falling snow, I wore boots, overboots, and a one-piece climbing suit to bed.

In the morning the temperature was –2° F. My bag felt like a giant Coke bottle, but I was warm inside my waterproof garments, as were the others in their fluffy bags. As the first light hit Makalu, Everest, and Ama Dablam, we packed up to begin twenty frightening diagonal rappels back down the ridge, which overhung the south face most of the way down. Our loads grew lighter as we consumed almost all of our ice hardware to place anchors every 150 feet.

At the col Peter greeted us, recovered from a short bout with the flu, but still a bit weak. He joined us, and we continued our descent toward base camp. Just below the glacier we were met by a welcoming committee that included Al Read, his family, several friends, and our Sherpas. A "Welcome Home Cholatse Expedition" sign graced an arch of willow branches over a gate in the stone yak corral at the entrance to camp. The Sherpas were preparing a victory dinner and baking a cake for us.

A more idyllic return from a climb is hard to imagine. We were far off any trekking route, camped in a meadow eye-to-eye with peaks on the other side of the Gokyo Valley, sharing our joy with a few friends.

The next morning I walked over the hill to watch the clouds. Below me two figures were sitting by a rock—our Sherpas watching the same movements of land and sky. On the next hill three local herdsmen also sat looking. Each group was separate, yet motivated by similar emotions. None of us would have come here and shared this experience without our particular ulterior motives. Our Sherpas were hired hands on an expedition, the herdsmen were tending their family yaks, and our objective was to climb a mountain. Trekkers on a trail might have snapped a picture or two, but invariably they would have kept on walking instead of sitting down to silently soak in the world around them.

I saw how little the essential values of the Khumbu have changed with the recent onslaught of tourists. We were able to share the essence of these mountains with those who lived in them, just as the first Khumbu travelers had done thirty years before.

One of the reasons Sherpas integrate so well with Westerners is that unlike hill farmers or merchants, they have no single life purpose. They herd, they farm, they trade, they work for trekkers and climbers. A typical Sherpa family lives on an acre of land in a village within sight of the mountains. Their children walk to school with no fear of trouble on the way or in class. They raise their own livestock and grow their own vegetables. For part of the year the husband travels, making a better salary than in town. He brings things back from exotic places and tells exciting stories around the fireplace. While he was gone, his wife managed the land, the animals, and represented the family in frequent community affairs. Together they travel to other villages and visit their summer home in a high meadow.

An hour below our Cholatse base camp was a cluster of fields and stone buildings that comprise the summer settlement of Na. Called *yersas*, these Sherpa summer homes are set in high-altitude pastures where yaks and goats graze during the warmest parts of the year. In one building I had tea with Sonam Dorje, the eighteen-year-old son of a Sherpa from Phortse who has been on eleven Everest expeditions. All the Na yersas were owned by Phortse families. Sonam had worked on several commercial treks, but he told me he would not be doing such work for two more years. "I'll be staying here from March to August. Sometimes my father comes; sometimes I'm alone. When one of my four brothers is old enough to stay here, I'll go back to work as a trekking Sherpa."

With his previous earnings from trekking he could have easily bought a transistor radio, like many of the lowland Nepalese who now violate the quiet air of their villages. Instead, Sonam bought a pressure cooker to save precious fuel for cooking potatoes and vegetables at his 14,500-foot summer home. On the wall he had hung art paper with Tibetan characters which he learned to draw at school. Next to his work hung a Marlboro ad and a *Time* magazine cover.

The juxtaposition was not as disturbing as it seems. On another family's wall I spotted a picture from *Time* of the cellist, Rostropovich, and his wife. Since my mother knew Rostropovich, I inquired why the picture had been posted on their wall. I learned that the family had put it up simply because it captured an expression of love between husband and wife. They had no idea who the people were.

After a rest day, several of us decided to extend our trek home by crossing the Cho La, a 17,800-foot pass connecting the Gokyo Valley with Pheriche on the Everest trekking route. Our intent was simply to see more of the region around the peak we had climbed, but in

John Roskelley with ice tools near the top of the Southwest Arete.

another sense our urge to circle around a mountain meaningful to us was exactly what reverent Tibetan Buddhists do with landmarks that have special meanings in their lives.

How different our Khumbu experience was from that of the Russians on Everest. Their memories would be weighted toward months in a sterile world, while only four days of our month were actually on the heights. Those four intense days, however, had paid us wonderful dividends for an extremely low investment. By cutting corners in every way, our month's lightweight expedition and trek with a Sherpa crew and government-required liaison officer (kept warm and content in a nearby Namche Bazar guesthouse at our expense) ended up costing less than half the tariff of most commercial Khumbu treks. The entire expedition, except for Peter Hackett, reached the summit of an unclimbed peak, and more important, returned healthy and happy—the true bottom line of a successful expedition.

21

A Night Out on Fitz Roy

I instantly decided on Fitz Roy when the NATIONAL GEOGRAPHIC *book division asked me to write and photograph about the climb of my choice for the concluding chapter of a book to be titled* MOUNTAIN WORLDS. *No other peak that I knew of combined such visual presence with such great technical challenge and reasonable accessibility. A dirt road led within a few hour's walk of the base of the peak. Getting there down the spine of the Andes in rental cars from a thousand miles away was another story, which led to me falling in love with Patagonia and returning many times.*

Bivouacking standing up on an ice ledge just below the summit without sleeping bags was not only one of the wildest nights of my life, but also one of the most rewarding. As we climbed up to the summit at dawn, alpenglow finally struck the wild spires of Cerro Torre profiled against the blue-shadowed Southern Patagonian Icecap. The photograph I made with my camera braced on a rock became a double-page spread for MOUNTAIN WORLDS *as well as for an illustrated history of the National Geographic Society.*

During the summer of 1985-86 (winter in California), I led a small expedition to Patagonia. We traveled over 4,000 miles on relentlessly bad roads from the mountain resort town of Bariloche in Central Argentina to both coasts and to national parks in both countries. One day we would be in a desert, another on a glacier, and yet another swimming with whales in the ocean. Our primary goal, however, was the ascent of a legendary mountain named after Captain Robert Fitz Roy of the H.M.S. Beagle, which came to Patagonia with a young ship's naturalist named Charles Darwin.

Patagonia is not a nation or a state, but one of those regions of the world, like the Himalaya or Antarctica, that defies political boundaries because it is so well defined by its own geography. Patagonia straddles southern Argentina and Chile where the earth's two greatest oceans, longest mountain range, and fastest moving sky merge into the grand finale of the American continents.

Here the legendary gales of the Roaring Forties circle the globe, unchecked by land except for Patagonia, where all features are influenced by the wind. Trees are contorted. Mountains are sculpted into the wildest forms on earth. Because of its reputation for

Michael Graber approaches the upper face of Fitz Roy from the Italian Col.

harboring some of the world's worst weather, Patagonia has no Club Meds, few paved highways, and a relatively short, but highly impressive roster of explorers and adventurers. Among the best known, besides Darwin, were Ferdinand Magellan, Antoine de St. Exupery, Butch Cassidy, and the Sundance Kid.

We first saw Fitz Roy from a campsite fifty miles away. The scene was inestimably stark and simple: an arid plain, a clear sky, and an apparition of a mountain turned crimson in the sun's first rays. My wife, Barbara, rushed out of the tent with her camera, exclaiming, "It looks like a fantasy. It's like something out of the Wizard of Oz!"

That otherworldly quality was accentuated by the bizarre wildlife we were seeing. Guanacos, fleet wild relatives of the camel and the llama, glided across the plains with long necks held gracefully in the air. Ostrich-like Darwin's rheas darted in floating bounds, flightless wings held just above the level of an ocean of thorny calafate bushes. Darwin first described seeing these birds in 1834 during his celebrated round-the-world voyage.

Surveying Patagonia and its natural history was a major goal of Darwin's Beagle expedition. The ship's crew journeyed up the Santa Cruz River to a spot about a hundred miles from the sheer peak that now bears the name of their captain, whose mercurial moods matched those of his mountain namesake. The peak was christened by a later explorer. Whether Darwin actually saw Fitz Roy may never be known, although it is highly doubtful. His journal says, "We viewed these grand mountains with regret, for we were obliged to imagine their nature and productions, instead of standing, as we had hoped, on their summits." No one seeing Fitz Roy in the nineteenth century could have honestly imagined reaching its summit.

As we drove the last miles under cloudless skies, our course of action became obvious. Clear spells rarely last more than two or three days, and we were having a day of the kind expeditions waited months to behold. We needed to sign in with the Parque Nacional Los Glaciares, hire horses to carry our food and equipment, hike six miles up to base camp, and be ready to climb before dawn the next morning.

To best understand Fitz Roy's place among the world's wildest peaks, we need to travel back in time to the opening of Nepal in 1950. That year a young French guide named Lionel Terray was invited to join a major Himalayan expedition. None of the world's fourteen 8,000 meter (26,247-foot) summits had been climbed, but Terray's team succeeded on the first of these "impossible" giants in a struggle so epic that the name of their peak "Annapurna" instantly became a symbol of human courage and perseverance.

Terray, still in his twenties, was at the pinnacle of his sport. Annapurna was opening the door to a golden age of Himalayan mountaineering. It would have been natural for him to return the next year to try an even higher peak. Indeed, the ascent of Annapurna marked the start of a decade during which men topped all but one of the fourteen giants.

Terray's next expedition took him to a much lower mountain in the almost unknown southern Andes of Patagonia. Fitz Roy's mere 11,073 feet challenged Terray beyond his wildest expectations. Subantarctic storms constantly buffeted the peak with extreme winds in which their best tents couldn't last a night. Every flaw in the 2,000-foot final headwall of vertical rock was frosted with wind-borne ice and snow. After weeks of failure, Terray "fought on without much hope, more for the principle of the thing than anything else."

On February 2, 1952, Terray and Guido Magnone finally succeeded in making the first ascent of Fitz Roy with six companions in support. Years later, after making other first ascents of Himalayan giants such as Makalu and Jannu, Terray reflected, "Of all the climbs I have done, Fitz Roy was the one which most nearly approached the limits of my stamina and morale."

For more than a decade, no one else repeated Fitz Roy. Climbing at such a high standard was in its infancy. During the fifties, ascents of cliffs as large as Fitz Roy's final headwall were just beginning to be done in Yosemite, a tropical paradise compared to Patagonia. The Half Dome-sized granite face that culminates Fitz Roy sits astride an ice mountain as glaciated as Mount Rainier with a vertical rise that rivals Mount Everest (ten of Fitz Roy's eleven thousand feet rise from its base, compared to just twelve of Everest's twenty-nine).

Not until 1968 did Americans try Fitz Roy. After waiting out storms for months, five California climbers achieved a fine new route. They were friends I knew from climbing in Yosemite, and their vivid descriptions of the mountain and the singular beauty of its surroundings struck a deep chord in me. Fitz Roy beckoned as an ultimate dream climb, but seventeen years were to pass before I saw the mountain with my own eyes.

My group of six consisted of myself, Michael Graber, David Wilson, and our wives. Michael and I had been on major winter ascents in the California Sierra, as well as on the first expedition to attempt the West Ridge of Mount Everest through Tibet. David and I had climbed together for a third of his twenty-four years. He was already a veteran of expeditions to Nepal, Alaska, and South America.

Our plan was deceptively simple. Since Terray's time, equipment and technique had greatly improved. We hoped to climb Fitz Roy without placing fixed ropes for fast retreat or stocking camps with food and gear to wait out storms. We knew only too well the story of an Englishman who reported that without having an umbilical cord of thousands of feet of rope fixed to a lower Patagonian peak, "we would still be there somewhere on the mountain, hanging from the unprotected ridge like a side of frozen mutton."

Instead of taking enough food and gear to wait out a storm, we planned to do exactly the opposite. By going light our safety would depend on speed and judgment. At the first inkling of bad weather we would flee down to a base camp about six miles by trail above the highest road. Given a clear spell, we hoped to climb Fitz Roy in two days. The first day would get us to the base of the upper headwall; the second would follow Terray's route a short distance, then veer onto a more difficult and more direct buttress climbed only once before in 1984 by an Argentine party.

To prepare for Fitz Roy, David and I had climbed the 2,000-foot sheer face of Half Dome in Yosemite in a single day with several hours left to spare. Mike let us know that he was not convinced such speed and skill would get us through Fitz Roy's defenses. He joked, "It's better to be lucky than good," but he was only partly kidding. "From all I've heard about this mountain," he said later, "you agree to its terms, not your own. Only if it deals you the right hand do you have a chance."

Our first day of climbing did not go according to plan. The greatest difficulties were not with rock, ice, or storm, as we had imagined, but with human beings. At four o'clock

Michael was not with us, nearly 6,000 feet above our base camp. Though the worst of the deep snow was behind us, after climbing for ten hours with sixty-five-pound packs, we were about to trade post-holing for technical ice climbing up a narrow gully. The risk of a fall was not what was preying on our minds. Michael, who had traveled 8,700 miles with us, was about to be denied the climb at the last moment.

Our equipment had made it through various flights, taxi rides, hotel rooms, roof racks, and campsites, only to have the one item of a mountaineer's trappings that cannot be improvised or shared disappear on the last leg of the journey: Michael's boots. As we were loading packs at base camp, Michael found them missing and took off down the trail to search for them. When he didn't return by dawn, David and I began the climb, as agreed.

When we reached the point where the hard climbing began, Michael had not caught up with us. We were unsure whether to wait or go on. What if Michael never found his boots? What if we were in the only short clear spell of the month? Regardless of justifications for going on, we felt a pit in our stomachs not to be with our friend who had shared our preparations, our enthusiasm, and our long journey.

It would be dark in two hours. Because of our loads and the deep snow, we were likely to make it only as far as the Italian Col, a high pass where we would have to bivouac in the open on rock ledges. If a storm came up with high winds we would be caught out by the elements. Our plan had always been to dig a snow cave higher under the final wall.

Just as we started to pull our ropes up the most difficult section, David spotted a figure far below. We were overjoyed to spot Michael coming, but it begged even more questions. Do we really know he has proper boots? Should we wait or climb the steep ice? Can he reach us by nightfall? Should we leave our rope in place over the hardest part? If we do and Michael doesn't make it tonight, will we be stopped from going for the summit tomorrow because we have to retrieve our two ropes well below our bivouac on the col?

Long before we could hear Michael's voice, he gave us arm signals that all was well. We fixed the rope and hastened hundreds of feet above to set up camp and start boiling water for hot drinks and freeze-dried dinners of lasagna and shrimp creole. The sun set behind the icy blade of Cerro Torre in a burst of gold mist just before Michael arrived with an incredible story to relate: "I couldn't find my boots anywhere, but I knew I'd seen them start out on the horses. I searched all the way to the road and then knocked on the gaucho's door in the middle of the night. His story didn't add up, and I was sure that he had taken my boots and hidden them. If I accused him directly, I risked never getting them back, so I let him save face and help me "find" them. I got back to base camp late this morning and headed out to catch you guys at noon."

"Do you feel good enough to go for the top tomorrow?" I asked.

"Of course!" Michael answered with a ready smile, reminding me how often personal limits have a curious way of expanding to meet the uncertainty of an adventure.

The morning dawned clear with a cold breeze. At six o'clock we started climbing toward the headwall. During the first hour, clouds began to blow past Fitz Roy at a furious rate and our sharply-etched snow ridge became a hazy form that blended into a ground blizzard. We turned around.

Overleaf one: Wild horses run through a meadow directly beneath Fitz Roy with Cerro Torre at far left.
Overleaf two: Cerro Torre at dawn from the summit of Fitz Roy.

At the time we had planned to be on the top, we reached a frozen lake above base camp. There we met the three women, still scanning the peak with binoculars. Barbara said, "I spotted you going up this morning, but I never saw you descending and I didn't see your camp. Did you see that yellow tent up there?"

"What yellow tent?" we asked in unison, totally surprised.

"It's just below the ridge crest. Here, take a look." We indeed could see a speck of yellow in a cave under a boulder, invisible from above and just minutes away from the base of our route. We continued on down to base camp in a thick beech forest near timberline, where eerie green light seeped through a tight canopy of leaves overhead. The wind, howling like a turbine on the peaks, was barely rustling the leaves on the forest floor. Around us were several crude huts, walled with leaning logs and roofed with plastic tarps weighted down with sticks. In another place such structures would be called a shantytown, but here they fit with the fantasy of a hobbit-world where twisted trees that seemed alive climbed up toward an ultimate mountain.

David, who remodels fine California homes, couldn't resist applying his talents to our hut. We all pitched in to raise the ceiling, seal the roof, and rebuild the crude fireplace. Beyond the forest a veil of snow was blowing horizontally without sticking to the ground. The prospect of storms that last for weeks was bringing out the same primitive need within us that had obviously affected other climbers here. Instead of living in the clean, portable, high-tech environment of our tents, we found ourselves drawn toward structures that were relatively permanent, wholly unmovable, but crude in the extreme. We were forsaking modern equipment designs, honed by years of attempts on great peaks, for a Neanderthal life of elemental shelter and fire.

I was reminded of what Yvon Chouinard, leader of the 1968 American Fitz Roy climb, told me just before we left California: "Don't do as we did. Don't wait out the weather in a snow cave up high. Stay in base camp and watch your altimeter. It can be your most important piece of equipment. When the elevation drops [an indication of high pressure], pack up and go for it even if it's storming worse than ever. You'll have a head start on the clear spell."

Two nights after our first attempt, the sky cleared and the altimeter dropped 140 feet. Before dawn we were on the mountain, but as we neared the Italian Col, winds were blowing and clouds were moving at tremendous speed. The rope we had coiled and carefully cached at the col was gone, blown away by winds that must have exceeded 150 miles per hour. Also gone was a food bag and a bottle of stove fuel.

We rappelled down the ice gully and found ourselves in the lee of the wind on a still night. In bright moonlight we glissaded down slopes of light powder snow over a firm crust. Seventeen hours after we started, we returned to our forest home.

The next day was almost good enough to climb. When the clouds cleared momentarily, we kicked ourselves for not being up there, but when the winds howled we knew we had made the right decision. That night the altimeter jumped down yet again, but when my alarm went off at four a.m. the weather was worse than ever. At five the wind was howling with snowflakes in the air. We fell back asleep.

At eight the sky was perfectly clear, and we rushed for our packs. By evening we regained the 6,500 feet to the ridge crest and found Barbara's yellow dot to be a tarp tied across the mouth of a small cave that opens directly onto a 2,000-foot cliff. Behind it, frozen into a wall of ice, was an expedition's full equipment: ropes, hardware, pots, a stove, a shovel, bags of food, sleeping pads. Whoever left it must have been desperately fleeing for their lives.

We christened our cramped chamber "The Yellow Submarine." After I crawled into my down sleeping bag, I tied myself to a piton so that I wouldn't slip away in the night. I set my wrist alarm for 3:30, tucked it under my cap next to my ear, and went to sleep under an absolutely clear, still sky.

Sunrise caught Michael working his way up a questionable cable ladder fixed on the first hundred feet of the wall. It listed at a crazy angle out of a vertical sheet of ice, so he attached his rope to anchors in the rock to protect himself. David then came up Michael's rope on mechanical ascenders. I followed with a heavy pack of equipment. Halfway up, the rope slid sideways off a bump of ice. In an instant I was flung sixty feet through the air in a wild pendulum arc around an overhanging corner. I screamed, not because of the swing, but because I saw my taut rope dragging across a sharp edge that could easily have severed it.

Everything held as I spun in circles, ten feet out from the wall and two thousand feet above the glacier. Adrenaline surged through my body, and my hands began to shake. I regained my composure and got my priorities straight: First, take photos; then finish climbing the rope.

David led the next section with a merger of ice and rock techniques. While one hand was jammed in a rock crack, the other drove an axe into ice. The going was slow because of the unusual amount of ice, and by midmorning I felt that we couldn't make it to the top and back in a day. David and Michael felt the same, but nobody discussed it. We each came to terms with continuing in our own way, aware that if we didn't wish to do so we would have to speak up soon.

David thought of it as a tradeoff: to make this climb we must be willing to spend a night without bivouac gear. Michael reminded himself how he vowed never to climb up that miserable gully leading to the col again; to keep that vow, we must keep going. I searched the sky for excuses, but found none: no clouds, no wind, no lighter blues on the horizon hinting of moisture in the air. There were no places to sleep on our wall with every ledge plastered in with steeply angled ice.

Late in the afternoon we decided to veer off the Argentine route onto virgin terrain. We knew the other way had put the Argentines into a desperate spot, but ours proved no better. The long shadow of Fitz Roy began to stretch across the valley, and we were in it. My fingers stuck to metal in the cold. As I led an overhang, they went numb and I fell, with the rope stopping me after eight feet. I tried again with a nylon ladder attached to my highest anchor, made it, and regardless of the impending night, a sense of well-being flowed through me. I was exactly where I wanted to be, exploring new ground in one of my planet's grandest settings.

By the time Michael led the next section, the sun was down. When it was my turn, I couldn't see beyond the overhangs above me. I tried to traverse an icy ledge and couldn't

Above: Michael Graber climbs unroped to catch up with his partners just before sunset at the Italian Col.

Below: Dave Wilson on the face.

make it. In growing darkness, I climbed directly up the overhang and chopped ice out of a crack at the lip. Moments later, I stood up on a snowfield with ice underneath that sloped back toward the summit, just a few hundred feet above me. With a sigh of relief I anchored my rope to a rock sticking out of the ice. For the first time that day, I was able to stomp a small platform big enough to sit down. Michael and David found one big enough for two.

We had nothing to look forward to until sunrise, an eternity away. We just stood there, shuffling, wiggling fingers and toes, sometimes sitting and shivering, sometimes running in place, watching our watches, waiting for the dawn. Tonight we would have no sleep, no warmth, no food, and no liquid. We were lacking those basic aspects of human existence, yet we had come to this by our own choosing; for us it was a privilege to stand the night away near Fitz Roy's summit in clarity and stillness.

When the full moon rose, we joined in a corny rendition of "Harvest Moon" as we stomped up and down in place to keep warm. This action reminded Michael of another kind of music, and his sudden, impromptu Tina Turner imitation of "Private Dancer" had us laughing uncontrollably and stomping ever faster.

Under the stars, hours seemed to pass like light years. Our attention turned to the constellations of the southern hemisphere. We recognized only Orion near the horizon and the Southern Cross well above. At three a.m. a tiny breeze chilled us to the core. We could only imagine what a real wind might do.

Dawn brought all the rewards at once. We could see, we could start moving, and as we moved, we warmed up. We reached the summit just after sunrise as the moon was setting over two hundred miles of continental glaciers that fill the western horizon—the Patagonian Icecap. To the east, treeless pampas stretched as far as our eyes could see; nearby were the jagged spires of Cerro Torre and the great lake, Viedma, fed by an arm of the icecap that calves icebergs into its waters.

The power of the view came from within us. It would not be same from an airplane, or if we had ridden to the summit of Fitz Roy in a gondola. Thought and vision became hopelessly intertwined. On top of such a dominant point of the earth, reached under our own power, we felt a strong connection between what was before our eyes and the knowledge of our inner selves that we had gained by the pushing the outer limits of our endurance. The time we spent on the summit became locked in our deepest memory, something never to be forgotten.

Our happiness was restrained, however. Only when we were safely down the mountain would we dare celebrate. It took seven hours and fifteen rappels to bring us back to the safety of the Yellow Submarine, which only yesterday had seemed a desperate place. After the climb, it was a palace with everything our hearts desired: warm sleeping bags, hot chocolate, freeze-dried stew, gallons of powdered orange drink, fine company, and sleep.

As we descended the next morning, clouds filled the sky and the wind was blowing yet again. By afternoon we reached our last obstacle: the frozen lake. Cracks radiated over the ice, so David and I scrambled along the cliffs next to shore. After Michael calmly walked across the lake in a beeline for the trail, David commented, "Michael, I think there is a very cold swim somewhere in your future."

Down where the forest met the arid plain, berries were just beginning to ripen on the calafate bushes. Legend has it that a person who eats this fruit returns to Patagonia. The pungent taste gave me pleasure, something like the land itself.

Many people believe that Patagonia's ferocious climate and distance from urban centers will keep big parts of it primeval forever. I know that I have not been alone in discovering there an elemental purity of environments—mountain, forest, pampas, ocean, and sky—exceeding anything in my experience. Like other wild and scenic mountain regions—Yosemite, the Alps, and Nepal, Patagonia–will first draw adventurous souls, then commercial enterprise, and finally the general public in increasingly sophisticated transport and comfort.

I'm thankful to have seen it first when I did.

David Wilson, Galen Rowell, and Michael Graber on the summit of Fitz Roy at dawn.

22

The Highest War

The highest war in history began in 1984 when Indian troops suddenly occupied the Siachen Glacier, where I had skied in 1980 under the auspices of Pakistan. Two years later, my wife, Barbara, and I came to Pakistan on a NATIONAL GEOGRAPHIC assignment to do a cultural story on Baltistan, the frontier district of Kashmir that includes K2 and all the high peaks of the central Karakoram Himalaya. Sometimes called Little Tibet, much of the region remains uninhabited, yet troops were facing each other off in permanent camps at elevations up to 20,500 feet.

When we met Pakistan's late President Zia ul Huq, I told him that since much of the area we were assigned to cover was closed, it would appear to the world as if India controlled it all, if our story had no photographic coverage. He made us his guests of state and assigned military helicopters to escort us into all the major parts of the war zone for six memorable weeks. As this new edition goes to press in 2002, the Siachen Glacier war smolders on.

Politics and war were the furthest thing from my mind during the winter of 1980, as I made the most remote journey of my life 285 miles across the uninhabited heart of the Karakoram Himalaya. With three companions and no native porters, I traversed four of the longest glaciers in the Himalaya through a region that we all had believed was part of Pakistan. We had good reason for this assumption. Pakistan had issued our permit and no foreign expedition had ever applied to India for travel on the Siachen or Baltoro Glaciers since Pakistan became an independent nation in 1947. Also, our U.S. Army U502 map clearly indicated the border east of the Siachen in line with Pakistani claims.

The crux of our route was the lack of a connection between the great Siachen and Baltoro Glaciers at a point about twenty miles east of K2. Conway Saddle, which sits at 20,500 feet on the rim of the Baltoro basin, does not lead directly to the Siachen. Instead, it butts up against Sia Kangri, a 24,350-foot peak east of the Gasherbrum Range. Coming from the Siachen, we reached the saddle after a wild two days negotiating an icefall at 22,500 feet on Sia Kangri's west face with Nordic skis and 120-pound loads in temperatures that dropped to –32° C.

Pakistani soldiers man an anti-aircraft machine gun placement below the Gasherbrum peaks in the K2 region of the Karakoram Himalaya.

When camped on Conway Saddle, it seemed to me one of the most serene places on the planet. We were totally apart from the civilized world, without even an airplane passing overhead for weeks. From our great height we could see well over a hundred miles in the clear winter air without a hint of human presence. Behind me, Sia Kangri rose into the sky. In front were the four Gasherbrums, each over 26,000 feet, holding court over the Baltoro Glacier far below.

Even in my wildest dreams, I would never have imagined how different Conway Saddle would be on my next visit, six years later. Pakistani soldiers in North Face down suits occupied the highest year-round camp in history, equipped with Chinese anti-aircraft machine guns and American Stinger missiles bought from European arms dealers to defend their position—and the entire K2 region—from Indian soldiers in Swiss-made down suits with Soviet Sam-7 shoulder-to-air missiles on the Siachen Glacier.

I viewed the scene from a French helicopter that hovered at 21,000 feet right over the saddle so that I could photograph a Siachen Glacier now controlled by five thousand Indian troops. The world's highest war continues to be fought here, little known to the outside world. As a guest of Pakistan's late President Zia, I was the first foreign journalist allowed within the Pakistani war zone that continues to close off thousands of square miles of Karakoram peaks, glaciers, and villages.

The Indians, however, chose an entirely different tactic. Instead of following the normal Asian policy of sealing off war zones to all visitors, they opened up the Siachen Glacier region to joint expeditions with military escorts in order to legitimize their land claim by the ongoing presence of expeditions with travel permits from India. When I flew to Conway Saddle in 1986, a group of Americans attempting Sia Kangri through India had just given up because of overwhelming objective danger: Pakistani mortars were landing all around them.

I first learned of the conflict two years earlier in the spring of 1984, as I was trekking out from a climb of Lukpilla Brakk on the Biafo Glacier. On the trail I met Reinhold Messner, who was heading up the Baltoro to traverse Gasherbrum I and II as part of his quest to climb all the world's 8,000-meter peaks. We knew each other, and I asked him the obvious question: "Any news from the outside world?"

"There's a war going on right here," he replied. "The Indians just seized the entire Siachen Glacier. All the valleys east of there are closed."

"That's incredible," I exclaimed. "The Siachen is the most remote place I've ever been in my life."

"Was the most remote," corrected Reinhold with a surprisingly keen ear for tense in a language that was not his own. What he didn't know then, was that his coming experience, too, would soon lose a measure of its remoteness. Although he later succeeded on his remarkable traverse of two 8000ers, by the following spring the traditional Gasherbrum Base Camp at 17,500 feet had become a military camp, supplied by helicopters and hordes of Balti porters. Other military camps stocked with troops, aviation gas, North Face VE-24s, AK47 rifles, and 12.7mm anti-aircraft machine guns cropped up in villages and rest stops along the classic K2 trek to the base of the world's second-highest mountain.

Early in 1986, I returned to Pakistan to make arrangements to photograph and write for *National Geographic* with my wife, Barbara. My assignment was the modern culture and geography of the ancient kingdom of Baltistan, now a district of Pakistan's "Northern Areas" where lies K2. I found a third of the Maryland-sized district closed to all visitors because of the war.

I made a business arrangement with an old friend, Nazir Sabir, to handle all my trekking and travel logistics. Besides owning a trekking company, Nazir has done rather well on high peaks, having climbed not only K2, but also Gasherbrum II and Broad Peak, the latter two with Messner. Two months before the start of my assignment, my wife, Barbara, and I attended a large government tourism conference in Peshwar with Nazir who told us, "The doors will never open for you unless somebody very high grants you permission. The Tourism Department doesn't have the authority to let you visit a war zone."

As we sipped tea at a governor's lawn party in Peshawar, a helicopter dispatched an unannounced guest flanked by military officers. When President Mohammed Zia-ul-Haq stepped onto the grass, Nazir whispered, "Now's your chance. He's probably the only man who can do it."

With cameras dangling around my neck, I moved up to photograph Zia greeting each important guest. Meanwhile, Barbara caught his eye and struck up a conversation. She told him that we were working for the *National Geographic* on a story about Baltistan. When a break came, she introduced me and asked if I could possibly chat with him for a minute sometime before he left. He wanted to know why, and his eyes widened when I mentioned that I had skied the Siachen Glacier under the auspices of Pakistan. I knew my trip had strategic significance, because the Pakistan Army had requested my published article as evidence of their formal control of a region that neither troops nor citizens had ever actually occupied. As I told the President that the *National Geographic* published only current photography with rare exceptions, he instantly understood my not so subtle hint that if my coverage deleted the closed third of Baltistan, it would appear to the rest of the world as if India controlled it. He turned to an aide and said, "See that these people meet with me before they leave the country."

At Zia's request, a C130 flew us to Rawalpindi for a private meeting at his home. He quickly put us at ease, and we found his soft-spoken manner, obvious intelligence, candor, and flexibility quite refreshing compared to that of many politicians in our own

Afghan freedom fighter in a Peshwar bazaar ignores the presence of a woman veiled in a traditional burqa—Barbara Rowell.

country. One revealing incident came at a later meeting when the President couldn't find a map of the Siachen Glacier area to discuss with me. He rung for an aide, who told him that all his maps were at army headquarters. "Bring me a piece of paper," he asked. I sat transfixed as I watched a man who had never been to the Siachen sketch me an accurate map of where each side glacier, pass, and military camp lay.

"You and I know the area belongs to Pakistan," the President told me. "If I let you visit the war zone, I hope you will tell the world how India came in and took a region that has been ours since the formative years of our nation."

"The Siachen region borders China, your enemy until recent years, and on India, always our enemy. We didn't think it wise to let foreigners run around near our most sensitive borders. It never occurred to us that India would steal icy, uninhabited mountains from us. We don't understand why they never made a separate claim for this region in the past. Their logic just isn't consistent with their actions. They say the 1949 Cease Fire Line from our first war over Kashmir was never officially extended through the mountains beyond the point known as NJ9842, and that we improperly extended it to include the Siachen region. If this is true, why, after they won two wars against us in 1965 and 1971, didn't they ask for the line to be repositioned above its present boundaries in their favor? There was plenty of fighting nearby in Kashmir, and after each war the United Nations worked with both armies to renegotiate the position of the Cease Fire Line, now called the Line of Control, and to put U.N. observers in the field. Yet India never made a separate claim for the Siachen, and the U.N. has never been authorized to monitor that area. You see, we really were taken by surprise."

On the other hand, Pakistani officials overlooked the significance of published reports in the mountaineering press that Indian Colonel Narinder "Bull" Kumar had led a 1978 expedition up the Siachen to make an ascent of Teram Kangri II. In 1980 another Indian expedition led by Brigadier K.N. Thadani climbed 23,396-foot Apsarasas with an advance base camp on the Siachen Glacier right where I had camped a few months earlier in the same year. The 1981 American Alpine Journal ran the item with the following footnote by H. Adams Carter, the very worldly editor who had organized the first expedition to climb India's Nanda Devi: "It is surprising that an Indian Army force should have crossed the Cease Fire Line and entered into what is generally held to be Pakistan, although the Indians would dispute this."

In 1981, Colonel Kumar returned with a major expedition of ninety Indian soldiers that penetrated the entire length of the Siachen Glacier to Indira Col, Sia La, and Turkestan La. They climbed 24,350-foot Sia Kangri and 25,400-foot Saltoro Kangri, both first ascents. This was something more than mountaineering. The Colonel had been sent on an official mission by the Indian Army in great secrecy to explore and lay claim to land India believed should be theirs.

It is not easy to understand why India would seize such seemingly worthless, uninhabited terrain, and why Pakistan would fight bitterly over it, unless one has a feeling for the bitter hatred between these two young nations. When the British left India in 1948, they drew a clear line of demarcation between what was to become the officially Moslem

Overleaf: A Pakistan Army helicopter flies past a 5,000-foot granite wall in the upper Bilafond Valley, closed to climbing even before the war due to its proximity to Indian-controlled territory.

nation of Pakistan and the new Hindu-ruled nation of India. Several million people died during the ensuing holocaust, as uprooted Moslems, Hindus, and Sikhs began great migrations to settle on the proper side of the new border. However poorly the British prepared their subjects for this chaos, imagine how much worse things might have been if the British had not drawn a clear line to separate the two nations. This is precisely what happened in the Siachen Glacier region.

Where the line stopped at Kashmir, the British left instructions that areas of Moslem majority should go to Pakistan, while areas of Hindu majority should go to India: Simple in theory, but in practice impossible to execute. Baltistan had been virtually all Moslem, with one little hitch. The Moslem Maharajah of Baltistan was under the rather loose suzerainty of the Maharajah of Kashmir, who was Hindu. The people of Baltistan declared, "We are Moslems, we belong to Pakistan." The Maharajah of Baltistan declared, "We are Moslems; we belong to Pakistan." The Maharajah of Kashmir declared, "Baltistan belongs to me. I hereby cede all of it to India." The Maharajah did the same with the Vale of Kashmir, also a place of Moslem majority. Thus India and Pakistan fought their first war over Kashmir in 1948, and the region was split in two by the Cease Fire Line.

Brigadier Aslam Khan was one of the leaders of the 1948 Moslem resistance that kept Baltistan under the Pakistani flag. He fell in love with Baltistan, and when an Orient Airlines DC-3 crash-landed in the Skardu Valley in 1958, he bought the hull and hired 400 Balti natives to drag it with yak-hair ropes to its present location beside a mountain lake. He named the place Shangrila, because of its similarity to the imaginary Himalayan paradise in James Hilton's 1933 novel, *Lost Horizon*, into which a DC-3 crash lands with a group of Westerners. In 1982, Brigadier Aslam opened the Shangrila Tourist Resort with the redecorated plane as a honeymoon suite amidst a group of modern chalets.

On a spring morning in 1986, Barbara and I awoke at Shangrila to the loud sound of engines right outside our room. Two French Alouette III helicopters, each with the English word "Army" in huge letters, were hovering over the lake. They landed a hundred feet away, and out stepped a Pakistani brigadier and a colonel. When a waiter bearing morning tea came to our door, I asked, "What are the helicopters here for?"

"I think they want to talk to you, Sahib," came the reply.

Soon we were having tea with the commanding officers of the Siachen Glacier War at a table on a manicured lawn in the heart of the Karakoram Himalaya. I felt as if I had been transported into the time of the British Raj. But time soon moved into fast forward as Barbara and I flew side by side in separate helicopters passing in an hour a village that had taken me a week to reach on foot in 1980. The narrow trail I once followed was now a jeep road. Ancient villages housed military camps. The road continued up from the last village of Goma into the Bilafond Valley, where we had once seen a great herd of ibex. The pilots told me that the herd was there when the soldiers came in 1984, but had since been shot for meat and target practice.

One by one, we visited the remote passes that Zia had drawn for us, each one dead-locked with Pakistani troops on one side and Indian troops on the other. We were sworn to secrecy about the exact details of what we saw below us for strategic reasons, until the

information on our photographs and notepads would be out of date. Over a period of six weeks we flew almost all of the major glacial valleys of the region well before any story could be published in the *National Geographic*: Chulung, Gyang, Bilafond, Kondus, Baltoro, Abruzzi, plus the Deosai Plains and the eastern sector of the Indus Gorge. Around and above us were hundreds of unnamed, unclimbed spires in greatest granite range on earth. Often we would put down in a remote valley for several hours, while I interviewed soldiers and took photographs. The most commonly shared feeling was that of boredom.

"What do you do here?" I asked at a camp at 17,500 feet on a splendid snow-covered glacier below Conway Saddle.

"Play cards, race around on the snowmobile, listen to music, and wait for mail," came the answer. Minutes later a snowmobile arrived in camp with a long bundle wrapped in a sleeping bag. As troops transferred it to one of our helicopters, I saw a soldier turn away in tears. The body was of his friend.

"This is our fourth death from high altitude pulmonary edema at Conway Saddle," the camp doctor said with sadness and frustration. "The only sure cure is rapid descent, but it was storming yesterday, and the chopper couldn't fly. He died during the night, and we brought him down this morning, first by sled, then by snowmobile. That's a 20 percent death rate at this camp since it was established fifteen months ago. It would be even higher if we hadn't choppered out some other victims who survived."

When I later flew to the 20,500-foot camp on Conway Saddle and on the return hovered even higher in the powerful Lama helicopter above a shoulder of Sia Kangri to look down the Siachen Glacier toward Indian military camps, I had no idea that an American expedition was pinned down by artillery fire below me. Mountain Travel USA had advertised "The Third Pole Expedition: Ascent of Sia Kangri 24,350 feet," in their glossy catalog for $8,000 per person. Arrangements were made through Colonel Kumar as a joint expedition with Indian Army climbers. Outraged Pakistan tourism officials lodged a complaint with the U.S. State Department. A trip leader for Mountain Travel in Pakistan had told me the expedition was canceled. At the last minute, Mountain Travel's owner, Leo LeBon, gave the go-ahead and came along.

As the Mountain Travel expedition neared the end of the Siachen, they began to hear rumbling sounds that they first mistook for avalanches. When artillery shells began to

Barbara Rowell shoots an AK-47 at an army camp on a high pass near the Siachen Glacier.

land around them, the American contingent holed up for a week, while the Indian soldiers continued on under fire that lasted until they got above 22,500 feet. LeBon sent a radio message to the Indian Army, asking them to negotiate a ten-day cease-fire so that his party could climb the mountain "in the name of international mountaineering." No answer came. The Indians reached the summit, and the Americans went home.

The expedition could hardly have walked into a more sensitive situation. Colonel Kumar had officially retired from the Army and began pushing Siachen travel as part of his private trekking business. In 1985, he attended an international mountaineering meeting in Tokyo, where he announced that the Indian government was opening up sixteen peaks in the eastern Karakoram to foreign mountaineers. Virtually all of them were around the Siachen Glacier in territory where all previous mountaineering permits to foreigners had been issued by Pakistan. The Colonel sent out notices to foreign outfitters offering to book expeditions through his company.

The representative from Pakistan returned home and gave the story to the press. It appeared on the front page of the national newspaper with one small error. Instead of saying that the Indians had opened up climbing to foreign expeditions in the Karakoram, the article said that K2 had been opened up for climbing through India. Tourism and military officials were incensed. Even though the story was quickly found to be in error, the Pakistan Army decided to put a series of military camps up the Baltoro Glacier, both to prevent Indians from coming anywhere near K2 and to protect the dozens of international mountaineering expeditions to neighboring peaks that bring a flow of foreign exchange into the country every year.

"We are fighting two enemies," a young captain told me as we flew over the mountains together. "India and Allah. I think Allah is winning."

"What exactly do you mean?" I asked.

"Maybe it is against Allah's will to live in these mountains. Temperatures drop to sixty below in winter. Even in summer, storms drop several feet of snow in a single day. Only a few soldiers die from bullets. The others fall into hidden crevasses, get sick from the altitude, or die from exposure. India is not winning, either. We are both losing to Allah."

When I returned to climb Gasherbrum II in 1989, I found the situation virtually the same. About ten thousand troops were stationed by both sides on or around the glacier. Little strategic ground had been won or lost, and a third of Baltistan remained closed to visitors. A major Pakistani offensive in 1988 failed to gain a pass with a loss of fifty lives.

Colonel Kumar confided to friends that he wished the whole affair had never happened, yet neither government would lose face by consenting to give up land to the enemy. In the final assessment, men might as well shoot at each other on the Moon as stand on the pristine heights of the Earth, gasping for breath, with weapons in hand. By comparison, mountaineering appears totally sane.

23

The John Muir Trail in Winter

Weekend winter trips into the roadless southern Sierra whetted my appetite to someday ski the entire 211-mile John Muir Trail. In 1987, I proposed a NATIONAL GEOGRAPHIC story on the trail and arranged both summer and winter coverage. With two companions, I set off in February 1988 for the summit of Mount Whitney, where the trail officially begins. Seventeen days later, we arrived in Yosemite Valley, having traversed the longest unbroken wilderness trail in America and, more important to us, having had it all to ourselves.

The southern terminus of the John Muir Trail is at a most unlikely spot: the summit of 14,496-foot Mount Whitney, highest point in the forty-eight contiguous states. On an equally unlikely morning—February 2, 1988—I set out with Rob Mackinlay and David Wilson to climb Whitney by the eleven-mile tourist trail that links the Muir Trail to the Owens Valley. Our goal was to ski 222 miles to Yosemite Valley through three national parks, one national monument, and two national forest wilderness areas through the heart of the High Sierra without crossing a single road.

I wanted to experience the entire trail in all its seasons, first and foremost as a personal quest related to my family history, but more immediately as the subject of a *National Geographic* story on the trail that I had been recently assigned. The more I researched the history of the trail, the less certain I was that the entire trail had ever been continuously skied during the winter months without coming out for supplies, and to this day the written history seems vague on that point. The half-dozen or so modern trips I knew about before ours had all been done in spring conditions, finishing as late as May, when I'd once jogged across the range in running shoes atop hard snow in the mornings and bare rock ridges in the afternoons.

The first ski traverse of the trail was made solo by Orland Bartholomew between December 1928 and April 1929. He made two planned detours over the crest to restock supplies, appearing as a bearded and long-haired apparition to the townspeople of the Owens Valley. According to his biographer, Gene Rose, Bartholomew was given "a royal sendoff by the people of Bishop [as] he headed back into the high country in fine spirits."

Beneath a full moon at dawn, ski mountaineers glide across the Kern Plateau,
one of the few long level sections of the 211-mile John Muir Trail.

Rose, a Fresno newspaper reporter, says that much of his impetus to research and write a book about Bartholomew's journey "came in 1970, when during a visit to a Fresno sports shop I met three young mountaineers who claimed to have made a 'first' winter crossing of the Sierra on skis."

I had met the same group in 1969 as they planned their adventure in an old cabin near Bishop. I recall seeing a well-worn copy of Hal Roth's 1965 book on the John Muir Trail, *Pathway in the Sky*, which includes a description of Bartholomew's trek, along with mention of eleven food caches placed the previous autumn. They were well aware of the earlier trip and had decided to place far fewer caches for their journey that would end in May with lots of running water and less need to melt snow with a stove.

Their discussion with Rose was probably a misunderstanding, but their wondrous tales of their successful journey became one of my main motivations to attempt the trail lighter and faster in true winter conditions. Whether or not it had been done that way before, I wanted to experience the heights of the whole southern Sierra in the dead of winter, rather than later in the spring when many of the slopes were already bare.

John Muir, for whom the trail is named, never did the route in either summer or winter. He died on Christmas Eve in 1914. Soon afterwards, the Sierra Club convinced the State of California to appropriate $10,000 for construction of a memorial trail from the summit of Mount Whitney to Yosemite Valley. Not until 1938 was the last section of the "Golden Staircase" finished behind the rugged Palisade Range of what was soon to become Kings Canyon National Park.

Before I set off to repeat the trail, I visited someone who had also been there before it was completed, a very special woman who traversed its entire length in sections during the summers of 1923, 1924, and 1925. Margaret Avery trekked as much of the present route as possible with her sister, Marion, and six friends. When they reached Evolution Valley, they made the first ascent of a sharp rock peak called The Hermit, which has such a sheer summit block that today the official register is placed below it and most parties never go to the true top.

As I looked through her ancient scrapbook crammed with photographs of lakes, mountains, and mule trains, I felt her youthful exuberance return. She spoke in the present tense about "summers that mean more to me than anything in my whole life," and I wondered if anything else in the life of a woman born in 1900 could have remained as much the same. Had the scrapbook contained pictures of school years, relatives, or hometown scenes, she would be thinking about them in the past tense, but the landscape in her scrapbook existed for her and for me virtually unchanged from the day she first set eyes on it.

Such is the legacy of John Muir. By using the weight of his fame and the muscle of his prose to help legislate protection for his favorite Sierra wildlands, he created a kind of immortality that few human beings ever achieve. The world of his writings, unlike that of most all his contemporaries in the American West, is alive and well. The trail created in his memory further preserves that legacy.

Overleaf: Pitching a tent on a spur of Mount Whitney at over 13,000 feet on a sub-zero February evening.
Opposite: Aerial winter view of the route of the John Muir Trail from the upper basin
of the Kings River to Mount Whitney on the horizon.

When I commented that the pages of the old scrapbook didn't show anyone carrying a backpack, the old woman said, "Of course we didn't have backpacks. We'd never heard of a 'backpacker.' All those light tents, clothes, sleeping bags, packs, and foods you carry now hadn't been invented. We had a choice of day hikes between cabins, overnight hikes, or using a pack train for anything longer. Doing the trail when I got out of college was a once-in-a-lifetime experience that I thought I could never afford again. The mules cost so much! We couldn't rent them, so we bought them outright for sixty dollars each."

She did return to a section of the Muir Trail in 1951 with her husband and ten-year-old son as part of a more tame Sierra Club outing. Mules carried everything for 111 people to a camp beside Lake Ediza for two weeks. Hired staff cooked and led hikes. Her son, undeterred by the crowd, felt as if he had entered paradise when the narrow trail beneath his feet delivered him into that primeval world of lakes and flowers set beneath sharply-etched peaks of rock and snow. As he watched his mother joyfully reunite with her youth and the natural world, the boy began a lifelong love affair with the High Sierra.

I am that son. Thirty-seven years later, I returned to my mother's scrapbook for another look before skiing the trail in winter. I carefully planned my trip to start on the day before the February full moon, so that when we pitched camp high on Mount Whitney, we would watch the moon rise in the east at sunset; then watch it set in the west at sunrise.

After our first long day on skis climbing from 8,600 feet to 13,500 feet, we set our tent on an icy ridgetop so narrow that its edges overhung steep cliffs on both sides. The temperature dropped below zero as the western sky shifted from orange to crimson, and then into a rose-purple glow that slowly filled the entire sky until a blue sliver of the Earth shadow peeked above the mountains to the east and the full moon rose into it. The snowy scene looked far more like the Himalaya than the "gentle wilderness" John Muir roamed in summer so long ago.

We slept fitfully, all too aware of not rolling toward one of the edges. At dawn, the light show repeated itself with sun and moon in opposite positions in the sky as we packed up and continued on to the summit of Whitney, windblown and almost devoid of snow.

By mid-morning we were skiing down the Muir Trail onto the vast Kern Plateau, from which no human habitation was visible. Our uphill effort of the previous day was now released into a long downhill glide from the barren heights through a mystical timberline forest of old foxtail pines. Far along the plateau, we set up a second camp beside dead pine limbs poking out of the snow. They were burnished and twisted by the elements, and as we thought about how cold and sweaty we were after suddenly stopping, someone said aloud what we all were thinking: "Let's not build a fire; these dead trees are too beautiful."

The next morning we started skiing toward cliffs where the trail had been blasted into the rock. The long switchbacks up 13,000-foot Forester Pass were entirely blown in with snow. We decided to climb a steep couloir to the left, carrying our skis over the final cornice with the aid of special ice picks that attached to the handles of our ski poles. From the top of the pass, we skied down soft powder toward Bubbs Creek and Bullfrog Lake, where we had left a food cache high in a lodgepole pine in a sealed, dark-green plastic barrel. Taking out what we needed for the next long section, we resealed the barrel and planned to retrieve it in the early summer, when I would hike the trail for another part of my story, supported by a pack train.

Through Sixty Lakes Basin the trail was entirely buried and impossible to see, except for rectangular blazes cut into the bark of trees here and there. We passed through a forest in which every tree had been freshly broken off fifteen feet above the ground by a massive avalanche. Luckily for us, the weather was holding and we had yet to experience a storm. Our metal-edged, cross-country skis with climbing skins were an ideal compromise for carrying forty-pound packs uphill, then removing the skins for skiing down powder slopes facing north. Though some parties have skied from north to south, we much preferred the idea of skiing down north-facing powder and skiing up south-facing slopes that had settled in the sun.

Day by day we crossed passes—Glen, Pinchot, and Mather—until we camped behind the Palisades, a range of 14,000-foot peaks where all of us had done extensive climbing. At Muir Pass we came to a stone hut built in John Muir's honor in 1930 before the creation of Kings Canyon National Park. Erecting our tent inside the hut, we spent an unusually comfortable night with a fire in the fireplace, thanks to wood left by summer visitors.

The next day we reached what for me and many other experienced travelers is the culmination of the range: Evolution Valley, named by Theodore Solomons long ago. Though Mount Whitney may be the highest point, it is here that the range comes together into its grandest form.

The original idea of a "crest-parallel trail through the High Sierra" had nothing to do with John Muir. It began as the dream of fourteen-year-old Theodore Solomons, who worked on a cattle ranch within sight of the peaks. Being far more of a cowboy than a hiker, he imagined a route that could be traveled by stock parties. Eight years later in 1892, Solomons set out to explore a route from Yosemite Valley southward with one partner, two mules, a rifle, a Dutch oven, and a big 8 x 10-inch camera loaned by Carlton Watkins, the famous pioneer photographer of Yosemite. Solomons got only as far as Devils Postpile, twenty-five miles south of the present boundary of Yosemite Park, but returned two years later to push a hundred miles south from Yosemite to where his mules were stopped in their tracks by a rampart of high peaks above delicate meadows surrounding what he called "Evolution Lake." Before turning around and giving up his quest, he named the surrounding mountains Darwin, Huxley, Wallace, Fiske, Spencer, and Haeckel because the grand setting reminded him of "the great evolutionists, so at-one in their devotion to the sublime in Nature."

My mother especially loved this part of the trail, where the valley, basin, and a lower meadow were also named "Evolution" on the new USGS map published the year she began her hike along the trail. From this point north to Yosemite, the trail has a decidedly more gentle character, both because the mountains are gradually lower with no more 14,000ers, and because the northerly half continues to follow the basic route of Solomons' wanderings with his mules over ridges and valley bottoms. In contrast, the newer southern half was engineered and blasted by hired crews to more directly pursue the goal of a trail along the High Sierra crest.

The original Muir Trail passed through a single piece of private land at Blayney Meadows near Evolution Creek, but it has now been rerouted to skirt the Muir Trail Ranch, open in summer only as a guest ranch for about twenty-five exclusive guests. In my mother's day, Clark Gable and Carole Lombard stayed there. The ranch was created by filing a claim for 200 acres of wetland around two natural hot springs made possible by an obscure "Swamp and Overflow Act" passed in 1896. In 1924, the year my mother passed through, the government reclaimed one spring because of an error in the ranch's survey.

We found the two springs to be as different as one could possibly imagine. The "rich man's spring" beside the guest buildings trickles into a tiled tub surrounded by finely crafted wood, to be used only by ranch guests. We couldn't sample it because the water had been diverted in winter to prevent freeze damage. Instead, we soaked in the 98-degree water of the "common man's spring" on the other side of the fence—a chest-deep mud hole even in winter as its heat melts the surrounding snows.

For the first 160 miles we saw no one. Then we met a caretaker at Reds Meadows Pack Station, beside Devils Postpile National Monument, which was closed for the winter. From there, two more days of skiing brought us to Tuolumne Meadows in Yosemite National Park, where we dined with winter rangers Tory and Brent Finley in their snug cabin on our fifteenth night. As we relaxed in front of the television, network news brought the day's highlights of ski events in the Winter Olympics into one of the few American living rooms where skiing meant basic transportation, rather than recreation or competition.

We were still twenty-four miles from the end of the trail at Yosemite Valley. Though we could have skied it in a day, we set up camp early in the afternoon beside Cathedral Peak. At sunset, we stood on its summit, then rushed down the icy slabs and cliffs to the comfort of camp in growing darkness and increasing winds. A major wind storm hit us the next morning as we traversed into the canyon of the Merced River in a ground blizzard, often unable to see our skis in front of us.

That afternoon, we checked into the plush old Ahwahnee Hotel, hoping for a quiet, comfortable night. When we went downstairs for dinner, we thought we had entered a homeless shelter. Hundreds of people were huddled with blankets against the walls. Seventy-mile-per-hour winds had blown a tree into a Yosemite Lodge cabin, killing an occupant and prompting evacuation of the lodge, tent cabins, and nearby campgrounds. More than once it occurred to me that I would rather be out there in the snows sleeping in a tent than in a noisy hotel crowded with people. Though in one sense we had returned to civilization, in another we were still very much in the wilds of the High Sierra.

Photographic Notes

When I began photography to record the adventures I was having in Yosemite and the High Sierra, 35mm cameras seemed too large and cumbersome. In 1965, I bought a tiny Kodak Instamatic 500 with a fine Schneider lens that accepted cassettes of Kodachrome film of a slightly smaller format than 35mm. My goal—then as well as now—was to record the peak moments of my adventures in the natural world with as little interference as possible. One day I watched Ansel Adams teach a workshop at Olmsted Point and decided then and there that I never wanted to shoot a large-format camera in the wilderness. The size, weight, and slow operation seemed far too limiting for the broad range of subject material I wanted to photograph.

In 1968 I bought a Nikon FTn and soon had lenses from 24mm to 400mm. As the decades have passed, I've continued to use Nikons and to figure out ways to maximize image quality by using the slowest, finest-grained films, quality lenses, and state-of-the-art digital printing.

My early experiences with a camera in the High Sierra backcountry taught me how to pursue meeting places of magical light and form as if I were following clues on a treasure map. Today's even lighter Nikon models further the process, so that when I head out by headlamp before dawn with a camera and a couple of lenses, I might come back with a

Leif Patterson celebrates the sight of green grass at Urdukas after months on the sterile heights of K2.

fabulous wide-angle sunrise, as well as a telephoto of a wary wild creature, plus some images of a climbing adventure, with or without companions. If the light fails me or something else stops me from getting the kind of images I'd hoped for, I still return happy and renewed by a personal connection with the wilderness. That's what motivates me.

I only photograph what I'm passionate about. If I'm not moved by what's before my lens, why should anyone else be? On the other hand, I may feel deeply moved, but snap a casual photograph that fails just as surely as if I felt nothing. The power of photography is to communicate the special way in which one human being has seen the world to another. It's not the objects themselves that we respond to in a photograph, but the way they have been assembled for us to re-interpret a scene through the mind and eye of another being. When viewing someone else's photograph, we often say, "That doesn't do anything for me," no matter how technically sharp and well-exposed the image may be.

Some of the images in this new edition are being published for the first time, using the latest digital imaging technology to preserve and restore detail that would have been lost by earlier printing techniques. There have been no additions or subtractions to image content, and the goal has been to match the original transparency as closely as possible, with corrections limited to exposure, pre-existing color, and damage to older transparencies from scratching or fading from too much projection. The Kodachrome I used until the late 1980s is actually five times more sensitive to light (as in projection) than newer Ektachromes or Fujichromes, though it remains the most archival color film in dark storage. Since I learned this in the 1980s, I began using Ektachrome duplicate slides exclusively for lecturing.

For every image in this book, silver-halide photographic prints, exposed by light from scanning lasers in a digital enlarger, were created and proofed multiple times as color guides for the printing of this book from the same digital files. Fine prints of these images are available through Mountain Light Gallery in Bishop, California or on the web at www.mountainlight.com.

GALEN ROWELL
Bishop, California

Index

Abruzzi Glacier, 174-175, 209
Adams, Ansel, 14, 34, 221
Ahwahnee Hotel, 220
Akbar, 163
Alaska Range, 87-88, 93, 111, 113, 135, 142
Alaska, Gulf of, 114
Alps (Swiss), 20
Ama Dablam, 180, 185
American Alpine Journal, 133
American Fitz Roy Expedition (1968), 197
American Dhaulagiri Expedition (1973), 163
American Karakoram Traverse Expedition (1980), 170
Ancient Bristlecone Pine Forest, 73
Anderson, George, 65
Anderson, Pete, 143
Andes, 190
Ansel Adams Wilderness, 34
Antarctica, 14
Apsarasas, 208
Arches Direct, 38
Argentine route, 198
Asay, Dan, 169, 173-177
Avery, Margaret, 216
Baltistan, 203, 205, 207-208
Baltistan, Moslem Maharajah of, 208
Baltoro Glacier 149-150, 153, 155, 159, 165, 167, 169, 174-175, 203-204, 209, 211
Bard, Alan, 133-135, 137-138
Bariloche, 189
Bartholomew, Orland, 213, 216
Basically Absurd Technology (aka "Datso"), 60
Basque sheepherder, 109
Bat hooks, 58, 60
Bat gadgets, 60
Bat tents, 60, 62, 65
Batso, 60
Beagle, H.M.S., 189
Bear Creek Spire, 25, 29, 31
Beck, Eric, 52, 54
Beckey, Fred, 45-49
Bell, George, 163
Berkeley, 25, 33-34, 51
Beyond the Vertical, 51
Bhutto, President, 163
Biafo Glacier, 169, 172, 176, 204
Bilafond Glacier, 173, 209
Bilafond La, 173
Bilafond Valley, 207, 209
Bill, Sandy, 88
Bishop, 25, 73, 106
Blanc, Mont, 17
Blanchard, W.E. Smoke, 22
Blayney Meadows, 219
Bonington, Chris, 88
Boulder Camp, 71
Boysen, Martin, 162
Braldu River, 155
Bridwell, Jim, 93
Bristlecone #WPN-114, 106-108
[British] Alpine Club, 20
British Columbia, 67
Broad Peak, 159, 169, 205
Brower, David, 14
Brown, Joe, 159, 162
Bubbs Creek, 218
Buckskin Glacier, 91
Bugaboo Lodge, 67, 71
Bugaboo Mountains, 67
Bugaboo Range, 67-68
Bullfrog Lake, 218
Buscaglia, Lou, 163, 165
Buttermilk Road, 30
Buttress, East, 137
Callis, Pat, 46-49
Camp Four, 30, 33, 35-36, 51, 55

Canada, Alpine Club of, 69
Carter, H. Adams, 208
Cassidy, Butch, 190
Cathedral Peak, 220
Cease Fire Line, 208
Central Karakoram National Park, 149
Cerro Torre, 17, 191-200
China, 207
Chitina River, 14
Cholatse, 184, 186
Chouinard, Yvon, 39, 52, 58, 87-88, 91-93, 197
Chulung Glacier, 209
Cirque of the Unclimbables, 17, 123-131
Clevenger, Vern, 180, 184
Colliver, Gary, 58
Concordia Amphitheater, 149, 157, 175
Conness, Mount, 96
Conway Saddle, 169, 173, 203, 209
Cook Inlet, 114
Cook, Frederick, 114, 134, 141
Craig, Bob, 159
Crockett, Davy, 130
Crowley Lake, 73
Crowley, Aleister, 20, 163
Currey, Donald, 106
Curry Village, 82
Darwin, Charles, 189, 219
Dawn Wall, 20
de Saussure, 17
Denali National Park, 119
Denali Pass, 145
Deosai Plains, 209
Devils Postpile National Monument, 219
Diamond [the], 96
Dickey, Mount, 113-114, 116, 119-120, 137
Direct Northwest Face, 20
Dogleg Cracks, 52
Dolt Tower, 36
Don Sheldon's Mountain House, 138
Dorje, Sonam, 186
Dunge Glacier, 166
East Buttress, Mount Mc Kinley, 137
Eastern Sierra, 29-30, 95
Ediza, Lake, 217
Egger, Toni, 17
Eiger, 54
El Capitan, 17, 26, 33-34, 38, 40, 43, 58, 81-82, 123
Ellesmere Island, 134
Everest, 184-185
Everest Base Camp, 180
Everest, Mount, 17, 149, 180
Evolution Creek, 219
Evolution Valley, 216, 219
Faint, Joe, 64, 81-83
Fairbanks, 143
Farrell, Mike, 106
Feagin, Nancy, 20
Fender, Tom, 36, 39-40
Finley, Brent, 219
Finley, Tory, 219
Fiske, 219
Fitz Roy, 189-191, 196, 200
Fitz Roy, Captain Robert, 189
Foraker, Mount, 141, 146
Forester Pass, 218
Four Mile Trail, 52
Frémont, John C., 105
Frost, Tom, 52, 88, 91
Gable, Clark, 219
Gallwas, Jerry, 34, 38
Gasherbrum Base Camp, 204
Gasherbrum Glacier, 174
Gasherbrum I, 174
Gasherbrum II, 174, 205, 211
Gasherbrum III, 174

Gasherbrum IV, 159, 174
Gasherbrum Range, 169, 203
Geist, Valerius, 138
Gifford, Nigel, 146
Gillette, Ned, 133-139, 141-147, 170, 173-177
Glen Pass, 218
Godwin-Austen Glacier, 153, 163, 175
Gokyo Valley, 180
Golden Age of Yosemite, 38
Goma, 209
Graber, Michael, 189, 191, 196, 198-201
Gray Matter, 60
Great Arch, 58, 62
Great Basin, 47, 74, 103, 105
Great Basin National Park, 105
Great Gorge, 114, 138
Great Roof, 39
Great Trango, 163, 167
Great Trango Tower, 159, 162, 164
Great White Throne, 45-47
Greenland, 14
Gunsight Pass, 137
Gyang Glacier, 209
Hackett, Peter, 179-187
Haeckel, Mount, 219
Haji Ali, 176
Half Dome, 26, 34-35, 57-58, 64-65
Harding, Warren, 20, 35, 38-43, 57-65, 95, 103
Harlin, John, 54
Heart Ledge, 54
Hennek, Dennis, 159, 163, 167
Hermit, The, 216
Hetch Hetchy Dam, 81
Hetch Hetchy Valley 81-82
Hidden Peak, 159
High Sierra, 29, 33, 55, 96, 213
Hilton, James, 208-209
Himalaya, 13, 25, 153
Hindu Kush, 153
Hispar Glacier, 169, 177
Howser Towers, 67-68, 71
Hudson, Cliff, 88, 91, 135, 138
Huntington, Mount, 113, 137, 139
Hunza, 177
Hussain, Mohammed, 163, 164
Huxley, Mount, 219
India, 203, 207, 211
Indira Col, 208
Indus Gorge, 209
Indus River, 154
Italian Col, 189, 196-197, 199
Jannu, 191
Janus, 60
Jensen, Jay 74-77
Jerry Gallwas, 34
John Muir Trail, 106, 213-220
John Muir Wilderness, 25
Jones, Chris, 68-69, 83-85
K2, 149, 154, 157, 169, 175, 203, 205
K2 National Park, 149
Kahiltna Glacier, 13, 135, 139, 141, 147
Kahiltna Pass, 135, 147
Kain, Conrad, 68-69, 71
Kangchenjunga, 159, 163
Kantega, 180
Karakoram, 149, 154-157, 166, 176, 211
Karakoram High Route, 169
Karakoram Highway, 149
Karakoram Himalaya, 149, 150, 169, 203, 209
Karstens, Harry, 120
Kashmir, 203, 207-208
Kashmir, Maharajah of, 208
Kathmandu, 180
Keeler Needle, 95, 100
Kern Plateau, 213, 218

Khan, Brigadier Aslam, 209
Khan, Pervez, 150
Khumbu, 180
Khumbu Icefall, 184
Khunjerab National Park, 149
Khunjerab Pass, 149
Kingdom of Nagar, 177
Kings Canyon National Park, 216, 218
Kings River, 216
Kleine Scheidegg Hotel, 54
Kondus Glacier, 173, 209
Kor, Layton, 38, 43, 51-55
Kumar, Colonel Narinder "Bull", 208, 210-211
Latoks (the), 169
Last Chance Ledge, 48
Leaning Tower, 39
LeBon, Leo, 210
Leonard, Dick, 14
Lhotse, 184
Liliwa, 155
Line of Control, 207
Little Lakes Valley, 26, 31
Little Tibet, 203
Lloyd, Tom, 143
Logan Mountains, 123
Logan, Mount, 13-14, 17, 22
Lolofond Glacier, 173
Lomba, Dave, 106, 109
Lombard, Carole, 219
Lone Pine, 100
Lost Horizon, 208
Lotus Flower Tower, 88, 123
Loughman, Mike, 34
Lukpilla Brakk, 204
MacCarthy, Albert, 14
Mackinlay, Rob, 213
Magellan, Ferdinand, 190
Magnone, Guido, 191
Makalu, 184-185, 191
Mango Brangsa, 176
Mather Pass, 218
Matterhorn, 17
McBrien, Mount Sir James, 126
McCarthy, Jim, 87-88, 91, 123-129
McGonagall, Charley, 143
McKinley's West Buttress, 142
McKinley, Mount, 13, 22, 87-88, 114,
   133-135, 141, 143, 145, 174
Merced River, 40, 65, 220
Merry, Wayne, 36
Messner, Reinhold, 204-205
Methuselah Tree, 108
Middle Cathedral Rock, 54
Miller, George, 74, 106
Monument Valley, 45
Moose's Tooth, 87-88, 92, 123, 136-137
Morrissey, Jim, 163, 165
Mount McKinley Great Circle Expedition, 134
Mountain Light Gallery, 222
Mountain Travel Nepal, 180
Mountaineer's Route [The], 103
Muir Pass, 218
Muir Trail, 213, 218-219
Muir Trail Ranch, 219
Muir, John, 14, 30, 57, 65, 81, 120, 138, 216,
   218-219
Muldrow Glacier, 137
Mummery, A.F., 20, 22-23
Mustagh Tower, 159, 172, 174
Na, 186
Nameless Tower, 162, 167
Nanda Devi, 208
Nanga Parbat, 154
National Park Service, 51
Navajo sandstone, 46
Needle, Keeler, 97
North Howser Tower, 68
North Pole, 134
Northwest Territories, 123, 130
O'Connor, Bill, 180, 185
Ogre (the), 169, 177

Overland Pass, 106
Owens Valley, 25, 29, 31, 71, 74, 77, 213
Pakistan, 149, 155, 203, 208, 211
Pakistan Air Force, 169
Pakistan Army (soldiers), 202-204, 207, 211
Pakistan Forest Department, 155
Palisade Range, 216
Parque Nacional Los Glaciares, 190
Parrot Beak Peak, 124
Patagonia, 25, 189-190, 201
Patriarch Grove, 73, 75, 79
Pearl Peak, 108
Peary, Admiral, 134
Pellisier Flat, 74
Peshwar, 205
Peters Glacier, 133, 135, 137
PG&E, 82
Phortse [the] family, 186
Photographic Notes, 221
Piana, Paul, 123
Pinchot Pass, 218
Pinchot, Gifford, 81
Pine Creek, 29
Pine Creek Canyon, 29
Pine Creek Tungsten Mine, 25
Pivetta Spiders, 55
Pratt's Crack, 29
Pratt, Chuck, 52, 58
Proboscis, 123, 131
Purdue, John, 146
Qamar, Tony, 67-69
Rawalpindi, 150, 162, 165, 207
Read, Al, 180
Reds Meadows Pack Station, 219
Roaring Forties, 189
Robbins, Royal, 38-39, 51-52, 62
Roberts, Dave, 111, 113-121
Robinson, Doug, 106, 111
Roper, Steve, 35, 51
Rose, Gene, 213, 216
Rose, Mount, 77
Roskelley, John, 163-165, 167, 179-186
Roth, Hal, 216
Rowell, Barbara, 190, 197, 205, 209, 211
Ruby Mountains, 105, 108
Ruth Gap, 139
Ruth Glacier, 114, 137-139
Ruth Gorge, 120, 138
Saint-Exupéry, Antoine de, 190
Sabir, Nazir, 205
Salathe Wall, 51-52, 55, 123
Saltoro Kangri, 208
Saltoro River, 170
Saltoro Valley, 173
Santa Cruz River, 190
Sasquatch sightings, 143
Schaller, George, 149-150, 153-157, 176
Schmitz, Kim, 163-164, 173-177
Schulman, 79, 108
Schulman, Edmund, 78-79
Sella, Vittorio, 174
Sentinel Rock, 52, 54
Seventh Rifle, 67
Shangrila Tourist Resort, 208
Sharp, Dave, 74-75, 78, 106
Sheldon, Charles, 120
Sheldon, Don, 114, 138
Sherpas, 186
Sherrick, Mike, 38
Shiprock, 45
Shipton, Eric, 49
Shyok River, 170
Sia Kangri, 173, 204, 208-209
Sia La, 208
Siachen, 207
Siachen Glacier, 169-170, 203-204, 207-208, 211
Siachen Glacier War, 209
Siachen Glacier, 169
Sierra Club, 34, 67, 81, 216-217
Sierra Club Rock Climbing Section, 34
Sixty Lakes Basin, 218

Skardu, 154, 162
Skardu Valley, 150, 208
Skinner, Todd, 123
Smith Creek, 109
Smith, Mount Harrison, 126, 129
Solomons, Theodore, 219
South Buttress, 139
South Face of Half Dome, 58
Southern Patagonian Icecap, 189
Southwest Arete, 186
Spencer, Mount, 219
Steck-Salathe Route, 54
Steve Roper, 35
Stump, Mugs, 93
Sundance Kid, 190
Swamp and Overflow Act, 219
Tacoma Mountain Rescue Team, 46
Talkeetna, 87-88
Taylor, Billy, 143
Teapot Dome scandal, 134
Tenaya Canyon, 57
Terray, Lionel, 190-191
Thadani, Brigadier K.N., 208
Thamserku, 180
the Nose of El Capitan, 33-36, 38
The Vertical World of Yosemite, 57
Thompson, Snowshoe, 130
Thyangboche Monastery, 180
Tilden Park, 34
Tioga Pass, 26
Traleika Glacier, 137
Trango Tower, 166
Trango Towers, 159, 165, 169, 174
Tri-clops Eye, 60, 62, 64-65
Tuolumne Meadows, 219
Turkestan La, 208
Underhill, Robert L. M., 97
United Nations, 207
University of California Barcroft Research
   Laboratory, 77
Upper Baltoro Glacier, 172
Utah, 45, 47
Vandiver, Chris, 95-96, 100-101, 103
Viedma, 200
Virgin River, 46
Wallace, Mount, 219
Wapama Rock, 81-83
Ward, Ed, 113-116, 119-121
Washburn, Bradford, 121, 141
Washington Column, 96
Watkins, Carlton, 219
Weins, Doug, 133, 135, 137
West Buttress, 43, 135, 141
West Face (Sentinel Rock, Yosemite), 52
West Ridge of Mount Everest, 191
Westgard Pass, 79
Wheeler Peak, 105, 108
Whillans, 17
White Mountain Peak, 78
White Mountains, 29, 73-74, 79, 103, 106, 108
Whitmore, George, 36
Whitney, Mount, 17, 77, 96, 100, 103, 213,
   217, 219
Whitney, Stephen, 107
Whymper, [Edward], 17
Wilson, David, 191-201, 211
Wilson, Woodrow, 81
Wiltsie, Gordon, 96-97, 100
Windy Corner, 142, 147
Woudworth, Harry, 46
yersas, 186
Yosemite, 13, 29, 31, 33, 35-36, 51, 57, 81, 83
Yosemite Falls, 43
Yosemite Lodge, 43
Yosemite National Park, 25, 219
Yosemite Valley, 13, 20, 25, 34, 57, 81-83,
   213, 219-220
Zia-ul-Haq, President Mohammed, 203-205
Zion, 45-47
Zion Canyon, 45